George Sanders

An Exhausted Life

George Sanders

An Exhausted Life

Richard VanDerBeets

MADISON BOOKS
Lanham • New York • London

Published by Madison Books
4720 Boston Way
Lanham, Maryland 20706

3 Henrietta Street
London WC2E 8LU England

Distributed by National Book Network

5   4   3   2   1

Library of Congress Cataloging-in-Publication Data

VanDerBeets, Richard.
   George Sanders : an exhausted life / Richard
VanDerBeets.
     p.   cm.
     Includes bibliographical references.
     1. Sanders, George, 1906-1972.   2. Motion
picture actors and actresses—Great Britain—
Biography.   I. Title.

PN2598.S33V3 1990
791.43'028'092—dc20   [B]   90-34432 CIP

ISBN 0–8191–7806–3

The paper used in this publication meets the minimum
requirements of American National Standard for
Information Sciences—Permanence of Paper for
Printed Library Materials, ANSI Z39.48–1984. ⊗™
Manufactured in the United States of America.

British Cataloging in Publication Information Available

For Margaret
with admiration and affection

"When a man says he has exhausted life,
you may be sure that life has exhausted him."

—George Sanders, as Lord Henry Wotton
in *The Picture of Dorian Gray*

Contents

Photographs follow pages 80 and 160.

Preface

The French windows of the darkened boudoir shatter. George Sanders catapults from a ladder and bursts into the second story room amid a shower of splintered glass. The beautiful blonde woman screams; her half-clad Latin lover flees into the dressing room. George, tanned and bearded, blue eyes flashing, strides to a desk, picks up a portrait of himself and tears it to shreds.

While this dramatic confrontation might have come from one of the hundred films George Sanders made during his long and active career, it was in fact a real-life episode. No such scene in a movie drama would have ended on the note which followed:

Breathing heavily, now looking pale and unsteady, he turns toward his wife.

"What's the matter, darling," a concerned Zsa Zsa Gabor asks, "are you sick?"

"My dear," George replies, "I'm an old man. I've absolutely no business climbing ladders."

"Come downstairs and have a drink."

"Well, perhaps just one."

This curious mixture of rage and ironic detachment captures one facet of the complex personality of George Sanders, an actor who carried his on-screen cynicism and aloofness into his private life and put them—in the mask of The Cad—to his own uses. It was a personality that fascinated both filmgoers and friends for over three decades, the more compelling when presented fully and accurately in the context of the life experiences which shaped his mind and heart.

As as actor, George Sanders was the best of a vanishing breed of movie villains: the elegantly mannered, exquisitely dressed, silken-tongued cad dripping verbal venom; the lordly, cynical scoundrel oozing malice. To those who knew him off the screen he was a complex, contradictory, immensely gifted man. ("Just look at that fellow," Noel Coward once exclaimed, "he has more talents than any of us, but he doesn't do anything with them!") He was also fundamentally insecure and introspective. Only by examining the gradual merging and synthesis of these two "lives" can an understanding of George Sanders be formed.

George Sanders: An Exhausted Life is an authorized biography written with the approval and assistance of the only surviving family member and heir of George Sanders' estate, his sister Margaret Sanders Bloecker, without whose gracious and valuable cooperation this book could not have been written. There have been two previous works treating the life of George Sanders: his own *Memoirs of a Professional Cad* (1960), a witty but uneven and regrettably incomplete anecdotal history (neglecting, for example, to mention his first marriage or to discuss the film roles for which he is best remembered), which of course does not cover the last twelve years of his life. The other is Brian Aherne's *A Dreadful Man* (1979), less a biography than an unstructured gathering of reminiscences scattered among a collection of unannotated letters between the Ahernes and George and his third wife, Benita, during the period 1958—1972, vague on many particulars, careless with dates and details, and rather self-serving in its treatment of its author's own career. "I personally don't think Brian knew much about George's private life at all," Zsa Zsa Gabor has told me.

This book makes use of all essential biographical sources and adds a significant amount of original material in the form of interviews, unpublished letters, and manuscript journals to provide as complete an account of its subject as possible: birth and childhood in St. Petersburg, Russia, with disclosure of what has recently been termed "the long-guarded secret" of the Sanders ancestry through the paternal line; youth and school days in England after the Russian revolution, early experiences which profoundly affected his later life; travels and adventures in South America as a young man, including a pistol duel; the mask of the Cad and the man behind that mask; his four marriages (secret first marriage, second to Zsa Zsa Gabor, third to Ronald Colman's widow Benita Hume, and fourth, briefly, to Magda Gabor) and his two relationships late in life with women not previously discussed publicly; his lengthy experience with psychiatry and therapy; the disastrous financial venture in Europe; the physical and mental decline; the ultimate failure of the mask; and his suicide, the reason for which revealed in a letter never before made public.

In addition to biographical materials, this book incorporates an in-depth consideration of George Sanders' film career and representative individual films, with analyses of his principal roles, discussion of every significant production in which he appeared, and previously unpublished comments by costars and supporting players. An appended filmography lists principal cast, crew, production company, and running time for each of his films.

George Sanders appeared in over one hundred pictures, with title or lead roles in thirty, and won an Academy Award for his supporting performance in *All About Eve* (1950). It was a career in most ways comparable to those of other talented and popular actors of Hollywood's Golden Age. A full and accurate rendering of his life off the screen, which accounts for the intertwining of that life with his carefully cultivated screen image, speaks to us as perhaps no other can today, when we recognize in ourselves both the vulnerability of the individual and the strong attraction of the protective mask, however fragile and ultimately destructive that mask may become.

Richard VanDerBeets
Aptos, California

Acknowledgments

To Margaret Sanders Bloecker, who generously provided letters, journals, family photographs, and memorabilia as well as her personal recollections in extended interviews, grateful acknowledgement and thanks are here made; to Lorraine Chanel for her reminiscences and use of letters and photographs; to Zsa Zsa Gabor, Eva Gabor, Joan Fontaine, Charles Kidd, M.W.D. Jones, and E.A.M. MacAlpine for biographical interviews; to the actors and actresses listed in the Bibliography, co-players who offered their recollections in correspondence interviews; and to the Reference and Loan departments of the Clark Library, San Jose State University, for assistance in the gathering of materials.

Unless otherwise credited, all photographs are courtesy of Margaret Sanders Bloecker.

Europe: 1906–1936

1 "My Father Came in the Mail"

George Sanders, who played so many kings and princes in such convincingly royal manner during his long film career, began his life July 3, 1906 in St. Petersburg, Russia, and ended it unaware of any connection between his family and the Russian royal family or the likelihood that he was himself descended from a Russian prince. "It came to light only after his death," his sister Margaret relates. "He would have been absolutely fascinated." Concerning his family, George once observed that "it was from forebears of solid social position and impeccable respectability that my mother came," and this was indeed the case: Margaret Kolbe Sanders was the daughter of wealthy industrialist Robert Kolbe, who owned large cotton mills in Narva, Estonia, homes in St. Petersburg, and country estates in Finland. This side of George Sanders' family was descended from the Thomas Clayhills of Dundee, Scotland, who had emigrated to Estonia in the early seventeenth century. But of the paternal line George could only remark facetiously that "to the best of my knowledge, my father came in the mail."

To the best knowledge of all three Sanders children—George, Tom, and Margaret—their father Henry had been orphaned at an early age, his father presumably a Paul Sanders born in London about 1840, and the Sanders family in England distant relatives on their father's side. Recent disclosures, however, indicate that Henry Sanders was illegitimately born to a Russian noblewoman of the Czar's court on October 20, 1868, that his real father was "a prince of the house of Oldenburg" married to a sister of the Czar. At the time of Henry's birth, there was an Anglo-Russian family living in St. Petersburg named Sanders whose mother, Dagmar, was a lady-in-waiting to the Dowager Empress, and by means of this court connection Henry was placed in the care of the Sanders family who, although comfortably well-off, were also given substantial funds for his keep and education. "Only in recent years, and through a chance remark," Maragaret reports, "did the truth of our father's background eventually come to light."

The complete story was confirmed to her by Mara Sanders, the youngest daughter and last surviving member of the Anglo-Russian Sanders family, who "gradually came to the conclusion that since all concerned were now no longer alive, she need no longer keep the secret." Mara had been closely connected for many years with the Russian nobility and in England was aide and companion to the Grand Duchess Xenia at the "grace-and-favor" Hampton Court residence given her after her escape from Russia. In addition to the facts of the paternity, Mara remembered a portrait of Henry's Russian mother hanging over his bed when he lived with her family and also recalled that he had been taken out frequently on excursions by the Prince's brother, together with his own children. This account of Henry Sanders' paternity would explain the small gold medallion left to Margaret by her father and still in her possession: it is engraved with a red crown and a blue crown on either side of the entwined red and blue initials of Prince von Oldenburg and his wife, sister of the Czar.

While he knew nothing of this ancestry, George was well aware that he had been born into "a world of clinking champagne glasses, colonnaded private ballrooms, and heel-clicking, monocled princes in gorgeous uniforms." It was a world that would soon disappear, but it lasted long enough to provide him an early childhood of peace and happiness. "If it is true that a man's character develops for the good in proportion to the degree of happiness and the amount of bountiful love he experiences in childhood," he wrote in later years, "then I must have the most noble and wonderful character in all the world," adding, however, that "a surprising number of people think otherwise." George was the Sanders' middle child; his brother Tom was born September 15, 1904 and his sister Margaret October 27, 1912, both in St. Petersburg. George was, by his mother's recollection, "a strong, healthy baby, wide-shouldered." She added, "Vaccination put a temporary stop to George's development, [for] it 'took on' very badly and he was quite ill for a considerable time after. It left him rather sickly and terribly shy. He only wanted to know the closest family, and the arrival of any visitor brought floods of tears and howls." Once past that early setback, his life was a childhood idyll: "When I look back on my childhood, it seems to me that all of my activities consisted in swimming, canoeing, sailing, skiing, tobogganing, skating, and listening to my father play the balalaika."

Henry Sanders was in fact the most accomplished amateur balalaika player in St. Petersburg and the trainer of the English Colony's Balalaika Orchestra, which was preparing for a grand concert at Konanoff Hall in 1902, the year George's parents met at a formal ball. Margaret Kolbe had been told by the hostess that "the famous Henry Sanders would be there and would bring his balalaika, that he was 'marvellously good-looking' and that after talking to him for half an hour one fell in love with him." They danced one waltz together, and although she was not impressed—Henry "was not a particularly good dancer"—she found him otherwise talented and quite charming, and at the Konanoff Concert some weeks later he proposed and was accepted.

They were married in December 1903. The British Consulate Entry of Marriage certificate lists Henry's occupation as "Assistant Director of rope factory" in St. Petersburg; it seems he had been taken straightaway into one of the family businesses, Hoth Ropeworks, and the couple moved into a flat which her mother arranged for them, complete with cook and maid. There followed several "care-free years with the usual routine as in my own childhood," the bride wrote, "winters in St. Petersburg, summers at my mother's place in Hungerburg, Estonia." This was the life which George enjoyed as a young boy, "as normal and quiet a family life as anyone could wish for," his mother reflected. "The children playing in the garden or on the beach, my mother, sister, and myself sewing while Miss Nye read to us." Miss Nye was the English governess and tutor employed for the children, who were educated privately at home until 1915. "Apart from their lessons, she taught them truthfulness, manners, and abolute obedience. They adored her, especially George."

In the spring of 1909 it was decided that George and Tom would go to England with their mother for the summer, and they stayed with relatives in Brockley and Kingsgate. "George got quite fat and so sunburnt and sturdy that everybody on our return to St. Petersburg said it was difficult to believe it was the same child," his mother reported. From that time on, George enjoyed vibrant good health uninterrupted by serious illness or injury of any sort until the last two or three years of his life. "He never ever had anything," his sister remembers. "Tom and I had everything—appendectomy, tonsillectomy—and George didn't have anything." This uncommon freedom from infirmity would, by the contrast, render the afflictions common to advancing age he might otherwise have accommodated much more devastating.

George's life-long love for the sea, especially evident during his early Hollywood years, began in childhood. At age five he and Tom were invited to play with the children of Grand Duke Michael; during tea the Grand Duke talked to the children and asked George what he was going to be when he grew up. According to his mother, George replied, " 'A naval officer.' The Grand Duke asked: 'English or Russian?' Promptly came George's reply, with a strong accent on the last word: 'English, of course.' " Three decades later, asked by a Hollywood interviewer what he would be if not an actor, he replied, "I'd be a seaman. I've spent my thirty-six years changing my mind, but I'll never change my mind about the sea. I've a boat of my own for weekends and spend many happy hours aboard it scraping and polishing . . . I'd do the same on someone else's deck." He had named his boat *Frustration*.

The summer of 1912 was passed with relatives in Imatra, Finland, and the spring of 1914 the family spent on the Italian Riviera, with side trips to Nice and Monte Carlo. "It might not be too much to say," George reflected later in life, "that my family epitomized the decadence of the upper classes under the Czar," perhaps recalling the "favorite pastime" of one of his uncles: "From his great, carved bed, a .22 caliber pistol in his hand, he would shoot flies that had gathered to eat the jam he had smeared on the ceiling. Liveried footmen stood by with champagne, extra rounds of ammunition, orange marmalade and strawberry jam."

Soon after the family's return to St. Petersburg in May 1914, war broke out. Robert Kolbe bought an estate at Mustamakki, Finland, and they spent that winter and the summer of 1915 there, away from the turmoil of St. Petersburg. George and Tom were scheduled to begin formal education in September at Dunhurst, a preparatory school in Hampshire. Henry thought it wise that his wife and young daughter Margaret accompany them to England and stay for a year or so "until the position in Russia became clearer. There had been private warnings and rumours from friends in the interior that a serious revolution was brewing." Concerning the revolution, George would later and only half-jokingly lament "the appropriation of trust funds that various affluent uncles and aunts of mine had set up to insure for me the sort of life that would have suited my indolent nature. The Czar had signed away our inheritances, our gilt-edged future, an action for which I, personally, have never forgiven him."

The two boys—Tom, age eleven, and George, nine—settled in at Dunhurst, and their mother and little Margaret moved into a furnished house until the next summer. Then Henry wrote his wife from St. Petersburg "saying that there seemed to be no sign of the expected revolution and that it would be quite all right for me to return with Margaret." The boys were put up in a vicarage near Salisbury with a clergyman and his wife until school resumed, and with some delay and difficulty, owing to wartime conditions, their mother and Margaret made the trip back to St. Petersburg.

In December 1916 Rasputin was killed and his body thrown into the Niva River not far from the Sanders' home. Henry was asked by police to supply dunnage from the Hoth Ropeworks to cover the corpse, an event which over the years developed into a colorful family story that the rope used to strangle Rasputin was of Sanders manufacture. Within a few days rumors circulated that the Empress was in hysterics, the Grand Duke Dimitri Pavlovich sent into exile, Prince Ussoupov reduced to the ranks and sent to the front. Henry, his wife, and Margaret left the city for Mustamakki and spent Christmas there. Soon after the beginning of the revolution, in February 1917, Henry decided to send his wife and daughter back to England. It was an arduous journey, part of which was spent in the cattle-hold of a merchant ship, evading German patrol boats. From London she went immediately to the vicarage to be reunited with her sons after a year's separation. "Tom had grown enormously and was so tall I had to look up to him. George had not grown as much but had broadened out. It was lovely seeing them." Henry, who had removed to Finland during the revolution, eventually joined his family in England at a newly purchased home near Maidenhead. George and Tom completed their two years at Dunhurst in June 1917 and prepared to enter Bedales School at Petersfield in the fall.

Although school records list their father's occupation as "Director of Company," Henry was in fact at loose ends in England and without real income of his own. His father-in-law, Robert Kolbe, had fled to Switzerland but with investments outside Russia was able to provide some financial support for his surviving relatives. In fact, Henry "never did much in business after leaving Russia for England," his daughter recalls. "Mother's family had money." Henry's dependent situation from this time onward was the root of what became George's life-long equation of wealth and self-worth, a perception which profoundly affected both his business and personal relationships. "I wouldn't have a wife who made more money than I," he declared in an interview twenty-five years later. "A wife should have only a little pin money, so that she can't make her husband feel inferior." For the present, however, George was experiencing insecurity and feelings of inferiority as a foreign-born schoolboy in England and had begun constructing a protective mechanism, a calculated persona born of shyness and intellectual contempt, which over the years he would gradually refine and shape into the mask of The Cad.

2 "A Sense of Utter Worthlessness"

Reflecting on George's experiences at Bedales and Brighton some twenty-five years afterward, his brother Tom remarked pointedly on "the vulnerability of his school days." In his own recollections George declared that "my parents sent me to the wrong schools," explaining that "environment and inherited talents create needs which are not always catered to by institutions of learning. These needs may lie dormant in an individual, repressed by fear of failure. Years later, he has become a square peg in a round hole." The two boys' letters during their school days validate these later perceptions. As the eldest at age thirteen to George's eleven, Tom wrote most of the letters from Bedales home to their mother with news of them both. In September 1917, the start of their first term, an early letter suggested a precarious situation: "Everything is so unsettled . . . There are several nasty boys here who go about teasing." Moreover, they felt neglected because their mother failed to write them as often as they wished. "I have not received a letter for some time," Tom complained to her in another note, and later in the year he wrote, "I have not had a letter this

11

term." Her visits were also infrequent and subject to change. "I had engaged some rooms at Steep," Tom wrote in 1918, "but as you aren't coming down I will cancel them."

During these two unsettling years at Bedales the brothers found refuge in school plays. "George and I are acting in a play called 'One-eyed Joe's Last Cargo,'" Tom wrote proudly. "I am One-eyed Joe, the famous smuggler, and George is Roving Tom, one of my accomplices." George's first role on stage was, appropriately, a supporting one. In a subsequent letter Tom reported that "the play came off fairly well, except that in the funny parts the actors laughed." The boys also found escape from the pressures of school by play-acting in the surrounding countryside of Hampshire. One of Tom's letters confided that they had "made a simply topping little hut in the woods near here, absolutely away from civilisation, and we go about scouting and stalking game and moor hens with bows and arrows and spears" and wished that their little sister Margaret could be there "to mess about in it and play in the woods and cook our food for us over the campfire."

It was at Bedales that George also found an outlet in sketching, a talent he would develop in later years. "Do you know that if you encourage George a bit," Tom wrote to his mother in 1918, "he will take on something quite big in the way of drawing." George was also able to give expression to his abiding interest in ships and the sea. "George is going to make a boat and I am going to make a turbine for it," Tom wrote in anticipation of an upcoming visit home, "so that we can let her go about by the sea-shore in the holidays," adding wistfully that they wished to vacation "at a place where we can run about bare-foot and do what we like, like in Mustamakki." From Bedales the boys matriculated to Brighton College, an institution, George later reflected bitterly, he would leave after four years "with a sense of utter worthlessness."

Although he later described himself as "a poor student" at

Brighton, in fact he consistently earned high marks throughout his years there. In his first term he reported to his mother that "I was top in English last week with 37 of 40. I have been top in French as well. I find the work fairly easy." In another letter the same year he wrote, "The exam week has finished and I have done very well. I never thought I'd do so well." The next year, 1920, he proudly announced, "I have been moved up Eighth Form this term!" And Brighton records show that for the academic year 1921 he "won the French prize for his class" and "won the class prize for German" in 1923, his last year. George's "sense of utter worthlessness" could not have derived from his performance as a student.

Nor could lack of athletic ability have been a source of feelings of inadequacy. Although he began his years at Brighton smaller in size than the average student (at age thirteen he told his mother about a boy who "won the running championship and he only is about my height"), he excelled in both team and individual sports, eventually concentrating on the latter in order to be independent of others for success.

He competed in cross-country, track and field, swimming, billiards, and boxing. "Yesterday there was the trial for the cross-country run," he told his mother. "I daresay you won't believe it but I beat Tom hopelessly." The next year he reported that "The cross-country is over—seven miles of hard running— lots of people were sick and had to be taken back by bus. I came in about 50th out of 300 people competing." Later that spring he wrote home, "I'm in the final for the high-jump (open) and in the semi-finals for the 220 and hurdles." He developed a proficiency at billiards—in 1921 he won the first round of the school competition—which he would use to good effect four decades later in the 1964 film *A Shot in the Dark*. In the summer term of 1921 he was also on the Durnford House swimming team, winning the high dive and taking second in springboard—another talent which proved useful several years afterward when he leaped into the Thames and swam to the rescue of a drowning man, an act for which he received the medal of the British Humane Society.

It was at boxing, however, that he most excelled. Brighton records indicate both his match progress and his physical development. He began competing as a lightweight at age thirteen, winning his first match but losing the second. Summer term of 1922 he fought as a middleweight and was undefeated until the final match. In 1923 he competed for both his house and school teams as a heavyweight, winning his final match against rival Lancing College. His physical growth continued until he reached six feet-three inches in height and weighed 200 pounds. In 1929 he and his brother were reunited after a six-year separation. "George had grown until he was two inches taller than I and was much broader," Tom recalled. "I asked him what had happened and he merely said, 'I guess I got rather tired of being the short brother.' "

George found time for other activities at Brighton as well. School records show he was active in the Officers' Training Corps, was promoted to Lance Corporal in October 1922, appointed Physical Training instructor for the Corps in 1923, and was eventually made Drum Major of its guard of honor. He sang in the chorus of Noblemen of Titipu in the college production of *The Mikado* in the spring of 1922 and the next year played two roles (the King of the Pirates and one of the policemen) in *The Pirates of Penzance.* Just how busy and productive his last several years at Brighton were is indicated in a letter to his mother in October 1922: "I shall not be able to take private tuition this term as my time is absolutely full up. I have boxing three times a week in the evening, and choir practice, and practice for 'Pirates of Penzance,' and all sorts of things. I was also asked to sing at a concert—it's in aid of charity—next Tuesday week. It ought to be rather good fun."

Successful both as a student and an athlete and active in a

variety of extracurricular events, George gave no direct expression during his school years of any feelings of worthlessness. What, then, engendered the bitter and distorted perception some thirty-five years later that he had been sent to "the wrong schools," that Brighton College was "an austere and somewhat moth-eaten second-rate public school," its students "the flotsam and jetsam of lower middle-class families"? The answer lies scattered throughout the boys' letters to their mother during those years.

In his very first letter to his mother from Brighton, thirteen-year-old George writes in a postscript, "Do send us some money." In December, before the holidays, he begins a letter with "Do buck up and send our money." Another letter implores, "Please don't forget to send the cash quick and as much as you've got down your stocking." And again later, "What about the cash? Are you bankrupt or something?" Before Christmas the next year he begins, "The chief reason for my writing arises from that fact that unless you send me some money pretty soon I shall have to stay here for a couple of weeks longer." In a letter written in his fourth and last year at Brighton, George still found it necessary to ask his mother to "send the money in your next letter, and send a good stockingful won't you," closing the letter with "Am in a hell of hurry so must say adieu, but don't forget about the money, will you dearie."

Money, specifically the lack of it, was a persistent concern throughout George's years at Brighton and a recurring theme in both boys' letters. "The money thing is a beastly nuisance," Tom wrote at the start of their second year. "After the journey and library subscription we had 5 shillings left and tonight we had to give 2 and 6 each to the school mission. That leaves us broke, and the sooner you can send us some more the sooner will we be happy." In another letter he complained that "both George and I are run out in funds. I do not know if it is possible but we would be awful bucked up if you would send us a little more."

Finding themselves chronically short of money in the company of fellow students who apparently had no such problem was a continuing source of embarrassment, often expressed indirectly: "There is a boy here named Loveday whose father is evidently a millionaire," George wrote his mother. "He has a motorcycle and his father said that he could buy himself a launch for his birthday." Their own concerns were more fundamental: "My everyday suit is miles too small for me," George wrote in September 1920. "The sleeves come out below my elbows. Still don't you worry about it. I can manage through this term all right." Tom experienced similar problems: "The Chief said my tweeds were too tight to wear at the College, but he did not mind me wearing it for a little while, so I may be able to get through the term." Shortly before their first Christmas holiday, the boys were informed that "if we go home in 'College Straws,' we would be a 'disgrace to the house,' so when it approaches the end of term, may George and I get an order for some kind of head gear, that is have it put down on the bill?" They were not spending their money frivolously: "Thanks awfully for the £1, we were very much in need of it," Tom on one occasion acknowledged to his mother. "I got myself a pair of shoes for boxing with it, and George is going into town tomorrow for his collars."

When Tom left Brighton in 1921 and was preparing to embark for a job in South Africa, his father gave him a rifle, for which he was very grateful, he wrote Henry, "especially in our present financial position." The family situation was no better by 1923, George's last year. "I sold all my ties for 6d each," he wrote his mother. "I think it is a better price than what you would have got for me had you sold them to the second-hand shop."

The sudden descent from a wealthy and privileged early

childhood—of loving parents, governesses, winter estates, and leisurely summers abroad to the lonely, precarious, and often humiliating years as a foreign-born schoolboy from a family in limited financial circumstances engendered deep insecurity, especially in George, the younger brother. The fact that his father was unable to contribute materially to the family's resources added to George's correlation between wealth and self-worth another equation, that of financial independence and manhood itself. This was the basis of the legendary tight-fistedness of his early Hollywood years, of the threat posed to him by successful women, of the desperate schemes in the 1950s and 1960s to become a business tycoon, and possibly of the fact that, fearing similar failure as a father, he remained childless all his life.

On leaving Brighton, Tom sought both adventure and success by moving to Rhodesia to work at a cotton mill and later a mining operation; after three years he wrote his father that he was "pretty well fed to the teeth" with the undertaking, but stayed on in South Africa another five years, eventually having to borrow his passage home. Perhaps mindful of Tom's failure, George decided to stay in England to continue his schooling after Brighton, and in 1923 enrolled at Manchester Technical Institute to study textiles. He stayed on after a year's study to work at the Manchester Textile Company, a job "for which, even if I had been able to get the hang of my duties, I could not have demonstrated any aptitude nor any genuine interest." His motive in taking the job, he reflected in later years, was "to prove to my parents that I was capable of supporting myself." He proved the reverse, unfortunately, for his small salary had to be supplemented by an allowance from his mother. He was relieved when, after a year, he was "good-naturedly thrown out of the company."

At this point in his life, as a shy and insecure youth of nineteen concealing his feelings of inadequacy behind a pose of disdain for the world yet looking to prove himself adequate by succeeding in that world, George took an adventuresome step that would significantly alter his life and determine to a large extent the proportions of happiness and tragedy which comprised that life.

3 "We Men of Steel"

"It is extraordinary how rapidly events occur in the affairs of our scattered but ever-affectionate family," George wrote his father from Buenos Aires in June 1926, six months after his arrival in Argentina. "It seems but yesterday that I toasted with a stoup of port the receding cliffs of 'England green and pleasant land.'" He had signed on as a manufacturer's representative for the British and American Tobacco Company in South America and would remain there four years—the happiest, most carefree, and in many ways most beneficial period of his life. He acquired an abiding love of Argentina, its people, its music, and its language, developing a proficiency in Spanish so fluent that during his Hollywood years he could carry on extended conversations with Latin actors, on one occasion convincing Mexican-born Anthony Quinn that he had been born in Argentina. "He spoke Spanish brilliantly," Quinn recalls. During the filming of *A Date with the Falcon* in 1940, George was conversing in Spanish with Argentine actress Mona Maris, who suddenly exclaimed, "It's impossible to believe you aren't a Latin American. There isn't a trace of accent in your Spanish. It's perfect." His sister Margaret well remembers George's four years in South America: "He learned to speak fluent Spanish, was fascinated by the local music, and could sing many of their lilting melodies while accompanying himself on the guitar." Three decades later George would remark wistfully, "I miss the music of the country; I find it more moving than any I have ever listened to."

Although he was, as always, concerned about making money ("I should really like to try to put something by during my stay out here," he wrote his father, "and possibly possess an income-earning capital"), it was his physical fitness and glowing good health that most occupied and pleased him. "Life is hard and work is hard, but we manage to survive, we men of steel," he wrote three weeks before his twentieth birthday. "My trip round the province did me a world of good, and when I returned nobody recognised me, I was so brown and fit. Camp life fills you with steel, your fingers get a grip of iron, your mouth takes on a firm line, and your face becomes a shield of bronze that hides more effectively your emotions."

His work at the company factory in Buenos Aires went well, and his superiors were pleased with his progress. He wrote his father something of the conditions of his life at that time: "I live in a *pensional* situated in the most central part of town, but 35 to 45 minutes away from the factory. The food is ghastly, there is no furniture, one has to walk through the rain to get to the bathroom." He had spent months "looking for digs nearer the factory" but found it "far too expensive for my paltry means." His "programme of daily life" began with rising at 6:30 in the morning, breakfasting on rolls and tea, and doing exercises: "alternate short and long-arm press-ups on the table, knee bending, and deep breathing." After a morning spent among consignments, branch shipments, and sales statistics, he lunched and then "hit the punch-ball for 15 minutes in order not to lose the famous short-jab." The workday ended at 6:30 in the evening; he had dinner at 8:00, often talked with friends in Spanish about "international politics and the reincarnation of the soul,'' then retired at 10:00. Sunday mornings he spent exercising on the roof of his building, then took long walks in the afternoon. "I have become like a watch," he wrote his father, "and I don't want anything to interfere with its smooth running."

This well-regulated life continued for a year, until he was sent by the company into the provinces and eventually to Patagonia to conduct a customer survey and promote the sale of the company's brands of cigarettes . From Buenos Aires he traveled to the railroad's end at Ingeniero Jacobacci, then with an Indian guide who spoke Guarani, the native language, he plunged "into the wilds of Patagonia." And wilds they were: no roads, no electricity, no hotels. Food and shelter were to be found only at privately owned sheep ranches, where travelers would be received hospitably if they arrived before sundown. "Because of the numerous bandits in this area, ranchers had a discouraging habit of opening fire with Winchester rifles on anyone approaching their property after dark." On those occasions when he and his guide arrived at a ranch after sunset they made camp, first digging a circular trench and filling it with the dried dung of the guanaco, a llama-like animal native to Patagonia, and then lighting the dung to smolder all night, providing them warmth and protection from wild animals. In this fashion, George made his way from ranch to ranch for almost six months.

Although he observed that Patagonia "has a stark, moon-like topography, dusty and lonely," he nonetheless "thoroughly enjoyed" his travels through the wilds: "At times I felt almost like an animal. My senses became more acute, and I virtually glowed with good health. I lived and ate simply and slept soundly. The robust state of health I was in and the kind of life I was leading would produce in me an appetite so ravenous that I would drool at the mouth like a wild beast at the smell of food." Sitting in a circle of ranchers and other travelers around lamb roasting on a turning spit, he drank *yerba maté* from a gourd ("in Patagonia they all drink out of the same cup," he remarked in an interview decades later, "but they are a healthy people and don't have germs"), then with his knife would cut off a large slab of meat and, as was the custom, eat it with his fingers. It was, as he later declared, "a primitive existence in Patagonia. I was in perfect health and savored everything I saw and experienced." This persistent theme— "glowing good health," "robust state of health," "perfect health"—runs throughout the letters and recollections of this period in his life. As a consequence he had begun to formulate a rudimentary life-philosophy: "From this experience I arrived at the conclusion that we all need periods of living as nearly like an animal as possible. To enjoy one's life to the fullest, one must build contrast into it. And the more extreme the contrast the fuller the life." It was a philosophy which, in a manner he had neither intended nor anticipated, would ultimately betray him the last several years of his life.

George remained with British and American Tobacco for three years, when his association with the firm was summarily ended. The circumstances were these: the company manager had become engaged to the daughter of an important Argentine industrialist, who was hosting a small celebration dinner party to which George was invited. "Unconcerned about the need for punctuality since I was, after all, in a Latin country," he arrived at the dinner an hour late to find that the guests numbered thirteen without him and, superstitiously, had been unable to sit down to dinner. The manager viewed George's belated arrival as a personal insult and "succeeded in having me thrown out of the company."

He was unemployed only briefly. Taking a train across the Andes to Chile, he landed a job in Valparaiso promoting sales for another tobacco company, essentially the same sort of work he had been doing in Argentina. "I was rather sad about leaving the Argentine," he reflected in later years. "I had engaged in a lot of youthful high jinks there." These included swimming in his dinner jacket across a lake in a downtown park and keeping a pet ostrich in his apartment, but it was in Chile that his most unusual, and on one occasion most harrowing, "high jinks" took place.

Sent into the north of the country to determine methods of improving the company's share of the cigarette market, George discovered that the area was little more than a string of nitrate mining camps each, however, with its own small theatre where amateur theatricals were put on. Here he struck upon the idea of producing and directing little shows, admitting free of charge anyone who showed a package of one of his company's brands. He hired "two guitarists and a broken-down conjurer," put together a show, and began a tour of the camps. The project was not a success, failing to increase demand for the company's products, and he was "recalled in disgrace" to Valparaiso.

Given another chance by the company and sent this time into the south of Chile, George found himself among farmers rather than miners and conceived another scheme to promote sales: flying over the countryside and dropping small parachutes with cigarette samples attached to them, together with leaflets addressed to the farmers. From a small military field near Temuco, his base of operations, he hired an old World War I Bristol biplane, had the machine gun removed from the gun cockpit so he could fly standing up behind the pilot, and dropped his parachutes by hand. Despite turbulence over mountainous territory, which ended the mission before half his load was distributed and which also brought on airsickness—in desperation he threw up into his glove—the campaign created much interest, including newspaper coverage in the capital city of Santiago. The scheme was a success, and the company was pleased. This triumph notwithstanding, George's stay in Chile, and indeed in South America, was soon to be terminated.

He had been living in a villa on the outskirts of Temuco as "the house guest of a very charming widow," who happened to be engaged to be married to a gentleman in town. Late one night when George and his companion were abed, the fiancé arrived and began banging on the shutters of the bedroom window, shouting what George considered "totally irrelevant accusations of infidelity." Throwing open the window, revolver in hand, he remonstrated with the gentleman and suddenly found himself challenged to a duel. He promptly accepted, climbed out the window, dropped to the ground, and discovered that it was too dark to see his antagonist. When their bodies touched, they maneuvered into a back-to-back position, agreed upon ten paces' dueling distance, and began stepping away from each other. Being barefoot, George had the advantage, for he could hear the crunch of the other man's shoes on the gravel path. "I turned and pressed my trigger in the direction of the last crunch. I stood my ground but there was no answering shot." Walking back, he found the man lying on the path with a bullet wound in the neck but bleeding very little. To George's great relief, the gentleman recovered within four days. "I have not owned a gun since then," he declared decades later, "and never will. It was a hairsbreadth escape for both of us."

In summoning a doctor for the wounded man, the widow had described rather too fully what happened, and the telephone operator called police. George was arrested, taken to jail, and locked up overnight. When the company learned of the escapade, they sent down a representative who, after some difficulty, secured his freedom. The upshot, George reported, was that "I was not only thrown out of the company, I was thrown out of South America."

He returned to England in December 1929 and saw his sister Margaret for the first time in six years. She had just come down with a case of measles, so their visit was a short one, and she left for art school in Vienna shortly afterward. It was Tom who recognized the great difference in their brother. "George had changed," he remembered. "He was much more cosmopolitan than when I had left. He spoke fluent Spanish and he even danced a wicked tango. And since then, he has always gotten out of trouble with the most amazing ease." Both were at loose ends, "so we thought we'd see what we could find in the way of jobs. I was anxious to get started at something," Tom recalled. "George," he added, "drifted into acting."

4 "And Never Looked Forward Since"

George's movement toward acting as a profession might indeed be characterized as drifting. Having returned from South America "in disgrace," as he put it, he was able to find a position after a time and with some difficulty, but it was work far removed from the stage: a "humiliatingly short period" of employment with L.I.N.T.A.S., the advertising branch of Lever Brothers in London. Hired to service various agency accounts, George spent more time socializing with and amusing his fellow workers, one of whom was "a beautiful redhead" named Greer Garson, than attending to the needs of his clients. This inattention to duty did not pass unremarked by his superiors, and after a few months he found himself "unceremoniously thrown out of the company," an experience by this time depressingly familiar. The redheaded young lady, however, belonged to an amateur theatrical group and persuaded George to read for a part in one of its plays.

At this point George's Uncle Sacha, who emigrated to England from St. Petersburg, where he had sung in amateur operatic productions, learned that George was unemployed again and insisted on giving him lessons to train and develop his voice sufficient to take up singing on the stage as a means of livelihood. Six months of study and practice eventually produced what George described as "a fairly deafening baritone"—in fact, a rich and resonant bass-baritone. To the unlikely pair of Uncle Sacha and Greer Garson, then, must go credit for altering George's drifting course, heading him finally in the direction of show business.

One evening in 1932 he was singing and playing the piano at a party where a producer heard him and offered him a job in a revue he was putting together." I promptly accepted," George remarked, "and have never looked forward since." The revue was called *Ballyhoo* and was George's first appearance on a professional stage. He sang and also played as one of a three-piece piano act. Unfortunately, his part required that he sing a song from one of the boxes high up at the back of the theatre, and the distance from the orchestra pit was too far for his sense of pitch. "The result was that I sang the whole song off-key every night to long-suffering audiences and a management less willing to suffer. They finally threw me out of the show," he recalled, adding that "subsequent appearances I have made as a singer were less painful to the audience though hardly any more successful."

Thirty years later he would reflect indirectly on this particular experience: "It is one of the bitter ironies of fate that singers by and large are not gifted with a very keen sense of pitch. There are very few who can read music and fewer still who have what is known as 'perfect' pitch." Of singing generally he observed that "of all the roads to public acclaim in show business the hardest of all and the one that seems to many the easiest, is that of a singer" for "there is no more unreliable instrument than the human voice. After years of training and study, singers develop such a keen appreciation of the subtle fluctuations in tonal quality their voices are capable of undergoing even during the course of a single day that their lives become a veritable torment of uncertainty." Rather than perform publicly, he advised, the trained singer would be wiser to "go on learning and improving and to walk through life with the inner conviction that if one ever did put one's vocal powers to the test it would cause a revolution at the Scala Milan." This in fact would be George's course from 1934 until 1952, when he ignored his own advice and bitterly regretted having done so.

After his failure in *Ballyhoo* he found refuge in the faceless anonymity of radio and spent a year with the BBC acting parts in radio plays, eventually appearing in more than fifty productions, experience he credits with training him in reading lines. At the same time he did nightclub work in London, then ventured onstage again in a 1933 musical called *King's Ransom*, starring Dennis King and Jeanne Aubert, in which he sang a song and played the guitar in his one scene. The show was not a success and closed "before the director really had a chance to throw me out." Nonetheless, he persevered. His first stage appearance in an important production was in Noel Coward's *Conversation Piece*, which opened February 16, 1934. Douglas Fairbanks, Jr., who knew George in London at this time, remembers having seen him in the production: "He was one of a very amusing male quartet singing 'Regency Rakes.'" George actually had two roles in the play, as the Earl of Harringford and Lord St. Marys. A photograph accompanying the London *Daily Telegraph* review of February 17 shows leading lady Yvonne Printemps at center stage, Noel Coward to her left, and George standing far left. After a fairly successful London run, the play was taken to New York, where it languished and soon closed.

On his return to England George was given his first starring role on stage, the male lead opposite Edna Best in *Further Outlook*, which opened October 29, 1935. He played to uniformly good reviews: "The part of Cavanaugh, the young airman, is played by Mr. George Sanders, whose charm and good looks were outstanding in 'Conversation Piece' both in England and America. Women in the audience will be convinced that it is his engaging smile and voice which are responsible for 'Kim's' heartbreak and 'Delia's' extravagant emotion"; and, "George Sanders as the young airman pilots the 'D.O.2' and the emotions of the audience with equal skill and enthusiasm"; and, "Mr. George Sanders has the rather thankless task of making Cavanaugh a hero and manages it skillfully."

Despite such positive reviews, George would not appear on a theatre stage again for over thirty years. "A really good evening in the theatre," he later declared, "an evening when the actor and his audience are in perfect rapport, is mathematically improbable. Consequently, the actor who strives for the ultimate is by and large engaged in a futile quest for the end of the rainbow." He remained active with the BBC, and in 1936 took a leading part in their production of *Black Vengeance*, which one review termed "very well acted, especially by Leon Quartermaine and George Sanders." His first appearance in films, a bit part, was the same year. As he moved from stage and radio performer to screen actor, the drifting ended. At thirty years of age he had found his profession.

The Man Who Could Work Miracles, adapted by H. G. Wells from his imaginative fantasy-comedy, stars Ralph Richardson, Roland Young, and Joan Gardner in the story of a bored group of celestials who decide to give a mild draper's assistant the power to work miracles. George appears only in the film's opening sequence, which required him, as one of the three gods, to ride half-naked and shiny with grease at four in the morning during the cold English winter on a horse also coated with grease. "I was the only one who didn't fall off," he recalled. Torin Thatcher, the god "Observer," and Ivan Brandt as "Player" are the other two greasy deities; the god George plays is named "Indifference." He has three lines to speak, the last of which refers to earth's inhabitants: "What is the good of them?" he demands archly of Player. "Squash them." It was an appropriate beginning to a career of playing roles in a manner that would come to be characterized as "indifferent, remote, and elegantly contemptuous."

George appeared in three other films released in 1936. In *Dishonour Bright*, a romantic comedy of misunderstandings in a divorce case starring Tom Walls and Betty Stockfield, he plays a small part, wearing his first moustache, as Eugene Pallette's assistant. *Find the Lady* has him supporting Jack Melford, Althea Henley, and Viola Compton in a story of two fraudulent American faith-healers who come to work their scheme in England. In *Strange Cargo* he has his first lead, as the son of a captain of an English cargo vessel which mercenaries are using to supply rebels in South America with guns and ammunition hidden in piano crates. George rescues an English girl (Kathleen Kelly) accused of murder, and together they expose the criminals on board and discover that one of them is the real murderer. *The Outsider*, although not released for three years, was filmed in 1936 and provided George another starring vehicle, this time the title role as Dr. Ragatzy, a European osteopath who attempts to cure the crippled daughter (Mary Maguire) of an established London doctor and in the process falls in love with her.

George found filmacting to be rather less demanding and far less threatening than performing in the theatre. "In the movies we do not have to cope with any of the problems of the stage. No ambitious understudy can ever hope to go in our place, and we luxuriate in the knowledge that his talents will never be discovered. We have no problem with audience response because our only audience is the director, who is paid to tell us that we are great." Film directors, he added, "are after all only photographing rehearsals which never have time to become scenes, but since the average audience is incapable of distinguishing between the first reading of a competent actor and what his highly polished performance would be if he worked on it for months, the arrangement seems to me to be quite satisfactory."

By 1936 he had been given a long-term contract with British and Dominion Studio, but when the studio burned to the ground in a disastrous fire, its assets were sold to Twentieth Century-Fox, which also took an option on all of its contracts, George's among them. Coincidentally at this time in Hollywood, Darryl F. Zanuck found himself in desperate need of British actors for his forthcoming production of *Lloyd's of London*. George was brought to California, where he was tested for and given the part of the haughty, imperious, cold-hearted Lord Everett Stacy. It was the role that determined the course and tone of his career and would move one film historian to reflect almost four decades afterward that with George Sanders' first American appearance "a major movie villain was born." George would in time realize that the persona of the elegantly refined villain was "oddly compounded of fact and fantasy," that "sometimes this curious sorcery produced a second man, a sort of sorcerer's apprentice, or marionette, who leads a separate, almost uncontrolled life of his own. Sometimes this marionette or mask is so intoxicating that the wearer becomes reluctant to reveal his less enlivening aspects to the public, and retires, inviolate, securely carapaced from the world by his mask." And, he adds, "sometimes he becomes indistinguishable from the parts he plays."

Hollywood: 1936–1947

5 "A Profound Sense of Unreality"

"I find it so pleasant to be unpleasant," George remarked in an interview after the release of *Lloyd's of London* in November 1936, commenting on his role as the haughty and sinister wastrel Lord Everett Stacy, the first unsympathetic part he had played in his short film career. "You see," he went on to explain, "I think that such roles require greater ability, more finesse, and are truer to life in their characterizations than are the romantic hero parts Hollywood hands out." The interviewer concluded by observing that with this role George Sanders had become "a new villain threat on the cinema horizon."

Although *Lloyd's of London* was George's first American film, the cast was, with the exception of Tyrone Power, almost exclusively British. The picture was an elaborate and ambitious project: there were over one hundred speaking parts, nearly three thousand players were used, and Zanuck's production budget was approximately $500,000. Appropriately, the real Lloyd's of London insured the picture for that amount against possible production delays through illness or injury to cast members or director Henry King. The story, which romanticizes the role played by British financiers in shaping England's history, follows the careers of young Jonathan Blake (Power) and his life-long friend Admiral Horatio Nelson (John Burton), chronicling the rise of English insurance underwriters at Lloyd's coffee house during the late eighteenth century. The romantic complication involves the triangle of Blake, Elizabeth Stacy (Madeleine Carroll), and her husband Lord Everett Stacy (George).

George's first lines in his first American film are directed to Sir Guy Standing, as Lloyd's founder John Angerstein, and they immediately establish the pose and set the tone of his on-screen persona of the elegantly malevolent Cad. Bewigged and attired in period costume of skin-tight breeches, cutaway morning coat with a puffy gathering of lace at the throat, walking stick in one hand and lace kerchief in the other, George purrs: "Permit me to introduce myself, Mr. Angerstein. Stacy of Cranford." Making a supercilious show of taking a pinch of snuff, he announces in a voice ever after characterized as silken, "I've recently come into a sum of money from my grandmother. Far less than I'd expected, I must own, but the old harridan was shamefully extravagant." He proposes to venture the risk of that money, incognito ("I've my name to think of"), in Lloyd's syndicate: "I understand some of you underwriters make preposterous profits." Lloyd's is not a gambling house, an offended Angerstein tells Stacy and quite rightly dismisses him as one of those young aristocrats who despises commerce as beneath his station yet who seeks to profit by it. Stacy exits in a dignified huff. George later sent his sister Margaret a studio publicity pose of himself sneering in full Lord Stacy costume, on the bottom of which he had lightheartedly penciled: "Answer to a maiden's prayer."

He has several more pithy scenes in the film, most of them with Power, and vindictively shoots him in the final one. In addition to creating his image as a villain and cad, *Lloyd's of London* also marked the beginning of a life-long friendship and a continuing on-screen antagonism between George and Tyrone Power. They would subsequently appear together, and oppose each other, in *Love Is News* (1937), *Son of Fury, The Black Swan* (both 1942), and *Solomon and Sheba* (1959), during the filming of which Power died and was replaced by Yul Brynner.

Reviews of George's performance in *Lloyd's of London* were uniformly favorable and indicate the impact of his unique blend of haughty disdain and villainy in the role of Stacy. The New York *Times* singled him out, observing that "the job George Sanders does with the villain of the story is the most entertaining in the film. Mr. Sanders manages to endow his character with more rudeness, heartlessness, foppery, snobbery, and downright hatefulness than we have seen lumped into one heavy in many a moon." *Film Weekly* found him "especially effective as the foppish, spiteful husband, the villain of the piece." When the picture opened in London in April 1937, the reviews were equally enthusiastic about George's performance. The London Sunday *Express:* "A newcomer, George Sanders, plays a nasty dandy with a polish reminiscent of Basil Rathbone"; the Sunday *Times:* "There is a fine study of a rascal by George Sanders"; and the Daily *Telegraph:* "George Sanders plays the villain with menace and a sense of style. We hope to see more of him."

More of George would indeed be seen, and hard upon the heels of this first portrayal of the Cad. Zanuck, quick to take advantage of George's sinister appeal, cast him at once for *Love Is News* with Power, Loretta Young, and Don Ameche. Several days after seeing the rushes of the picture, Zanuck signed George to a long-term contract, and there quickly followed villainous supporting roles in *Slave Ship* (1937), in which he plays a sinister slaver at odds with Wallace Beery and Mickey Rooney, and *The Lady Escapes* (1937), a marital farce which casts him opposite Gloria Stuart as a suave and caddish playboy sued for breach of promise. Even in his first starring role, as Lt. Michael Bruce, the hero of *Lancer Spy* (1937), George was able to nourish his reputation as a villain, as the story calls for him to play a double role: Bruce bears an uncanny resemblance to Baron Kurt von Rohbach, a German officer captured by the English (and also played by George), whom Bruce is called upon to impersonate in Berlin while spying on Prussian aristocrats planning the big push of 1918. This second role gave George the opportunity to make impressive use of his fluency in the German language, and the part became the prototype for a string of Prussian and Nazi characters he would later develop into a specialty of sorts. In presenting George to the public as one of its new stars, the studio appended the following announcement to the end-credits of *Lancer Spy*: "This picture has introduced to you a new Twentieth Century-Fox screen personality, Mr. George Sanders."

Between 1936 and 1937 George was making important contacts as well as significant career strides. In August 1936, Mary Pickford gave him a letter of introduction to producer Walter Wanger, writing in a cover letter to George that "I have told him what splendid picture possibilities I believe you possess." George's star was on the rise, yet his diffidence and sense of detachment limited what was expected of him in the way of self-promotion. As he would reflect decades later, "I had had since the beginning a profound sense of unreality about my newly acquired profession which the atmosphere of Hollywood did nothing to dispel." It was a perception that would never entirely leave him.

He led a quiet, almost reclusive life, refusing to seek publicity or notoriety by haunting night clubs or dating a succession of starlets. Fox, notorious for promoting "romances" among its stars, made strenuous efforts to couple George romantically with a number of actresses on the Zanuck lot at the time: Alice Faye, Sonja Henie, Loretta Young, and Virginia Field were among the candidates. "I don't like night clubs," George protested, "and I don't like women. They bore me." He refused to allow what private engagements he did have to be used for publicity purposes. He was in fact involved at this time in a love affair with Dolores Del Rio, his costar in *Lancer Spy*, though few in Hollywood knew details of it, and he maintained the relationship for some time. "He used to ring her up from Leatherhead quite often" when visiting home in England, his sister Margaret remembers. "He called her 'Sorrows of the River.' "

To ensure his privacy, George took a cottage in the Hollywood hills on a street named, appropriately, Hermit's Glen. "Why should I stay up most of the night at clubs and be weary for a week when I can sail my sloop out into the Pacific or read a good book?" His circle of friends was small, and he once estimated their number at about six or eight. "I suppose one should really go around making new friends, but there's nothing wrong with the ones I already have. Anyhow," he added facetiously, "I only have eight chairs in my dining room." He submitted to occasional interviews by the Hollywood press corps, but his manner intimidated and alienated reporters. In 1943 the Woman's Press Club would vote him the year's "most uncooperative actor."

In 1938 he made two more pictures for Zanuck, *Four Men and a Prayer*, directed by John Ford and starring Loretta Young and Richard Greene, and *International Settlement*, once again opposite Dolores Del Rio. The next year was one of his most productive, beginning with the release of *Mr. Moto's Last Warning*, with Peter Lorre and Ricardo Cortez, and *So This Is London*, with Alfred Drayton and Fay Compton. Despite Fox's publicity build-up of George as one of their new stars, the studio lent him out to RKO in 1939 to play Leslie Charteris' sophisticated adventurer, "The Saint." Reflecting on that series in a 1951 interview, George called it "the nadir of my career," adding that "the titles of some of the pictures I made during that era will give you a notion of how repulsive they were: *The Saint in London, The Saint Takes Over, The Saint in Palm Springs, The Saint Fights [Strikes] Back.*"

Whatever George's reservations and opinion of the series, moviegoers loved him as The Saint and film historians of the genre today agree that "his sophisticated personality made him ideal for the role." The series also proved a profitable one for RKO. Charteris' *Saint* books had achieved an international audience by the mid-1930s, and RKO bought the rights and cast Louis Hayward in the first picture, *The Saint in New York* (1938). George took over the role from an unconvincing Hayward, who was better at playing weaklings and semi-villains, and made the next five films in the series.

His first Saint picture was *The Saint Strikes Back* (1939), based on Charteris' novel *Angels of Doom*, costarring Wendy Barrie and directed by John Farrow. It provided good mystery entertainment and guaranteed the return of the character to the screen. *The Saint in London,* also 1939, co-starred Sally Gray as a society girl enamored of Templar and drawn into an international currency fraud. This entry, shot in England, features a strong British cast. In *The Saint's Double Trouble* (1940) George again plays a double role in a story built around the striking resemblance between Simon Templar and "The Dutchman," a jewel thief. In one scene George The Saint, impersonating George The Dutchman, confronts George The Dutchman, who is impersonating George The Saint. Complete confusion was avoided by the RKO makeup department, which altered George's nose, chin, and hairline to give him a rougher and more sinister appearance as the villainous Dutchman. Both *The Saint Takes Over* (1940) and *The Saint in Palm Springs* (1941) bring back Wendy Barrie to costar, with returning supporting actors Jonathan Hale and Paul Guilfoyle (as Pearly Gates).

By this time, the series was so popular and George so identified in the public mind with the role that on the occasion of his presenting a plaque at an awards luncheon in Los Angeles, he was called upon by the assembled group to give them "the Saint's whistle," the melody Simon Templar whistles over the opening credits of each film and which one reporter in 1940 termed "almost as famous as Tarzan's yell." It was an embarrassing moment for George, who could not whistle very well and in any case would have been unable to give a true rendering, since that particular bit of business was done by someone else and dubbed at the studio.

The series ended over a dispute between RKO and Charteris, who grew dissatisfied with the Saint's screen exploits in plots only remotely related to the author's storylines. RKO then created a new hero named The Falcon, based on Michael Arlen's story "Gay Falcon," and George played the title role in the first four *Falcon* films. "I appeared in a series called *The Falcon*, built around *The Saint* character," George reflected some years later, "and nibbled my way through such hunks of film cheese as *The Gay Falcon, A Date With the Falcon, The Falcon Takes Over.*" The new series was indeed essentially the same as its predecessor, even to the extent of using *Saint* costar Wendy Barrie in the first two *Falcon* films. The similarity did not go unremarked by Charteris, who sued RKO and won an out-of-court settlement.

Of the films in the series that George made—*The Gay Falcon* (1941), *A Date With the Falcon* (1941), *The Falcon Takes Over* (1942) and *The Falcon's Brother* (1942)—only the last two are of any real interest, and for reasons outside the stories themselves. *The Falcon Takes Over* draws its plot from Raymond Chandler's *Farewell, My Lovely* and stands as the first filmed version of that novel. It costars Lynn Bari and features Ward Bond as "Moose Malloy." (Two years later the better-known remake, *Murder, My Sweet,* with Dick Powell as Philip Marlowe, was released.) At this point George, intolerably weary of the series, wanted out. RKO offered to contract for his brother Tom, whom George had earlier brought over from England and who had changed his last name to Conway, to take over the role. This was effected in *The Falcon's Brother*, wherein The Falcon (George) is called upon to investigate the disappearance of his brother Tom Lawrence (Tom). At the end The Falcon is killed by Nazi agents, and the role is consequently passed to Tom.

As would later be revealed, RKO wrote in Tom's part to persuade a balking George to do one last film in the series. According to producer Maurice Geraghty, "They gave George a glowing picture of how it would make a star out of his brother, but they had no such plans or hopes." The studio was, in fact, astonished when Tom was an immediate success and carried the series forward, even outgrossing the pictures George had made. Tom starred in nine of the remaining Falcon films, his last series role coming in 1946.

Owing to George's screen identification with detectives and mysteries and in order to provide increased publicity for a rising studio star, it was determined in the early 1940s that he should acquire a reputation as a writer of mystery novels. "Murder on a George Sanders set!" reads the blurb for *Crime on My Hands*, a title in Simon & Schuster's Inner Sanctum Series published in 1944. A condensation was serialized in the November and December issues of *Photoplay* magazine the same year. "In the midst of a shooting scene," as the premise summary recounts, "the star discovers an extra, Severance Flynne, lying dead, shot through the head with a .38. Since everyone else in the scene was carrying .45s except Sanders, who carried a .38, George decides, for the time being, to keep this information to himself while he seeks to trap the murderer." The author: none other than George Sanders himself. This book was followed in 1946 by another entitled *Stranger at Home*, also credited to

George. The attributions were widely believed at the time, few readers bothering to wonder how George might have found time to write two full-length novels during one of the busiest periods in his film career (between 1943 and 1945 he made eleven pictures, with lead roles in eight) or to consider the likelihood of his putting into his own mouth as a character such slang-ridden locutions as "Wanda, you're messing around in a dangerous situation. Why did you send out those phony stories?" or "I think I'll cinch it tonight. Your telegram tipped me to the identity of Lord Hake."

In any case, five years after publication of the second novel, George revealed the actual provenance of both books when responding to an interviewer's question about the publicity and reviews they had received. "Actually, old boy," George confessed, "I've never read them. They were written for me by some ingenious scrivener or other." This revelation apparently went unnoticed by the producers of The Unholy Four, a 1954 film which credits George Sanders for the original story, Stranger at Home, on which the screenplay is based.

Simon & Schuster will today neither confirm nor deny that the novels were ghostwritten, responding that the only information available is that the publishing contract "is signed by George Sanders" and that the books were "copyrighted in his name." George's sister Margaret, however, does "know for a fact that Stranger at Home was composed by a ghostwriter," for a copy of the book was sent to her by the person who wrote it, and she quite logically assumes that Crime on My Hands was also ghostwritten.

Cad, villain, spy, detective, "author": the initial years of George's Hollywood life and film career would prove crucial in reshaping his image and personality off-screen as well as on: the introspective, insecure, and reclusive resident of Hermit's Glen and the suave, disdainful, silken-tongued persona of the early films. Those two "lives," having begun on parallel courses but gradually narrowing under the pressures and "curious sorcery" of his life, were beginning to converge. Ultimately they would merge and he would withdraw, inviolate and securely carapaced from the world by his mask, indistinguishable from the parts he played.

6 "In the Strictest Confidence"

Considerable insight into George's state of mind as well as evolving personal values during his early and formative Hollywood years can be drawn from the manuscript journal he kept between 1937 and 1938. Ostensibly in the form of an extended letter to his father Henry ("To Dad," the prefatory page reads, "in the strictest confidence"), the journal consists of 270 numbered pages on 135 leaves of 6-by-10-inch heavy-weight scrapbook paper, hand-bound by George in thick red and blue cardboard covers with end papers. Written over a period of eight months, the journal ranges widely in both subject matter and tone, concluding with the observation that "I set out with the intention of making this letter funny, but as I was in a different mood every time I attacked it, the result I fear is incredibly unfunny."

The first section is concerned largely with money matters. Having achieved some success in films and the prospect of a much improved financial situation, George had begun to grow wary of being cheated or taken advantage of. His tight-fisted-ness during these early years would become legendary in the Hollywood colony and in retrospect serves as a gauge of his later compulsiveness in attempting to secure wealth enough to insulate him from the insecurity and sense of inadequacy acquired during his youth in England.

"It is evident that Mssrs. Hawes & Curtis have made another of their 'book-keeping errors' as there is no item in my wardrobe that could possibly be described as a dinner jacket," he complains on the very first page of his journal, referring to a bill forwarded to him from an English tailor. "When they first sent me this bill they included an additional item on it, a 'lounge suit' making the total in all about £30. I ignored this bill just as I have steadfastly ignored the many charity appeals, begging letters, & optimistic notes from racketeers that clutter up my mailbox every day. Mind you, I do not blame Hawes & Curtis for trying this stunt. After all they have made a good deal of money out of me in the past, and now that my orders have stopped perhaps they are not altogether unjustified in assuming that with the aid of a skilled accountant they might continue to make money out of me without bothering to send goods along with their bills." He then indulges a fantasy: "One of my favourite reveries is the idea of forming an institution from which you send out bills to people all over the world and then sue them when they don't pay. You get a commission from the lawyers your unfortunate victims employ to defend their cases. Most people are so timid or so jealous of their reputation that they would stump up without a murmur."

He concludes by asking that his mother be advised not to readdress and foward to him "advertisements or any letters that look as though they might contain charity appeals or other forms of graft without first reading them (I do not want to hear any more from British Equity), as the local mail I have to deal with is sufficiently voluminous without the intrusion of overseas whatnot."

It is the seeming instability and unpredictability of his profession that arouses some of his deepest concerns. "Getting ready for a picture is an odd sensation," he confesses. "You always wonder if it's going to be your last. Nobody knows how long their luck is going to hold up in this town. Some people stay on top for years, others never get there, and some get to the top and fall down to the bottom almost immediately. Even in the short time I have been here I have seen a few people come and go." He then returns to a familiar theme: "I sometimes wonder if it's worthwhile trying to get on top if all one's savings are going to be taken away by the government. High taxation is nothing more or less than a practical application of the communist theory. Everybody gets levelled out. When you add to the various federal & state taxes the commissions and what-not that are filched from your paycheck by parasites of the industry—Motion Picture Relief funds, Community Chests, Agents, Insurance—added again to the compulsory expenses such as wardrobe, transport, premieres, etc. you are finally left with a couple of half-pennies to jingle on a tombstone. I have an awful feeling that I shall be faced with the realization that I might just as well have saved myself the trouble and sat on my backside in Leatherhead all the time."

George was also dismayed to find early on that "the amount of intrigue involved in the social life here is often so tiresome, the amount of restraint, diplomacy, and bum-sucking that has to be done so nauseating, that there are times one asks oneself the question 'Is Success worth the price you pay for it?' This is a question I hope to answer in a few years." Over time— although measured in decades rather than years—he would have his answer. For the present, however, much of what he writes here seems intended less for his father than as a therapeutic working out of some of his own philosophical foundations. Developing a variation on the theme he had formulated during his years in the Argentine, he proposes that "a period of happiness can only be experienced by comparison with a cor-responding period of misery. The more intense the pain, the more exhilarating its subsequent alleviation." Yet, he decides,

"Peace of Mind, which can be won through the conquest of worry, is a thing of far greater worth than the sort of exultant happiness that must sooner or later be paid for in the hard currency of sorrow."

Anticpating a judgment he will validate almost three decades later by the experience of losing everything in a disastrous financial venture, George writes, "people who have absolutely no money at all worry less than those who have stacks of it, for to lose what you have furnishes the prospect of a positive blow; to lose what you have not, or have failed to acquire, offers purely a negative prospect." The hard realities of life intrude, however, when he observes that "One thing I know—I have never encountered a single obstacle that a sufficient quantity of money could not have overcome. I have never been faced with a problem that money could not have solved." This was a view he would hold until the last year of his life. Nonetheless, he is always generous concerning the welfare of his immediate family. "You went on my pay-roll at the beginning of the year at £20 a week," he writes his father. "I hope this money will be a help to you and that it may bring you a small measure of that Peace of Mind upon which I became so verbose."

George was also continuing his efforts to get his brother Tom into the motion picture business in England, with an eye to eventually coming to Hollywood. In offering advice regarding strategies for "breaking into pictures" he relates much of his own experience and in so doing reveals many of his otherwise unspoken attitudes about the profession he has chosen for himself.

"I got William Burnside & David Selznick to arrange with Alexander Korda to make a test of Tom in England if he (David) likes Tom's pictures. The kind of pictures he should send are ten by eight glossy prints of all face angles in big heads and some good unconventional poses in medium and long shots. It should be understood that Tom's *likeness* is not the thing we are after. Nobody is interested in what Tom looks like really. What Selznick wants to know is how he can be *photographed* and what sort of personality emanates from his picture. It's all a lot of crap of course, but it has to be done. If I succeed in selling David Selznick on the photographs, and the test is made, I will get the very best director for Tom—W.K. Howard has already agreed to direct the test. The fact that he has made an unsuccessful test before should not depress Tom. I have made plenty of unsuccessful tests, and so has everybody else in the business. And the fact that they said Tom didn't photograph well should be no cause for alarm since they said precisely the same thing to Ronald Colman." As for strategy ("I refer of course to subtleties and not to such practices as jumping into Producers' cars and trying to rub them up the right way—incidentally, jumping into Producers' beds and trying to rub them up the right way has been found to be infinitely more effective)," George confides that he has "been spared the more arduous forms of intrigue, as generally speaking I can sling the bull-shit faster than the other guy. But of course I'm knocking wood and hoping my luck will hold. The problem that has to be solved when you are under contract to a studio is to get the parts. It is an established fact beyond dispute that three or four bad parts in a row will ruin any actor's career. Now, good parts, which go towards bigger money and greater popularity, occur only at rare intervals. Bad parts occur all the time. Almost everybody eligible for the bad parts is eligible for the good. So whoever wins, wins, and whoever loses, loses, if you seen what I mean.

". . . Preparations for my next picture *Shanghai Deadline* [released as *International Settlement* in 1938 and not a 'good part' for George] are still in what I might call the pre-'Hell Let's Shoot It' stage, and consequently there are numerous story conferences at which tremendous attention to the minutest detail of dialogue & characterisation is paid by all concerned,

49

and advance scripts marked 'Revised Temporary Final' are issued to the principals. It never pays, however, to *read* these
scripts as the entire story is invariably rewritten on the set, the
dialogue improvised by the players, and the characterisations
remoulded by the Director in accordance with his day-to-day
moods, whims, & fancies. When the picture is finished most of
the scenes are retaken, and when these retakes are cut into the
picture it is trimmed, which means that most of your best lines
are cut. Then they find they have run over-footage and have to
take large chunks out of a picture now lacerated to a point
where the continuity is affected.

". . . Upon being cast in a part, you are called to the studio
for a totally unnecessary and incredibly boring interview with
the Producer (in the world of the theatre the words Producer &
Director are synonymous, but in the film-business the Director
is the fellow who directs the picture and his status is that of an
artist, whereas the Producer is the big-shot but his real function, outside of prodigious cigar-smoking, has never been discovered). The scene that takes place in the Producer's office
follows a set routine, something like this:

"You go in—you are offered a cigar—you accept with
alacrity, surprise, & gratitude, struggling for mastery in the
expression of your face, then boyishly, with a perfectly charming grin, you ask if you may smoke it later. You are offered a
chair—the chair looks comfortable, but you perch on the edge
of it, timorously, as would a maiden about to receive the favour
of her sovereign. Then after an impressive amount of throat-
clearing, coughing, spitting & belching on the part of the
Producer, the peroration begins. You listen to endless scenes
that won't even survive the 'Revised' stage let alone the 'Revised
Temporary Final' nonsense and to dialogue that is destined at
best for the cutting-room floor. Then just as your head is
beginning to nod, you suddenly realise that the whole thing is

over and you become alert again in order to take part in the following dialogue which invariably ensues:

The Producer (with the air of one about to receive the compliment of a lifetime): "Well, what do you think of the story?"

You (in accordance with the best rules of diplomacy, committing yourself to nothing except emphasis): "What do I think of the STORY???!!!!!"

The Producer (with a chuckle): "I knew you'd like it."

You (trying to get as many expressions as possible into your face at the same time): OH, MR. WURLZELHEIMER!!!!!!!

You leave, not altogether unimpressed with the proceedings. After all, you feel somebody has probably struck a blow for something or other, and that the whole thing is calculated to promote better understanding between Producer and Produced, and that at least it provides the former with the salutary if erroneous illusion that he is working for a living."

In early 1938 George reiterated his advice that Tom delay coming to Hollywood until he had secured a foothold in the English picture business. "I think it is terribly important for him to make a determined effort over a good trial period of say 6 months to get into British Pictures in however small a way, so that when he finally comes out here he will feel confident of his powers, be able to say that he has Motion Picture Experience, & show stills as proof." As a consequence, a significant portion of the journal is devoted to advice for Tom with that goal in mind and is in fact gathered under a heading, *How to Get into British Pictures.*

". . . Some years ago I made a picture for Fox-British at Wembley entitled *Find the Lady* [it begins]. If you ever have the misfortune to see this picture you will understand why the

51

Production Manager of the studio, Mr. Gartside (remember this name, it's important), raised strenuous objections to the connivance between the Casting Director (my good friend Mr. Burnside) & my London agent Bill O'Bryen in suggesting as inexperienced a player as myself for the leading role. The wrath of Mr. Gartside knew no bounds, however, when as a trump-card in my favour somebody made the tactless though extremely logical remark, 'You make lousy pictures, so you might just as well have lousy people in them.' But the fight was won despite the opposition of Gartside, as history has proved. I got the part. My performance in it justified Gartside's worst fears. But it was a toss-up as to which was worse—my performance or the picture. What has all this to do with Tom you say? Wait.

"Father Time, conqueror of all things, has changed the flavour of Gartside's utterances. For while Burnside is now a big shot in the Selznik outfit, and I am a big shot in the acting racket, and Bill O'Bryen is a big-shot in the agency field, Gartside is still turning out lousy pictures for Fox-British. And now it has come to my ears that Mr. Gartside has been seeking to gain stature in that company by claiming the credit of *discovering me*. Here therefore is one avenue which might lead to a break in British pictures."

What follows demonstrates the extent to which George's early Hollywood experiences had engendered in him a profound cynicism about not only the picture business but human nature—and a willingness to encourage duplicity and dissembling.

"... Tom should pay a social call on Gartside one afternoon [he advises] and say he was just passing the studio and thought he'd drop in—say he is my brother and a great pal of Sam Engel's (who is Gartside's superior of course). The visit should be purely social, and Tom shouldn't talk about himself at all but manifest a tremendous interest in Gartside, telling him how highly I have always spoken of him and that I feel that *he* was really the person who discovered me for pictures, and what a bulwark of the industry I feel him to be. Try to give Gartside the impression that I go about Hollywood saying nice things about him. Never a word about a job of course, and if pressed for details about his own affairs Tom should say that, while he is of course an actor by profession himself, he gave up acting a couple of years ago to attend to the family business but he is thinking of taking it up again, that he had an offer from the Selznick International outfit some time ago and that he will probably make a trip out to Hollywood to stay with me and look up some friends etc., and discuss the possibility of working in pictures for Selznick. All very casual and matter of fact, you understand.

". . . Never a word about *work*. Never talk to anybody in this world about what *you* need. Nobody cares a hang what *you* need. People are only interested in what they need *themselves*. But let them once get the idea that perhaps if they do something for you they might indirectly further their own interests, *then* of their own volition they will offer you on a silver salver the very thing you want. Getting a job is not a question of going to a prospective employer and standing before him, hat in hand, and humbly saying to him, 'Please sir, I need work, my wife and children are starving.' Why should he give you any work? What the hell does he care about your family? But give him the impression that you *don't* need work, that you've something up your sleeve, that you are a friend of so and so, that your services are not easily acquired but that if they are they might redound in profit of some kind to the acquirer—you may confidently expect a different result. It has taken me fifteen years to find this out, but some people *never* find it out and spend their lives in bitter complaint. If at school we were taught a little less about the proper way to conjugate Latin verbs and a little more about the art of human relations, there might be fewer disappointments in this world . . ."

In an apparent reflection on his own family's financial problems after the Revolution, George laments, "Classical study was all very well in the days when every father had a business for his son to go into. But nowadays when the thing is just one big fight it would be just as well to know *how* to fight instead of being obliged to get into the ring untrained, take all sorts of punishment from the more experienced fighters, and try to figure out which fist to use and when to use it before you get completely punch-drunk and go reeling about the ring for the rest of your life." Having offered Tom these reflections on the world-as-prize-ring, George returns to the campaign to get him into British films.

". . . Tom should then call on Lionel Barton at Denham. Lionel Barton is Casting Director for Tom Walls, but before he got this job he was an independent theatrical producer and it was he who put me in *Ballyhoo*. It was also he who cast me in the Walls picture *Dishonour Bright*. So you can well imagine how he would lap it up if Tom tells him that I am always talking about him as my 'discoverer' and how terribly clever and kind I think he is. Tom will have no difficulty in getting in to see these people if he says he is my brother and that he wishes to see them on my behalf. And their reserve will soon thaw when they realise he doesn't *want* anything except the opportunity to pay them compliments. The line to take with Barton is exactly the same as with everyone else—compliments, flattery, tremendously deep gratitude, admiration, and genuine interest. Above all an earnest desire to win his friendship and that of anyone else who may be knocking about the office or studio.

". . . Tom should next call on Lawrence Huntington (Director), a letter from whom follows. He should call on him to return on my behalf the scripts he sent me to read, which I think are absolute bilge but this is of course between ourselves, and tell him that I think they are simply marvelous and that I fought like hell to get the studio to let me do *Trap* [one of two screenplays Huntington sent George in January of 1938 in hopes of getting them produced in Hollywood; the other was titled *Jazz Doctor*] because in addition to my own liking for the story, I have such tremendous faith in Lawrence Huntington's judgment ever since he directed my picture *Strange Cargo* and that I feel that *he* and he alone 'discovered' me. Now then, these are all people to make friends of and through them make other friends in the industry. Then comes the Final Step.

". . . After spending plenty of time and money making friends in the industry, Tom should go and see Bill O'Bryen—again as the family ambassador, again the same line—flattery, compliments, lay great stress on my tremendous admiration for him, that it was *he* who discovered me, how clever and kind he is etc., and then only after persuasion from Bill admit he would like to work in pictures but only if he could be represented by such an able man as Bill O'Bryen etc. Now then, when Bill goes out to make the thrust and *sell* Tom, he will meet an industry that is more than receptive to the name of Tom Sanders, who will be glad to consider him for this or that part, who will sit up and take notice also because his brother in Hollywood can do them some good. And thus the magic process of getting a break in pictures will have been accomplished . . ."

Directly to his father George advises, "If you want to back Tom in pictures you must be prepared to spend time & money. You may remember that the profits I made out of *Conversation Piece* I invested in clothes. The profits I made in British pictures went towards financing the Hollywood venture, and only now after 6 years sowing am I beginning to reap. It should not take Tom anything like as long of course, because my career was all pioneer work. I hadn't the faintest idea how to go about anything. I was faced on all sides by actors with 20 years experience, considerable looks & ability, but starving. It took me a long time, to be precise some 15 years since I first started thinking about success, to figure out just *why* they were starving. Tom can profit by my mistakes.

"It is true that British pictures are in a hell of a mess and that there is not much doing, and that any company may fold up at any moment. But a certain amount of work is still available, and out of the thousands of people who are after that work, Tom must be the one to get it. If there are thousands after it in England, there are millions after it in Hollywood, and to come out here without any experience at the game at all, without any knowledge of the business side of it, and without any practice in the sort of studied insincerity that is a concomitant, is to handicap yourself for the *real* chance that Hollywood offers.

". . . As I said before, it will require finance. If you thought it worthwhile to invest £2000 in a business that at best could produce £1000 a *year,* would it not be worthwhile to invest £100 in a business that has been known to produce as much as £6000 a *week* (Constance Bennett in her prime got this). If you *push* and I *pull,* we might get somewhere. It is true that the picture business is speculative. It is true that film stars are the target for rackets of all descriptions. Film actors have the reputation of being fabulously wealthy, which of course is only true in some cases but the credit goes to all, and they are therefore regarded as an easy 'touch.' Incidentally, you had all better be careful what you do because if people find out you are related to a film actor, you too will become the target for charity appeals & rackets. But the picture business taken by and large is about the only business which offers returns that are quick enough to overcome the economic depression we have been suffering from since the Revolution before we all go to the grave. If Tom gets in on it and my luck holds, it is possible that we may all be able to have some fun together before the undertaker gets his first order."

As to the nature of the financial investment required for

Tom to have a chance to "get in on it," George is quite specific. "I suggest that Tom gets one good suit, one very nice tailored shirt, one nice tie, one pair of smart shoes (brown brogues) and wear this outfit to *all* the interviews. Margaret must choose all materials, in fact she must choose the whole caboodle in order to make sure all colours blend, etc. There must be no back-chat from anyone, least of all from Tom and you. Mother has a pretty good idea, but Margaret definitely *knows*. The tailor to go to is Leslie & Roberts of Hanover Square. The suit must not cost *less* than 14 guineas and the shirt, which should be tailored at Izod's Conduit Street, not less than two guineas. The tie may be obtained there too, or else at Hawes & Curtis. The tie must not cost less than 10/6. The final effect must not be too *townified* for the purpose for which the outfit is designed. A quiet (plain) Scotch tweed (but not a Glen-Urquhart check) is the thing to steer for. We are striving for an air of prosperity but not a townified prosperity suggestive of importunity (a sort of 'Have got to be at a cocktail party in ten minutes' effect), nor yet the other extreme—too much the retired gentleman farmer—but a point midway between. A gay prosperity, a sort of 'Just got back from St. Moritz' feeling and an 'I've got all the time in the world to sit here and chat with you' effect. I cannot stress too heavily the importance of achieving this effect, for if you don't achieve it none of Tom's interviews will ring true (Look Rich and You'll Get Rich)."

Despite all George's detailed advice and the suggested strategems designed to enable his brother to "break into the picture business," Tom did not get into pictures in Britain. Instead, he changed his name to Conway and began on the English stage, finding some repertory and then radio work, after which George brought him to Hollywood in 1940. His first film, *Sky Murder*, was released that year. He had an active if not distinguished career but was always overshadowed by George; both men were tall, suave, and handsome but Tom possessed much less personal style, wit, or charm. His leading roles in the "Falcon" series (1942–1946) proved a barrier to real success in Hollywood, for he was never able to break out of the detective stereotype. When the series ended, he played Bulldog Drummond for Fox, then appeared as detective Mark Sabre in the television series of the early fifties. As he aged and found it increasingly difficult to land parts, he began drinking heavily. As a consequence of Tom's alcoholism, he and George became estranged; in 1965, when his brother was discovered sick and destitute in a rundown Los Angeles hotel, George was unaware of his situation. Two years later Tom died of liver disease.

George also encouraged his sister Margaret to develop her talent as a singer, and a part of his journal offers advice to that end, again by way of their father and drawing on his own experiences. ". . . The news of Margaret's progress as a songstress is indeed gratifying. As soon as she acquires sufficient confidence I can easily get her an audition with C.B. Cochran. Whatever she plans to do with her voice, whether she plans to be a concert platform artist or an opera singer, or just sing at private parties for a fee, there is no better training ground than the chorus of the London theatre. I have been trying to sell you this idea for ages, but I know that you have prejudices left over from the days when chorus girls were prostitutes. The thing is definitely on a different basis nowadays. The profession of a chorister is a perfectly honourable one, and as a matter of fact it is about the cleanest side of the business. After all, if Winston Churchill had no objection to his daughter becoming a chorus girl, I see no valid reason why you should have to yours.

"If Margaret's voice is really good, Cochran will put her on to understudy the leading lady, and this is invaluable experience. The chorus also provides one with an opportunity to walk about a stage in front of a large, critical audience without the feeling that they are all looking at you (because you know damned well that they are looking at the leading lady) and without the sense of responsibility carried by the principals. Then you can begin to shoulder that responsibility by degrees and get used to the idea of being looked at. But if you try to get there all at once you'll do what I did in *Ballyhoo* and have to start again at the bottom just the same. I know that Sasha disapproves of chorus work on the grounds that it is a strain on the voice. But here again he is going back twenty years to operatic chorus work when every member of the chorus took his work seriously and tried to shout louder than the fellow next to him in an effort to be spotted by the director and perhaps be singled out for a principal part in the next performance. Modern musical comedy conditions, however, are vastly different. The chorus is only used four or five times during the whole performance—the rest of the time they sit in their dressing rooms and knit. When they *are* called to the stage they only appear for about five minutes at a time, and whatever they have to sing is frightfully easy. When you are tired you just move your lips and pretend to sing.

"But there is one very strong recommendation that I would like to make if Margaret starts to work in the theatre—she must not live in London. Her earnings would only be between £4 and £7.10 a week according to whether she had any lines to speak, or if she were put on to understudy anybody. Now then—this is not enough money to live on in London. I arrived at this amazing truth after years of nerve-shattering experimentation, as indeed I have had to arrive at most of the other things I know. She must get a cheap car and a chauffeur just like I did, and she will live in great comfort in Leatherhead and end up saving money. London is chock full of fancy restaurants, theatres & places of entertainment from all of which you are barred by an empty pocket—a fact which, whether you admit it or not, affects your sense of importance. We are taught to want things. The further you bury yourself in the country the fewer your needs. Leatherhead is not really country, but it is as close to it as you can get without hampering money-making efforts."

What follows, however, seems to derive less from financial considerations than a brotherly concern that Margaret remain at home in Leatherhead rather than live in a fast-paced metropolitan environment with its attendant perils for young, naive girls. George's experiences as a London theatre actor and man-about-town would have provided him reason enough to counsel against her moving to the city. "Most of the chorus girls live out of town, usually with their families, in much the same circumstances as Margaret's. The thing is perfectly feasible. It becomes rather a nuisance during rehearsals but after that it's plain sailing, particularly if she has a car. Most of the girls have trains to catch and if they are kept rehearsing after midnight, the Company is obliged by law to send them all the way home in taxis. But if Margaret has a car she can do the thing in great comfort. So let our motto for the time be—Live in the country and like it." Nothing ever came of Margaret's singing, however, for she subsequently met and married Ernst Bloecker, removed to Germany, and began raising a family. George's overprotective fears for her proved unwarranted.

Throughout the journal George returns time and again to the subject of money and success. "Money in its present form is the principal factor of our life, but if it is to change its form what other factor can usurp its position? It seems to me that the formula for success must always be the same—skill at games. Skill at the game of influencing people. Skill at the game of winning influential friends. Count up on your fingers the number of influential friends you have made yourself and upon whom you can rely to help you in time of need, and you know the extent of your intrinsic wealth. Money alone cannot be regarded as an accurate measure of security, since we have to depend upon the manipulative skill of insincere custodians into whose keeping we are obliged to entrust it for its proper management and care. Yesterday's savings should only be regarded as a measure of yesterday's skill. It is the skill of today that promotes the security of tomorrow. Political friendships, properly cemented, are not susceptible to stockmarket fluctuations, nor to fire, nor to theft, nor to acts of God, nor to economic disaster and are therefore a more solid indication of wealth than any other." In a metaphoric turn, George embroiders this theme: "Let's make friends with those who seek to overthrow our world so as to insure the reservation of ring-side seats for ourselves in the New World they'll create—and employ such skill as we may possess to consolidate friendships already made in case the Reformists score a miss. In short, let's run with the hare and hunt with the hounds."

To be sure, the journal is not all ruminations on economics or politics. George contemplates, for example, living aboard a boat. "For many months I have been considering the Pros and Cons of living afloat. An article which appeared in the press to the effect that I had purchased a houseboat and was living on it at Huntington was not founded in fact but in the fertile recesses of the publicity department. There is no smoke without a fire, however, and I am bound to admit that the idea in its original form came from me. The harbour of Santa Monica is closer to the studio than my personal abode. A radio-telephone can be installed on a boat for as little as $250—an efficient ship-to-shore service connecting you with any number you want at little extra cost. To live in a $5000 house is as dull as hell. To live in a $5000 boat is exciting. Living in a $5000 house means going *out* to have fun. Living in a $5000 boat means staying *in* to have fun. The thing that interests me most of all about the idea is that if the civilized world suddenly turns upside down, I can just up anchor and sail away to the South Seas (where I would perish of course). Another factor that influences me considerably is that Southern California is a yachtsman's paradise. So much for the Pros. Now for the Cons," he begins but then breaks off with, "Well, they're just a bore anyway." Within a few months of writing this he purchased a sloop and began living aboard it at Santa Monica harbor.

Given the love of Latin America he had acquired in the Argentine and his fluency in Spanish, it was natural that George's vacations would take him south into Mexico, trips he viewed as salutary retreats from the often depressing demands of life in Los Angeles. "I spent Christmas in Mexico on a quail hunting expedition," he writes, "reasonably free from the excessive consumption of alcohol that is involved in the Yuletide festivities of Beverly Hills. I found the atmosphere of Mexico a welcome change, a change that I needed. It was sleepy and dirty and delightfully free from the aura of ambition that Hollywood exudes from its every pore. At Ensenada—a fashionable bathing resort further down the Mexican coast—I sat on a cliff, a blade of grass between my teeth, and watched for the first time in my life the Christmas celebration of some killer whales that had found a playground in the calm waters of the bay. It was an impressive sight, and it led me to ruminate upon the helplessness of man without his mechanical devices. How easily can a man overpower and capture the largest denizens of the deep if he has the proper equipment. How helpless his task if he has not. I feel that gadgets, tools, & weezes must ever be the yardstick of human progress.

"I ate my Christmas dinner at the Rosarita Country Club and then went into the patio and joined the Mexican farmers and their wives, who had ridden in for the festivities, in country dances and guitar playing, and of course over-acting my part dreadfully, becoming more Mexican than any Mexican had ever been, but having a hell of a lot of fun in the process. I spent days lying on the beach in the sun and never even started to shoot the quail that everybody else was shooting. After all, if you want game you can save yourself the trouble of shooting it by going into a shop and buying it, but you cannot buy memories as easily."

These excursions and the memories they inspired—the trips to Mexico and Coronado or to Catalina Island on his boat—were but brief respites, and having to return seemed always to depress George: "Back in Hollywood again," he writes after one such return. "Back among the rackets, the bullshit, the sham." Yet that was where and how he earned his living. Hollywood was also where he would soon meet the first of his four wives.

7 "Women Are Strange Little Beasts"

In one of his first Hollywood magazine interviews, given early in 1938, shortly after the release of *Lancer Spy*, George was asked to list the attributes he would expect in an ideal wife. Prefacing his reply with a cautionary "it's a pity for a man to marry too soon" (the piece was titled "Ten Ways to Avoid Matrimony"), he answered that his ideal mate would have to be "a demure creature, red-haired, who plays a good game of golf." The woman he took two years later as his bride was neither a redhead nor a golfer, but she was demure to the point of insignificance. This was George's first marriage, which his family and close friends knew of but which was kept secret from the press and public.

The secrecy in part owed to George's long-standing insistence on keeping his personal affairs away from public scrutiny. Notorious among Hollywood columnists as a difficult interview, he would curtly change the subject when the talk came around to his private life or snap "None of your business!" or, as happened on several occasions, terminate the interview. According to his brother Tom, "George kept his marriage secret because he wanted to keep his life private. "And because of his career." Career might well have been a consideration, for "bachelorhood" was deemed critical in maintaining the popularity of a young actor being groomed for more romantic roles. "The reason I'm single is because I like to have my cake and eat it too. I like my freedom," George claimed in an interview titled "Hollywood's Most Baffling Bachelor" given in 1941, some six months after he had in fact married 25-year-old Susan Larson on October 27, 1940 at the Hollywood Methodist Church.

Susan Larson was the professional name of Elsie Poole, but no one used her real name, not George or his family or friends; she herself went by the name Susan. She grew up in Los Angeles, where her father worked as a carpenter at the United Artists studio. After graduating from Hollywood High School, she entered California Christian College to study piano and organ. After her father died in a fall from a ladder at the studio, she worked briefly at the Wilshire Brown Derby as a waitress; someone in show business noticed the 5'6", 125-pound blonde, got her a test at Fox, and she was put under contract. She had bit parts in several "B" pictures, among them *Walls of Gold* (1933) and *Three on a Honeymoon* (1934).

Susan and George met on the Twentieth Century-Fox lot in early 1939, while he was making *Mr. Moto's Last Warning*. During their eighteen-month courtship the two were never seen together in public, not even riding in the same car or talking at the studio. They would drive separately to a meeting place— often the boat on which George was living at the time, which was anchored at Santa Monica harbor. When they decided to marry they did so by simply strolling unattended into a church one afternoon. On the day following the marriage, Susan quietly withdrew from her connection at Fox, gave up acting, and virtually disappeared from public view. George would later explain that he kept his wife "in the background" because he

wished her to stay the way she was—simple and unaffected—
waiting for him when he came home to give him "serenity,
peace, reality in place of competition and artificiality."

As George's wife, Susan never attended a premiere or a
preview, never went out to dine and dance, never went to a
Hollywood party. George's English friend Brian Aherne met
Susan on a few occasions and recalls her only as "a quiet, timid
little soul who spoke little." Once Aherne noticed George alone
at a Hollywood party and asked why Susan had not accompanied him. "Oh, I can't bring her," George replied. "She bores
people." Joan Fontaine, Aherne's wife at this time, confirms
that George "never took Susan with him to social gatherings,"
adding that he once referred to her as "the girl who did his
laundry." The couple lived in George's West Hollywood home,
an English-style house with a pool and tennis court. He also
owned a beach house at Laguna. When he was working in a
film, Susan would deliver him to the studio in the morning and
retrieve him at night. His married life was "placid and calm,"
according to brother Tom, who was married at the time to
actress Lillian Eggers. The two couples would occasionally get
together at George's house for a swim, a game of tennis, or a
few rubbers of bridge.

George himself continued his customary, solitary routines:
on the set between scenes he would retire to his dressing room
or find a corner of the sound stage where he could read. He
usually lunched alone, seldom spoke to other members of the
cast or crew. The day's work done, he vanished. As for
George's life off the set, one columnist observed, "If he has any
friends in Hollywood or participates in any social life, no one
knows who they are or what it is."

During this period frustrated reporters and columnists
were trying to determine George Sanders' marital status. Con-
jecture and rumor abounded: "The story is that there is a
woman in his life, and only one," speculated one reporter in

1942. "It is said he may be married to her. No one has seen her; no one seems to know her name. Some say they were married before Sanders came to Hollywood. Others say there is no such woman, that she is a figment of Sanders' imagination, a rumor planted for the purpose of protecting himself from other women." And of course, "Sanders himself says nothing at all." George maintained the shroud around his personal affairs: "If people wish to write about my private life, let them. I merely reserve the right of refusing to make statements myself. What I do when I am not in the studio is strictly my own business." Another columnist alluded to "his semi-mythical marriage," but declared that "not one movie sleuth can swear that George Sanders is a married man or a bachelor."

A retrospective account of the marriage found it "unbelievable that a famous star could court and marry a girl under the nose of Hollywood—and have nobody know about it. It seems particularly hard to believe when you realize that the girl was also in the acting profession. Yet that is what happened." The studio, because of its bookkeeping and records needs, knew of his marriage but gave out the official story that "George lives very quietly by himself in Hollywood and admits to having skillfully avoided matrimony." Yet he would later dismiss the whole idea of a secret courtship and marriage as "nonsense. We lived with privacy—but not secrecy."

In any case, the marriage was finally revealed late in 1942. It was Susan herself, not George, who issued the public announcement. Once having made the disclosure, however, she disappeared entirely from sight again. The story was published in the September 1942 issue of *Movies* magazine: "Hollywood has done a lot of speculating about George Sanders' marriage," the piece began. "George wouldn't admit he had a wife but rumors persisted. Now at last the mystery is cleared up. There really is a Mrs. Sanders." The article identified Susan and the date and place of her marriage to George, adding "they are one of the town's happiest couples" because of "her adaptability. She falls in with her husband's moods, lights his cigarettes, and laughs when he makes one of his attention-getting remarks." The story was still newsworthy a year later, when a fuller account with additional details appeared in another magazine, claiming "months of tireless searching" in tracking down "authentic, never before published facts in the life of Hollywood's gay deceiver." Even after the facts were revealed, George would not elaborate upon or comment about his marriage to Susan. "His marriage is as everyone in Hollywood knows, a fanatically tabu subject with George," one reporter wrote in early 1943, citing his vehement declaration, "I will NOT discuss it. I am not putting out a story on my marriage."

His reasons for this continued reticence had less to do with his well-known insistence on the inviolate privacy of his personal life than it did with another secret, the tragic and closely guarded one that Susan had begun to exhibit early symptoms of mental illness. "Her mental trouble was inherited from her mother, who died in a mental institution," George's sister relates. Margaret had met Susan before the marriage, when the couple came to London for a visit in the late 1930s, and then later in California after the war. "She was in a very sorry state, in tears most of the time, very emotionally unstable." George's second wife, Zsa Zsa Gabor, never met Susan but knows from what George told her that "he had a very miserable marriage with that woman. He treated her very badly, like a peasant, and she was mentally not strong. She was in a mental home for quite a while."

George was distressed and frightened by the experience. "He was deeply upset by the whole mess with Susan," Margaret remembers. "I met him in Paris when the divorce was going on. He was very, very upset. The whole emotional thing got him down." It was at this point that George began therapy with a psychiatrist in New York. While the precise nature of

Susan's problem was never publicly disclosed, its early stages were characterized by "a monumental inferiority complex where George was concerned" in that she believed herself "inadequate emotionally and mentally" and had felt compelled to enroll in classes in grammar and other basic subjects during her marriage to him. Educated in the traditional British college curriculum, George was also extremely well read. "He was a man with a good deal of intellectual energy," recalls Henry Thoresby, a friend from the early 1960s. "He did after all read Shopenhauer in bed. He was a highly intelligent individualist who could be impatient of fools. I remember being astonished by the multiplicity of his interests. He was somewhat frustrated by the life that he had chosen to lead. I should imagine that he would have been perfectly suited to the existence of a rich and independent nineteenth-century princeling." George's reading included Shakespeare and other Elizabethan playwrights, as well as nineteenth-century British novelists and a wide range of works of European philosophy. He read German and French writers in the original and knew Greek and Roman philosophers and dramatists in translation. To Susan this intellectual background must have indeed been intimidating. Toward the end the marrige, her mental state "varied between depths of despair and depression and an almost unnatural degree of euphoria and high spirits," which suggests a manic-depressive condition.

George was shattered by the collapse of his marriage and by what happened to Susan, blaming himself for her mental problems. "I didn't give, you see," he told a friend. "I only took." The break-up came on December 10, 1946. To that point Susan had loved George devotedly, waited on him, and did everything in her power to please him and accommodate his every mood. He came home that December evening to find her in a state of profound anxiety and to learn that she would no longer be waiting for him at home, would no longer provide him the peace and serenity he needed. She was packing and told him that she was leaving him. Completely taken by surprise, George vainly attempted to argue her out of her decision even as she methodically finished her packing, called a taxi, and rode away out of his life. "You only have to see him and talk with him to realize how deeply he misses his wife," observed a columnist to whom George confided his feelings in an uncommonly candid interview, which concludes with this telling insight: "Susan Sanders appears to have always had great understanding for the man who for ten years had been a Hollywood enigma."

One evening some months before, George came home to Susan from the set of *The Private Affairs of Bel Ami* and without any preamble began reciting a mixture of lines from his part in the film and from the earlier *The Moon and Sixpence*: "Women are strange little beasts," he intoned. "They can be bought by a smile, a look, a compliment, anything that touches their vanity. Women strike me as incredibly stupid. It's impossible not to despise them." Another woman would have been infuriated. Not Susan. She understood. She laughed. And after a startled pause, George burst out laughing, too.

Perhaps this was why she had been so important to him, why he needed her, why he came to appreciate her only after she was lost to him. Perhaps, more than simply an adoring and disarmingly ingenuous wife, she had been able to see beyond the protective mask, past the defensive cynicism, the disdainful manner and scathing remarks, the carefully cultivated image which her husband presented to the world.

"Since the breakup of my marriage," George reflected, "friends have tried to console me by saying there are as good fish in the sea as ever came out of it. I wonder about that . . . I really wonder."

8 "Schweinehund"

"For a long time I was considered the ideal actor to play sneering, arrogant, bull-necked Nazi brutes," George remarked late in his career. "Nobody, it seems, could enunciate the word *Schweinehund* quite as feelingly as I." This particular bit of typecasting originated in his pre-World War II German characterizations, what might be termed the Hun or proto-Nazi parts, beginning with his double-role in *Lancer Spy* (1937).

The last American spy melodrama of the thirties to be set in World War I, *Lancer Spy* has been rated one of the best of that decade by historians of the genre. The story line, from the novel by Marthe McKenna, involves a British secret service scheme to take advantage of the extraordinary resemblance of Royal Navy Lieutenant Michael Bruce to Baron Kurt von Rohbach, a German officer of the imperial guard captured by the British. Bruce undergoes intensive training in order to impersonate the Baron, take his place in Berlin, and obtain details of an invasion plan that, if successful, could win the war for Germany. The ersatz von Rohbach fools all of the German high command, except intelligence officers Hollen (Sig Rumann) and Gruning (Peter Lorre), who assign agent Dolores Daria (Dolores Del Rio) to confirm their suspicions. She discovers the truth but in the process falls in love with the impostor. With her assistance, Bruce steals the vital plans and escapes across the Swiss border. The tide is turned for England, but Dolores is captured and executed for her collaboration.

With his head shaved on both sides and sporting a spiked Kaiser helmet, George plays the part of the Baron with a sinister élan. His convincing interpretation of the Englishman and his German double earned him unanimous critical praise. The New York *Times* thought it "only right that George Sanders (previously seen only in minor roles) should have been awarded stardom" in the part. *Variety* found that George's "subtle inclusion of British characteristics while impersonating the German lends a tang of impending danger to his performance." The use of a prop monocle added to the image of his Prussian nasty and became a trademark of the portrayal of the Hun. *Time* magazine would later describe George as "the only actor since Erich von Stroheim and Charles Coburn who can wear a monocle without looking as if he is going to drop it in his soup." In *Slave Ship*, released the same year, he played the part of a pirate and was told to wear a monocle. The film's producers ignored the fact that at the time in which the story was set monocles had not yet been invented, and George became a sneering anachronism as history's first monocled pirate.

Brush cut, spiked helmet, and monocle accompanied him in his role as Captain Heinrichs in *Nurse Edith Cavell* (1939). The screenplay is based on the true story of a woman who in the early years of World War I was executed for helping Allied prisoners and wounded soldiers escape Belgium and back to their own countries. Nurse Cavell (Anna Neagle), aided by three close friends (Edna May Oliver, ZaSu Pitts, and May Robson), creates an "underground railroad" which for months confounds the Germans, but she is eventually trapped by spies and sent to prison. As the cruelly dispassionate Heinrichs, George makes an example of Cavell: he assists in convicting her

of unfounded charges of espionage, personally and with pleasure informs her of her death sentence, and then marches her to
the waiting firing squad.

The film is a remake of the 1928 silent *Dawn*, starring Sybil
Thorndike as Cavell, which on its release created an international controversy, with a flood of protests from Germany and
a flurry of apologies from British officials. In September 1939,
however, World War II was underway and the New York *Times*
could remark in its review that *Nurse Edith Cavell* was " a deeply
affecting tale of individual heroism under the crushing influence
of modern warfare" and, moreover, "anti-German only in so
far as the Germans were pro-war." George's portrayal of the
arrogant, unfeeling Hun embodies precisely the "crushing influence" that dooms the heroine.

In his next German role, George plays a real jackboot-and-
swastika Nazi. *Confessions of a Nazi Spy* (1939) employs a quasi-
documentary format, with voice-over narration to string together fictional and newsreel sequences that tell the story of
espionage attempts by the German-American Bund in the late
thirties. The script, based largely on evidence gathered from
the 1938 FBI trials of Nazi sympathizers and organizers, focuses
on German-American zealot Curt Schneider (Francis Lederer),
who offers his services as a spy for German Naval Intelligence.
He attracts the attention of both Nazi spy organizer Schlager
(George, once more with shaved head) and FBI inspector Ed
Renard (Edward G. Robinson). Paul Lukas plays Dr. Kassel, a
Bund leader and amateur racial genealogist. Despite, or perhaps
because of, what has been called the film's "shrillness of tone,"
it was a commercial success in America and provoked German
diplomatic retaliation, which resulted in the banning of the
picture in eighteen countries.

In 1940, two other prototypical "ur-Nazi" roles served to
reinforce the equation of George with "bullet-headed Prus-
sians." *Bittersweet*, the second filming of the Noel Coward

operetta, finds him again with brush cut and monocle playing the villainous Baron von Tranisch, an arrogant Viennese officer who attempts to ravish Jeanette MacDonald on a dance floor and kills Nelson Eddy in a duel. Of George's performance (incidentally, his first appearance in a color film), *Time* magazine remarked that "George Sanders plays the villain as only George Sanders can. It's a pleasure just to watch him in action." He kept the short hair and uniform for his role as Gurko Lanen in *The Son of Monte Cristo*, in which he seeks to become military dictator of Lichtenberg by manipulating Grand Duchess Joan Bennett, only to be foiled by Louis Hayward, a masked rogue who turns out to be the son of Edmund Dantes. While the New York *Times* found the picture "just a routine retelling of a conventional sword-and-cape adventure tale" with Hayward "uninspiring" and Bennett "lackluster and droopy," it praised George's "hard-grained performance as the wicked general."

Man Hunt (1941), arguably the best of the films in which George appeared as a German or Nazi, was adapted by Dudley Nichols from Geoffrey Household's novel *Rogue Male* and had the distinction of direction by Fritz Lang. It tells the story of English big-game hunter Alan Thorndike (Walter Pidgeon) who in 1939 undertakes to stalk Hitler just for the sport of it. When, in Berchtesgaden, he gets him in the sights of his empty rifle, Thorndike suddenly decides to abandon the "sporting stalk" as planned and to load and fire. Before he can shoot, he is caught by guards and taken to the ruthless Gestapo commander (George), who tortures him to try to get a signed confession and use him as an international scapegoat. In the course of making a complicated and somewhat miraculous escape, Thorndike is aided by a Cockney seamstress (a streetwalker in the novel), played by Joan Bennett. The film was praised for its "keen and vivid contrast of British and Nazi temperaments" and "subtle psychological overtones." George "plays the Nazi better than any German could possibly play it," another review concluded.

Two 1943 productions reversed the usual plotline by having George play a counter-spy in Germany, but each part in fact gave him occasion to portray the usual Nazi role as part of the deception. *They Came to Blow Up America* casts him as an FBI agent of German parentage who trains with a group of Nazi saboteurs, a role he played with "his usual grace and aplomb." Anna Sten is the romantic interest, and Dennis Hoey handles the actual Gestapo duties. *Appointment in Berlin* finds him opposite Marguerite Chapman as a propagandizing Nazi broadcaster who is really a British agent. Onslow Stevens plays the real German officer in this one. An interesting bit of casting has George's screen father, Sir Douglas Wilson, played by his own father Henry. George had brought his parents to the United States to live with him during the war.

"By this time I had been typed," George later recalled. "I was definitely a nasty bit of goods." Yet, he added, "eventually I was allowed to do other things." It would prove to be these other things—strong supporting roles in four distinguished pictures and the lead in one other major production—that would make him one of the busiest and most popular actors in Hollywood during the period 1940–1947.

9 "Circumstances Beyond My Control"

"If I have occasionally given brilliant performances on the screen, this was entirely due to circumstances beyond my control," George reflected in 1960, some twenty years after his role as Jack Favell in *Rebecca,* a brilliant supporting performance in which he upstaged Laurence Olivier in each scene the two played together and was at the center of some of the best moments in the film. This uncommonly modest remark was consistent with his often expressed opinion of acting and actors: "Film acting is rather like roller-skating; once you know how to do it, it isn't particularly stimulating intellectually"; or "I am not one of those people who would rather act than eat. Olivier was born with a desire to act. My own desire as a boy was to retire"; and "Acting is for children . . . who else can take this posturing seriously?" Not George Sanders, as the recollections of several of his costars from that early period in his career suggest.

"He didn't seem to take himself, as an actor, very seriously," recalls Elena Verdugo, who played a Polynesian child-bride to George's Charles Strickland in *The Moon and Sixpence*

(1942). Anthony Quinn, with him in *The Black Swan* (1942), concurs : "He didn't take acting very seriously." Lucille Ball, George's leading lady in *Lured* (1947), believed he "never really cared about acting—just making a living." And Zsa Zsa Gabor confides that "he was ashamed of being an actor." George's outspoken disdain for his craft may have begun with his stint between 1939 and 1941 as The Saint, the RKO detective series which he thought the nadir of his career. His sister Margaret, whom he visited in London on occasion of the premier of *Lancer Spy* in 1937, remembers that "at that time he seemed very much to enjoy his profession and the success he was attaining, only later becoming somewhat disillusioned with the whole acting scene."

Once established, disillusionment took firm and permanent hold. In a 1957 letter he bitterly expressed what seemed to him an unhealthy interdependence in the profession: "I wonder which is the sickest, the audience which seeks to escape its miseries by being transported into a land of make-believe, or the actor who is nurtured in his struggle for personal aggrandisement by the sickness of the audience." His conclusion: "I think perhaps it is the actor . . . alienated from reality, disingenuous in his relationships, a muddle-headed peacock forever chasing after the rainbow of his pathetic narcissism." Nine years later, at age sixty, bitterness had been tempered by wistful regret: "It would make life much simpler if I could be content with my profession, if I could find within its confines the opportunities for creative satisfaction that I need and seek."

Whatever he thought of his own ability as an actor ("I can only provide mediocrity," he remarked late in his career), those who worked with him in films are generous in their praise of his talents. In recent interviews, costars and supporting players in pictures from 1940 to 1970 uniformly express admiration and respect for George as an actor. Douglas Fairbanks, Jr. and Vincent Price, who both appeared with him in *Green Hell*

George at age three,
St. Petersburg, 1909.

Henry Sanders,
St. Petersburg, 1900.

Margaret Kolbe Sanders,
George (left), and Tom,
St. Petersburg, 1909.

George and Tom in the Bedales
School play, Hampshire, 1917.

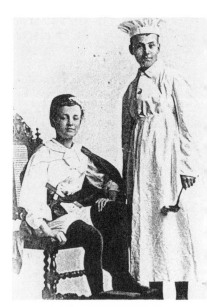

George in his first
year at Brighton, 1919.

In a college play
at Brighton, 1921.

College graduate,
Brighton, 1923.

First wife Susan Larson, 1939.

In Buenos Aires, 1928.

Tom, Susan, and George in Hollywood, 1941.

Susan, George, Lillian, and Tom at Laguna Beach, 1942.

Tom and George in Hollywood, 1943.

On the set of *Appointment in Berlin* with his father, Henry, and Marguerite
Chapman, 1943. (Courtesy Columbia Pictures)

Wedding day with Zsa Zsa in Las Vegas, April 1, 1949.

With Helen Hayes at the Oscar ceremonies, 1951.

In Spain during the early filming of *Solomon and Sheba,* with Gina Lollobrigida and Tyrone Power, 1958.

Between takes during the filming of *Village of the Damned,* with co-star Barbara Shelley, 1960.

George and Benita in London, 1966.

With Zsa Zsa in New York, 1969.

Wedding day with Magda Gabor in Indio, California, December 4, 1970.
(Courtesy World Wide Photos)

George and Lorraine Chanel
in Palma de Majorca, 1970.

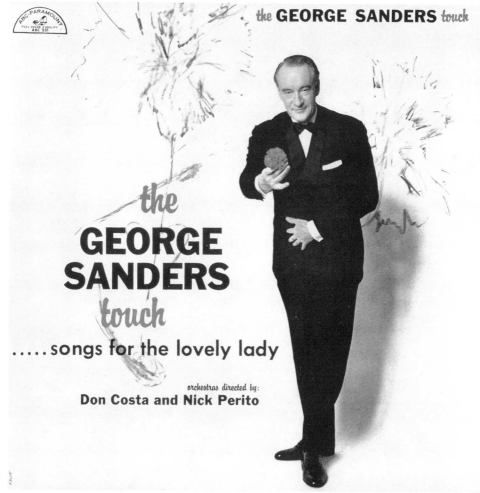

The George Sanders touch.

(1940), share the same high opinion: "an excellent actor," Fairbanks says unequivocally; "a natural actor," suggests Price, who adds this supporting anecdote: "Once when he told me he was going to do a film in Egypt, I asked if it was a costume pic or modern, he said, 'It all depends on how I hold my cigarette.' " Laraine Day, George's costar in *Foreign Correspondent* (1940), thought George personally "vulgar and unpleasant," nevertheless praises him as "a brilliant actor."

Marguerite Chapman, the leading lady in *Appointment in Berlin* (1943), describes George as "a fine actor," adding "It was a privilege and an experience to have worked with him. I learned a great deal." "A fine actor" is the phrase also used by Gene Tierney, who appeared with him in three films of the forties (*Sundown*, 1941; *Son of Fury*, 1942; *The Ghost and Mrs. Muir*, 1947). "Absolutely one of the finest," agreed Lucille Ball (*Lured*, 1947). Ella Raines (*The Strange Affair of Uncle Harry*, 1945) believes George was "unique in giving to other actors in his own quiet way . . . a highly disciplined actor." "He was consistently good as a performer and was a strong presence on screen," recalled Cornel Wilde, who appeared with him in *Forever Amber* (1947) and *The Scarlet Coat* (1955). Both star and supporting player in *Samson and Delilah* (1949) praise his ability as a performer: Victor Mature terms him "truly a great actor," and Mike Mazurki, who played a captain of the Philistines and knew George off the set, provides additional insight into his appeal: "He was born to act and was, in fact, the consummate actor. He had the physique, face, voice, intelligence and sense of adventure it requires, plus that little touch of the rascal that all fine actors seem to possess." Gary Merrill, costar of *All About Eve* (1950), the film for which George won an Academy Award, believed that he and George were "a lot alike in that we played parts that were kind of like us, parts that suited our personalities."

While she thought him "slightly intimidating to the other

actors" in *King Richard and the Crusaders* (1954), Virginia Mayo believes that George should be remembered as "one of our greats." Robert Douglas (*Ivanhoe*, 1952, and *The Scarlet Coat,* 1955) observes that "as an actor his range was immense, possessing a magnificent voice, great poise, and above all an unusual intelligence and approach to any part he undertook." "He didn't consider himself a great actor, but he really was," insists Zsa Zsa Gabor, who costarred with him in *Death of a Scoundrel* (1956), the only film in which they appeared together, adding "Laurence Olivier once told me he was one of the best." Asked which of George's abilities she most admired, Zsa Zsa answers, "frankly, his acting." Sister Eva, of the Gabors the most experienced and formally trained actress, "admired him greatly as an actor . . . absolutely the most brilliant. There was nothing he couldn't play."

"An actor with great concentration . . . he also gave a great deal to fellow actors," recalls Shirley Jones (*Dark Purpose*, 1964). Two players from *A Shot in the Dark* (1964) hold high opinions: "He was an excellent actor with superb comedic timing," observes Elke Sommer; among George's qualities, Herbert Lom most "admired his professionalism." Even as late as 1970 his work in *The Kremlin Letter* drew admiration from actors and director alike. Lila Kedrova: "He understood his craft as a film actor as well as anyone I ever worked with in any country around the world. He was a professional in the truest sense of the word." Max von Sydow: "George Sanders was certainly one of the outstanding artists of his generation." And from John Huston: "George Sanders possessed a sharp, driving intelligence that was reflected in his acting . . . There was a quality of perfection about him, a talent of precision. I admired him hugely."

Among his peers this was the reputation of the man who had declared "acting is for children." So why was it that a film actor of George Sanders' range and ability could find no contentment in his craft, no satisfaction for his creative needs? The answer lies, ultimately, in the cumulative life experiences which formed his image of himself. But at this point the "circumstances beyond my control" which produced the supporting performances in major productions of the period 1940–1947 should have strengthened, not weakened that image. The first of these performances was in Alfred Hitchcock's *Rebecca* (1940).

Adapted from Daphne du Maurier's 1938 bestseller, *Rebecca* was Hitchcock's first American film but remains a distinctly British work, set mainly in England with a predominantly British cast. It is the story of a naive young girl (Joan Fontaine) who marries aristocratic Cornish widower Maxim de Winter (Laurence Olivier) and is haunted by the image of his beautiful first wife Rebecca, whose presence fills the family home, Manderley. This presence is nurtured by the sinister housekeeper, Mrs. Danvers (Judith Anderson), pathologically devoted to the memory of her former mistress. When by chance the boat in which Rebecca had drowned is recovered and shows evidence of deliberate sinking, de Winter for the first time speaks to his wife about Rebecca, revealing that she was conniving and promiscuous, that he had hated her and, driven to rage by her taunts, had accidentally killed her. At the inquest, Rebecca's lover, Jack Favell (George), attempts blackmail with a letter that throws suspicion on de Winter but is thwarted when it is learned that Rebecca was dying of cancer. Mrs. Danvers then sets Manderley afire and dies in the flames, which also consume the past and the guilt, releasing de Winter and his second wife to begin afresh. An effective combination of romantic melodrama, gothic atmosphere, and murder mystery, the film earned the 1940 Academy Award for Best Picture.

The shooting script for *Rebecca* introduces and describes the character of Jack Favell, Rebecca's "favorite cousin" and lover, following an off-camera line ("Looking for me?"): "Sitting on the ledge of the open window is a very self-assured individual of rather obvious good looks, flashy but with a certain charm for women." George played the role "splendidly in character," as Frank Nugent put it in his New York *Times* review, and projects a frank indecency so complex and smooth that it attracts rather than offends. His interpretation of the character was apparently what author du Maurier had envisioned; many years later she still remembered "how well George Sanders played the part of Jack Favell."

George stole scene after scene from a relentlessly wooden Olivier, who chose to underplay the de Winter character as a colorless boor. Additionally, Olivier was unhappy with Joan Fontaine (his bride-to-be Vivien Leigh had been promised serious consideration for the part), and insulted his costar on the set. Her experience with the English cast of *Rebecca* may have been the root of Fontaine's long-standing dislike of George. She characterizes Englishmen as covered with shells of "external enamel." George had "several coats," she adds, and was consequently "a tied-up man." She may have resented George's friendship with her English husband Brian Aherne and their association with what she terms "the British Brigade," the colony of English actors in the thirties and early forties whom she regarded as having formed an impenetrable clique. (In fact, George remained something of an outsider even among the English colony, which apparently harbored a distrust of Englishmen born outside Britain). Fontaine's twenty-second birthday fell during the filming, and the only English actor to show up for the surprise cake and champagne party set up by the crew was Reginald Denny, who told her that the rest of the British cast (Olivier, George, Nigel Bruce, Gladys Cooper, among others) were in Judith Anderson's dressing room swapping stories, not interested in attending the celebration. To make matters worse, Hitchcock was up to his usual game of playing divide-and-conquer with the actors ("You know that Olivier doesn't want you in this role," he told Fontaine) and seemed pleased that some cast members disliked one another. In all, it was not a happy production, but for George the role of Favell was the first in a string of what he would later call "damned winning heavies," characterizations that over the years would provoke many leading men to complain that he "made his cads so fascinating that he drew attention away from the other characters."

Yet in his next film, *Foreign Correspondent* (1940), he played one of his occasional sympathetic roles, jolly-decent English reporter Scott ffolliott ("Double *f* at the beginning, old boy, and they're both small *f*'s," he explains to Joel McCrea. "One of my ancestors had his head chopped off by Henry the Eighth and his wife dropped the capital letter to commemorate the occasion"). Essentially a suspenseful spy melodrama spiced with comedy and romance, the story involves a newly assigned American correspondent (Joel McCrea) in Europe on the eve of World War II, the head of a pacifist organization (Herbert Marshall), who turns out to be a spy for the Germans, and his unsuspecting daughter (Laraine Day), whose friend (George) helps rescue a kidnapped Dutch diplomat (Albert Basserman). The story climaxes with the crash of an airplane into the Atlantic. Casting problems delayed production and centered, ironically, on Joan Fontaine and Brian Aherne: producer Walter Wanger told Selznick that if he would lend Fontaine for the female lead in the picture, her husband could have the male lead. The Ahernes, however, had plans to tour together with a play. The lead was then offered to Gary Cooper, who refused it. George's role as ffolliott had also been offered first to another actor, Rex Harrison, who turned it down.

Several on-set incidents during the filming involved George. Hitchcock, who claimed to dislike actors, ordered several retakes of the plane wreck because it apparently amused him to see McCrea and George floundering in the water. It was during these scenes, as the actors were struggling to get out of the windows of the flooded plane, recalls a still-annoyed Laraine Day, that "Mr. Sanders continuously tried to get his hands under my dress." This may have been simply a tasteless prank or an expression of frustration over the unnecessary retakes, for it seems less likely that George was overcome by lust and unable to restrain himself from pawing the lady while both were half-submerged in cold water.

The original ending of the film, a scene between George and McCrea enroute to America after the ocean plunge, occurs in the chronology of the script in September 1939; but at Wanger's insistence, because word from England suggested that the bombing of the country was imminent, the ending was re-shot. George does not appear in the revised ending; McCrea delivers a radio broadcast from London as bombs fall, violating dramatic logic by leaping eight months into the future. It was a prophetic revision: the new ending was shot on July 5, 1940; German bombing of England began on July 10. But by then George had moved quickly into yet another production.

This period was the most active of his career. The year 1940 saw, in addition to *Rebecca* and *Foreign Correspondent*, the release of *Green Hell, Bitter Sweet, The Son of Monte Cristo, The House of the Seven Gables*, and two entries in The Saint series (*The Saint's Double Trouble, The Saint Takes Over*). The next year he would appear in another six films, and in 1942 seven more. Film fans at the time may have wondered if more than one actor was using the name George Sanders. Most of these appearances, however, were in "B" pictures. His next support-ing role in a major production was in *Rage in Heaven* (1941), with Ingrid Bergman and Robert Montgomery. Adapted by Christopher Isherwood from the James Hilton novel, this ro-mantic drama tells the story of a manic-depressive psychotic (Montgomery) who marries his mother's secretary-companion (Bergman) and becomes insanely jealous when his friend Ward (George) comes to live nearby. He accuses his wife of carrying on an affair, attempts to kill Ward and then when his mind collapses entirely, concocts and carries out a plan to kill himself and put the blame for the "murder" on his friend. Ward is brought to trial and convicted but saved when evidence of the plot is uncovered. George is noble as the other man and has some very affecting romantic scenes with Bergman, which lend support to the story that this role, coupled with his performance opposite Norma Shearer in *Her Cardboard Lover* (1942), prompted Louis B. Mayer to propose that George be groomed as a romantic star. Invited to lunch with Mayer to discuss the matter, George declined both the meal and the opportunity to change his screen image: "Had I become a big-time romantic star I might now be a good deal richer than I am," he reflected decades later. "On the other hand it is quite conceivable I would no longer be around, professionally speaking: the mortality rate among stars is extremely high, whereas a good character actor is almost indestructible." He never wished he had decided otherwise: "I only regret having missed what would undoubtedly have been an excellent lunch."

George's last supporting performance in a major production during this period was as Lord Henry Wotton in *The Picture of Dorian Gray* (1945), although he is top-billed in the opening credits over the then unknown Hurd Hatfield, who plays the title role. Director Albert Lewin, who also wrote the adaptation of Oscar Wilde's wickedly elegant novel, had been an associate producer for such MGM "literary classic" productions of the thirties as *David Copperfield*, *Mutiny on the Bounty*, and *Camille*. To play the cynical and haughty Lord Henry, scattering Wilde's catty little bon mots, Lewin wanted George, for whom the part seemed to have been written. Many reviewers thought this choice Lewin's only sound one: in an otherwise strongly negative New York *Times* review, for example, Bosley Crowther writes that George "gives the only commendable performance" in the film.

The adaptation remains relatively faithful to the book: painter Basil Hallward (Lowell Gilmore) has captured the beauty and innocence of his young friend Dorian Gray (Hatfield) in a portrait. Dorian wishes always to look as he does in the picture and, encouraged by the amoral Lord Henry, vows to surrender his soul if the likeness will assume all the ravages of age and experience, leaving him still youthful. He gets his wish. Acting on Lord Henry's advice, "Don't squander the gold of your days, live! Let nothing be lost upon you . . . there is only one way to get rid of a temptation, and that is to yield to it," Dorian undertakes a career of dissipation and hedonism, causing in one instance the suicide of a young cabaret singer, Sybil Vane (Angela Lansbury). As the years pass he remains young and unchanged; the portrait grows old and hideous. When Hallward discovers Gray's secret, Dorian kills him. After twenty years, weary at last, Dorian resolves to make amends, and a new start, by destroying the painting. When he plunges a knife into the picture, he falls dead. The portrait recovers its original appearance of youth and beauty, and Dorian's corpse shows all the marks of his decay and dissipation.

"When a man says he has exhausted life, you may be sure that life has exhausted him," Lord Henry tells Dorian midway through the film, a line which could sum up the story itself. George's seemingly effortless delivery of this and other witty and wicked lines reinforced in the public mind the image of George Sanders the cynical but elegant and refined cad. It was the persona he would use to even greater effect during the next decade. During the period 1940–1947, however, he was kept busy with other supporting roles in films which were not major productions, second features in which he gave performances often lacking the "brilliance" he claimed was due to circumstances beyond his control.

In *Green Hell* (1940) he and Vincent Price support Douglas Fairbanks, Jr. and Joan Bennett in a studio-bound adventure about explorers seeking Inca treasure in South America. If for nothing else, the film is of interest as the first in which George sings, albeit very briefly: he and George Bancroft belt out an Anglo-American duet of "Home on the Range" as they float down the Amazon on a riverboat. Even in this odd set-piece, the quality of his strong baritone is apparent. *The House of the Seven Gables* (1940), an uninspired adaptation of Nathaniel Hawthorne's novel, undertakes the story of the cursed Pyncheon family, with Vincent Price accused by his grasping brother (George) of murdering their father. The love interest is a Pyncheon cousin, played by Margaret Lindsday, possibly but not likely an off-screen love interest as well: in an interview after the picture was released, George let fall that he was "once in love with Margaret Lindsay." If this were so, the relationship would have developed during the filming, a period when George was deeply involved with Susan and very near the time of their marriage. This was probably a bit of press agentry intended to publicize the film. Margaret Lindsay appeared mostly for Warners in the thirties and forties, playing leads in "B" films and secondary roles in more important productions.

Sundown (1941) gave George the chance to play another sympathetic role, this time supporting Gene Tierney, as a dark-skinned Arab beauty, and Bruce Cabot in assisting British troops in North Africa during World War II. He spends most of his time in this romantic action story running about in desert jackets and shorts. His next two pictures find him again playing the heavy. In *Son of Fury* (1942) he is Sir Arthur Blake, a nasty eighteenth-century English aristocrat who conspires to deprive Tyrone Power of his inheritance. Sir Arthur's daughter (Frances Farmer), loses Power to Gene Tierney, here a dark-skinned Polynesian beauty. In this film George has an opportunity to demonstrate another talent acquired in his youth, boxing: the opening scene takes place at the Bristol Sporting Club where Sir Arthur makes short work of his opponent in a bare-knuckle (and bare-chested) prizefight. *The Black Swan* (1942), a rousing adaptation of the Rafael Sabatini novel, once again pits Tyrone Power against George, who as Captain Leech is almost unrecognizable in a flaming red beard. Maureen O'Hara is the object of their attentions, and sword fights between George and Power abound. Some seventeen years later, they would play another dueling scene in *Solomon and Sheba* with tragic consequences.

From these two costumers George moved next into a pair of tuxedo romps, *Tales of Manhattan* and *Her Cardboard Lover* (both 1942). A collection of separate stories tied together by a tail coat which passes from owner to owner, *Tales of Manhattan* features an all-star cast, including Charles Boyer, Rita Hayworth, Ginger Rogers, Henry Fonda, and Charles Laughton. In his episode, George plays a haughty society attorney who exposes an apparently successful Edward G. Robinson as a skid-row bum. The film was directed by Julien Duvivier, with whom George would later work (and about whom he would complain) in *Captain Blackjack* (1950). *Her Cardboard Lover,* a rather slight comedy, is notable as Norma Shearer's last picture. She plays a society flirt who hires a lover (Robert Taylor) to make her fiance (George) jealous. Predictably, she and Taylor fall in love, leaving George in the cold.

Two very similar films in terms of cast, production crew, setting, and atmosphere, *The Lodger* (1944) and *Hangover Square* (1945), call upon George to play a detective tracking a psychotic murderer (Laird Cregar in both pictures) through foggy, gaslit London. The screenplays for each production were by Barre Lyndon and direction by John Brahm, with Merle Oberon in the former and Linda Darnell in the latter as the threatened female. George's last supporting role in a second feature during this period was with Hedy Lamarr and Louis Hayward in *The Strange Woman* (1946), a costume drama in which a scheming woman destroys the lives of three men.

In addition to these many supporting roles during the

period 1940–1947, George played the lead in ten other films (not including his title roles as The Saint and The Falcon). Only one was a major production, but it was a turning point in his career, one of the two or three films for which he is best remembered and the most significant in molding his image, both on-screen and off: *The Moon and Sixpence* (1942). "George was called off to do a scene with Herbert Marshall in which the two argued about women and love," reports an on-set interviewer during the filming. "Mr. Sanders' comments sounded more than a little convincing. Somehow, I could already hear the loud complaints that will come from women when they hear such disparaging remarks about ladies as a whole." And complain they did, as George remembered almost two decades later: "It was a remark I made in *The Moon and Sixpence* which resulted in my acquiring a reputation as an authority on women. In the film I said something to the effect that the more you beat women the better they were for it. I suddenly found myself in the center of a storm."

There were in fact many such lines that George delivered, for the film, an adaptation of W. Somerset Maugham's 1919 novel, is an interpretation of the life of French impressionist painter Paul Gauguin, who scorned all human relations in his demonic devotion to his art. The adaptation is a faithful one: living an orderly and dull existence, Charles Strickland (George) seems a commonplace, middle-aged stockbroker until one day at age forty he suddenly deserts his wife (Molly Lamont) and children, leaving them completely unprovided for, and goes off to Paris to paint. Geoffrey Wolfe (Herbert Marshall), the film's narrator, follows to urge his return, finds him in utter poverty, indifferent to everything but the desire to paint, and resolute about staying.

In Paris, Strickland is befriended by Dutch painter Dirk Stroeve (Steve Geray), a mediocre artist (but aware of Strickland's genius), who takes him into his home when he finds

Strickland seriously ill. Strickland is brutally indifferent to Stroeve but not to his wife Blanche (Doris Dudley), whom he paints in the nude and, despite his utter disdain for women and the shackles they represent, seduces. Recovered, with the affair discovered, Strickland is unmoved by Stroeve's pain and despair, dismisses him as a "fat fool" and makes ready to depart for the South Seas, cold-bloodedly telling Blanche she cannot accompany him. Shattered by remorse and grief, she kills herself. Strickland merely shrugs: he had taken up with her, he says, because he needed practice in painting the female figure and could not afford models.

In Tahiti he meets a fourteen-year-old native girl, Ata (Elena Verdugo), whose simple love and devotion touch a hidden depth in him. He marries her ("I shall probably beat you," he warns. "How else will I know you love me?" she asks), finds contentment at last and fulfillment of his artistic ambitions. The idyll is shattered when Strickland discovers he has contracted leprosy. He urges Ata to leave, but she refuses. Accepting his fate, knowing his days are numbered, he works furiously and creates his greatest paintings. When he at last succumbs, Ata carries out his last wish by burning their home, on the walls of which is his masterpiece, a mural of the Garden of Eden.

The Moon and Sixpence is more than the story of a tormented man's contempt for society, convention, and women; it attempts to explain what drives the artist in his relentless and often unscrupulous quest for beauty. George is contemptible, and ultimately touching, as Charles Strickland. It was one of the few parts he commented on approvingly, expressing "supreme satisfaction over having had the opportunity to play the role." If the film falls short of fully illuminating the soul of the artist, that is also true of the novel and probably of every attempt to depict the life of a creative genius. Filmgoers, however, seemed less interested in this theme than with the way

George's character treated women and his remarks about them in general: "Women are strange little beasts. You can treat them like dogs, you can beat them until your arm aches, and still they love you. Of course, it's an absurd illusion that they have souls . . . Love is a disease. A weakness. It interferes with one's work. I have no time for it."

Here the myth of George Sanders, Woman Hater, was born. "A whole mass of women were up in arms against me," he later recalled with amusement. "They were outraged. 'How could you have said such a thing?' they demanded with heaving breasts. 'It was caddish, brutal, and uncivilized.' I pleaded that I was only playing the part of Gauguin who, after all, was caddish, brutal, and uncivilized . . . I just spoke the words that were given to me." But he could not resist adding, "The fact that on this point Gauguin, Maugham, and I were in unanimous accord was, in my opinion, neither here nor there."

In any case, George decided to cultivate the image and perpetuate the myth, for it added an appropriate and useful dimension to the mask of The Cad. In a series of magazine and newspaper interviews he carefully embroidered on this theme. Knowing what sort of answers journalists expected, he did his best to provide them: "Mr. Sanders, what do you think of intellectual women?" "*Are there any?*" "Do you think that beautiful women make good wives?" "*They make better mistresses. All women make better mistresses.*" "Do you think a woman should be beautiful before breakfast?" "*It would never occur to me to look at a woman before breakfast.*"

And so it went. In three interviews in different magazines within a four-month period in 1942 he produced comments calculated to add to the image. "A woman's place is over the washtub, not the typewriter" (this to a lady journalist); "A woman's highest duty is to keep her husband's shirts pressed and the buttons on"; "The most attractive women are those who know their place and don't try to exceed their womanly rights and privileges." The most notorious 1942 interview was *Photoplay*'s "George Sanders Puts Women in Their Place." Here George issues such pronouncements as "The entire relationship between the sexes was founded on the premise that women are frailer than men. So they are. It is stupid, it is entirely futile to argue around that basic and irrevocable point. Being more frail, it follows, naturally, that she has greater limitations . . . The one thing that woman does superlatively well is to bear a child. This is her difference from, and her superiority over man. Why can't she rest her case on this unassailable rampart? Women should remain where they belong, in the boudoir and the parlor. Men should keep women subjugated. When they are subjugated, they are happy."

He was still nurturing the image in a 1951 interview: "Well, perhaps not actually little beasts, but they're definitely the inferior sex, and when they try to assert themselves the equals of men they become completely unendurable."

In 1961 he wrote a piece for *Good Housekeeping,* misleadingly entitled "There's a Lot to Like About Women," in which he facetiously suggests that it is women's weak points that have kept them strong: "Women don't really like men. What they want first is an escort rather than a companion, then a wedding rather than a marriage, followed by a home and children." By this time, the image of George Sanders the Woman Hater was one he could not have shed had he wanted to; indeed, it served as an essential part of the mask of The Cad for almost three decades after its genesis in *The Moon and Sixpence.*

The other films during this period in which he had lead roles were, with one exception, undistinguished productions. In *Paris After Dark* (1943) he plays a surgeon and head of the Parisian Resistance assisted in both capacities by nurse Brenda Marshall. This time the German colonel is played by someone else (Robert Lewis). *Quiet Please, Murder* (1943) is essentially a game of hide-and-seek in a public library with George as a book forger in league with Lynne Roberts. Both are foiled by Richard Denning, who also gets the girl of the piece (Gail Patrick). At this point, the grind of having made twenty-one pictures in three years was taking its toll on George. "Working as I do, in one film after another, I don't have time to think," he complained in an on-set interview. "In this script I have, let's see, 415 scenes. Because I am making too many pictures, too rapidly, one after another in blurring succession, I shall feel that the lines I say in every one of these 415 scenes are the same lines I said in the picture I have just finished, and in the one before that." And apparently the next as well: *Action in Arabia* (1944), a low-budget war drama with Virginia Bruce and Lenore Aubert, was one of the films George later claimed he was unable to remember anything about. "I find I made things like *Action in Arabia*, *Lured*, and *The Scarlet Coat*. I can only assume I was paid handsomely for them, but I am at a complete loss as to what action there was in Arabia, or who was lured where and why. As to the scarlet coat, did I wear it, and if not, who did?"

It is less likely that George forgot *Summer Storm* (1944), a sensitive filming of Chekhov's tale "The Shooting Party" in which he gives one of his better performances. Directed by Douglas Sirk and costarring a surprisingly adept Linda Darnell, it is a finely rendered drama of passion and decadence in pre-revolutionary Russia which deserves wider recognition. Olga (Linda Darnell), the illiterate, beautiful, and scheming daughter of a peasant woodcutter on the estate of Count Volsky (Edward Everett Horton), is married to the Count's overseer (Hugo Haas) but has dreams of wealth and a better marriage. Fedor Petroff (George), the district judge, becomes her victim and succumbs to the illicit love she offers, sacrificing his fiancée (Anna Lee) and career for his passion. The story's commentary on a tragic period is completed with the deaths of both Olga and Petroff. The performances in *Summer Storm* are uniformly good, with George excellent as Judge Petroff who, aware of and tormented by his weaknesses, cannot overcome them.

In *The Strange Affair of Uncle Harry* (1945), however, George is badly miscast as Harry Quincy, a small-town milquetoast who lives with his two spinster sisters. Driven to poison the neurotic sister (Geraldine Fitzgerald) in order to marry the woman he has fallen in love with (Ella Raines), he accidentally does in the other (Moyna MacGill). George's character is a sympathetic one, and because of the Hays Office edict that no screen criminal go unpunished, the ending was altered; the would-be killer wakes up to find his crime a dream, and the final fade-out is a happy, romantic one. This change so outraged producer Joan Harrison that she quit Universal. *A Scandal in Paris* (1946, later titled *Thieves' Holiday*) finds George back in costume to play Vidocq, the nineteenth-century rogue who became Paris chief of police. Signe Hasso and Carol Landis costar in this light comedy-drama. In *Lured* (1947), a minor murder mystery, he is his usual man-about-town, helping Lucille Ball and Scotland Yard clear up the murders of some beautiful women. Boris Karloff is the mad-artist villain.

George did not appear in any pictures released in 1948, for he had worked very little during the long and painful divorce from Susan in 1947. This was also the year that he met the woman who would become his second wife. Four months before that meeting, a beautiful Hungarian divorcée sitting in the darkness of a second-run movie theatre in New York, entranced by George's performance in *The Moon and Sixpence,* turned to her mother and said, "There is my next husband."

Hollywood: 1948–1957

10 "Cokiline"

"I always adored indifferent, unapproachable men. They were the great challenge of my life," Zsa Zsa Gabor confided to an interviewer shortly after she and George were married in 1949. Having watched him two years earlier move across the screen "like a disdainful prince, cool, remote, elegantly contemptuous of everyone," she began reading magazine interviews and articles on the unapproachable George Sanders but did nothing about meeting him in person: "I'm a fatalist and left it to kismet." Allah apparently smiled on her, for fate brought them together on April 29, 1947, at a party hosted by banker Serge Simonenko in New York City. Tanned and fit, elegantly attired in formal black silk dinner clothes and surrounded by admiring women, George sat "like a pasha" and seemed to her "as irresistible in person" as she had found him on the screen. "Take me to him. I must meet him," she begged her host—and then gushed, "Mr. Sanders, I'm madly in love with you." With a condescending smile George replied, "How well I understand, my dear."

At that moment Zsa Zsa Gabor was neither a celebrity nor an actress. Her only identity had been as the wife of well-known men: first of Burhan Belge, the Propaganda Minister of Turkey whom she had married in her teens in 1939 and had left, still a teenager, in 1941; then of millionaire hotelman Conrad Hilton in a marriage that lasted from 1942 to 1946 (she was six months pregnant with his child the day she saw *The Moon and Sixpence*; her daughter Francesca was born in March 1947, six weeks before the Simonenko party). At that moment, having made fifty-seven pictures, with leading roles in twenty-five, George was a well-known film actor, who once declared in an interview, "I wouldn't have a wife who was more famous than I." Had he known when he met her that within four years Zsa Zsa would acquire not only an identity of her own but international fame, he might have thought twice before leaving with her after the party that night.

Zsa Zsa suggested that George and his friend, author Erich Maria Remarque, accompany her home for a drink. When after several hours Remarque rose and prepared to leave, George coolly announced between bites of caviar and toast that he would be staying the night. "And by the way," he informed Zsa Zsa when they were alone, "I'll call you Cokiline from now on." The word was Russian, he told her. "It's just a term of endearment, Zsa Zsa. You're my sweet little cookie." Twenty-five years after this evening she would say "We always lived happily ever after—before the marriage, during the marriage, and after the marriage." In at least one sense that was so. They would become lovers and separate several times, they would marry and divorce, but throughout the turbulent relationship and the broken marriage there was one constant: in Zsa Zsa, George had found a life-long friend.

Both had been desperately unhappy in their recently ended marriages, and finding happiness so soon after with a new love was an unexpected emotional high for each, particularly Zsa Zsa: "I just adored him . . . I was just very much in love with him. I was very naive and very, very young mentally then. I think he really loved me. I am always very honest with people

. . . I think he liked that." George appreciated and later acknowledged that honesty: "Zsa Zsa is perhaps the most misunderstood woman of our times. She is misunderstood because she is guileless. She allows her vitality and instincts to spring from her without distortion. She doesn't disguise her love of amorous entanglements or jewels or whatever else catches her fancy, because her character is pure. She is whole-cloth." With a revealing use of his own metaphor of The Mask, he adds: "Not for her is the conventional mask of studied behavior . . . The mask is used by people who want either to remain inviolate from the assaults of public life or who need an invented glamour."

For two weeks they were together constantly, and Zsa Zsa was "walking on clouds." She thought they were perfectly compatible: "We had the same tastes, laughed at the same jokes, liked the same friends . . . George had a colorful background, had traveled a lot, knew all the countries I had lived in and understood my cosmopolitan attitude because he shared it. It was the ideal matching." George would later agree only in part with that appraisal: "We were able to make contact on some levels; for example, we both had the same approach to humor, and we understood one another in certain aspects of our analysis of social life. But on certain rather important levels—how to live, for example—we were unable to communicate."

When the two-week idyll ended, George had to return to Hollywood; a few days later Zsa Zsa followed. She arrived to find that he had withdrawn into a shell, distant and uncommunicative. Puzzled and hurt, she returned to New York. Several months passed, during which time there were occasional long-distance telephone conversations. "Mostly I called him. He was always nice, but very aloof and mixed-up." From the newspapers she discovered that he was going out with several Hollywood actresses.

Then suddenly one day George called to announce that he

was in New York and wanted to see her. He was having intensive sessions with his psychoanalyst, he said, and had learned that he was protecting himself from her to avoid being hurt again, that he knew he might get deeply involved and was afraid of the consequences. Zsa Zsa gradually came to believe that "the reason for his so-called indifference was plain unhappiness because he and his wife hadn't fitted together," that "the sickness of his ex-wife and his self-accusations had created a confusion within him. He was afraid to feel happiness while she was so miserable . . . What the public and columnists called a woman-hater was, in reality, a man with the most tender feelings even for the one from whom he had parted . . . It made me love him more."

Yet after only a few days together in New York they quarreled, and she fled to Palm Beach. More months passed. When they later met by accident at another New York party, George seemed to her different, somehow changed. His analyst had helped him to see things more clearly, he told her, but a week later he sailed for Europe, not quite certain, he confessed, why he was leaving. He stayed for two months. At last he called from London, begging her to meet him in Bermuda. Zsa Zsa, by this time hoping "to be cured of my passion for indifferent men," sought the advice of her mother. "It can't last longer than ten days," Mama Jolie told her. "But ten days of happiness in a woman's life is a wonderful and rare thing."

In Bermuda Zsa Zsa found George the most "approachable" she had ever known him. Two weeks later she moved into the Hollywood apartment building he owned on Shoreham Drive, and while he tinkered in his elaborate basement workshop with his inventions (an alarm that sounded when Zsa Zsa forgot to turn off the bath water was one of his ingenious but unmarketable creations), she cooked all his meals, did his laundry, and waited on him. "I'm marrying George Sanders if I have to hit him over the head," she told her family. It was Zsa

Zsa who proposed marriage. "You had better think about it twice," George responded cautiously. "I have many problems, Cokiline. I've been in analysis for years." His reluctance drove her to despair: "I am dying in love with him," she cried to her mother. "But with him it is nothing. He doesn't show emotion." Actually George, who described the courtship as a series of fateful "collisions," seemed to view their marriage as ultimately inevitable: "Finally in Las Vegas we collided with a minister who put an end to all this nonsense with a ring."

The date was April 1, 1949. The bridegroom had forgotten to make hotel reservations, and the wedding night was spent in a sparsely furnished motel room. At first "neither of us spoke," recalled the bride. "George was thinking of his lost freedom and I was thinking of my lost alimony." Under the terms of her divorce from Conrad Hilton Zsa Zsa had forfeited more than a quarter-million dollars by remarrying. Throughout her marriage to George and long after it was over she never expressed any regrets.

They returned to the modest little apartment in Hollywood where Zsa Zsa dressed herself in peasant outfits, cheerfully worked over a hot stove, and decorated the place with materials from the corner hardware store. "George never wanted me to have a career. He was adamant that I be a housewife—and that was it. I was so young, so insecure, I agreed." George had insecurities of his own: "I'm a very helpless man," he told her in a rare moment of exposed vulnerability. "I need a woman like you to mother me." Mama Jolie was outraged: "They went nowhere and did nothing. Every night they went to bed at nine and watched wrestling matches or movies on TV," she complained. "George had wanted a *hausfrau* and that's what my glamorous daughter became. She brought his slippers to him. She rubbed his back, she flattered his ego."

All this would change when Zsa Zsa, now accompanied by daughter Francie and her nanny, bought a Bel Air mansion with fourteen rooms and three acres of gardens. "Cokiline, I don't like big houses," George protested when he saw the place. "I would be lost here. I'm happy in my little apartment. I must have a place to commune with myself, and my workshop is there." They arranged what would prove a disastrous compromise: George would move some of his belongings to the house and keep the rest of his possessions in the apartment. George later claimed he was "allotted a small room in which I was permitted to keep my personal effects," but in fact he had his own rather spacious bedroom suite. When he "moved in," however, he arrived carrying in one hand a small overnight case and in the other a suit and clean shirt on a hanger. Whenever they quarreled George would punish her by removing himself and his "personal effects" to the apartment. Often Zsa Zsa would go days or even weeks without seeing her husband at home and found herself "commuting between my house and his apartment to cook and care for him." Once when he had moved out in a huff, she telephoned late at night and begged to see him. "If you bring me a sandwich and a glass of milk," George told her, "you can come here." She rushed to the refrigerator, fixed a ham sandwich, wrapped it in waxed paper, grabbed a bottle of milk, and at two a.m. drove the ten miles to his apartment. The next day he moved back with her.

This bizarre and frustrating cycle was interrupted by an offer George received to make a picture in Spain. He thought of it as "a sort of honeymoon" for Zsa Zsa, since they hadn't taken a trip since the wedding. She wanted to bring Francie along, but George resisted: "You know how uncomfortable I am with children. I find it hard enough to communicate with adults, but with babies . . ." Francie stayed home with her nurse. "He never liked children or animals," Zsa Zsa later commented, recalling the time she had persuaded him to take her rhinestone-collared gray poodle for a stroll on the streets of

New York City. "I don't know what people are thinking of me, walking this fag dog," he complained.

The film was *Captain Blackjack* (1950) and the director Julien Duvivier. The shooting schedule for the picture was set for eight weeks; it would be almost seven months before it was finished. They flew to Paris, went to Barcelona by train, and then by air to Majorca where most of the location time would be spent. Two decades later George would choose Majorca as his residence, but now as the filming dragged on he found the island monotonous and was convinced that "I was doomed to stay there for the rest of my life . . . the atmosphere surrounding the picture was somewhat deficient in what I might call the serious approach to movie-making." He had no contracted salary—the principal actors received travel and living expenses during the production but were to be paid out of the receipts of the picture —and as it turned out none of them was paid.

George had the title role, supported by Agnes Moorehead, Herbert Marshall, Patricia Roc, and Marcel Dalio. Although effectively directed and in many scenes strikingly photographed, the film was ruined by poor editing and a bad screenplay. George complained daily about the script: he was required to play an American adventurer named Mike Alexander and, despite his cultured British accent, was given dialogue studded with such "Americanisms" as "Is this on the level?" and "Wait for me, honey, I'll be back." Unhappy with the entire project, he escaped by eating and sleeping and as a result put on weight during the long months of production. The change is apparent in the film: scenes shot early in the schedule show him quite fit; in later ones he appears noticeably heavier. The new Mrs. Sanders held up well during her belated and extended "honeymoon," and looking back on the experience George reflected, "Whatever else could be said about Zsa Zsa . . . one thing is certain, she has a lot of guts . . . No one is a better companion on a trip."

They returned home in time to celebrate their first anniversary and for George to undertake a role that would earn him the Academy Award as best supporting actor for 1950: the portrayal of Addison DeWitt in *All About Eve*. It was a production that would create tension between him and Zsa Zsa. When George signed for the picture, she asked him to get her a small part in it, "little more than a walk-on in the last minutes of the film," as she described it. This can only be the role of Phoebe, the ambitious protege who, like Eve, pursues success at any cost. It is pointless to speculate on what turn Zsa Zsa's career might have taken had she played the part. For Barbara Bates, who did, the role led to a string of undistinguished appearances in "B" pictures and suicide in 1969. The part, with some 35 lines of dialogue, was rather more than a walk-on and not likely to have been given to an untried actress. On the other hand, there was no need for George's cutting response: "Don't be silly. Acting isn't for you." It was a judgment he would remember with chagrin less than two years later.

A more serious conflict arose from Zsa Zsa's insecurity and possessiveness at this point in their marriage. She admits to being "sick with jealousy" when George so much as shook hands with another woman, let alone kissed one, and the presence of both Marilyn Monroe and Anne Baxter in the cast of *All About Eve* made her "wretched." Although in the film he kisses neither, his contact on the set with Monroe, who had a two-scene role as his girlfriend, infuriated Zsa Zsa. "I lunched with Marilyn once or twice during the making of the film," George later recalled, "and found her conversation had unexpected depths. She was very beautiful and very inquiring and very unsure." Zsa Zsa thought otherwise and even now becomes tense speaking of it: "He kept coming home and saying to me, 'That poor little innocent girl, she sits there and reads poetry, and there was no place to sit in the commissary so she asked if she could sit with me.' I was furious . . . we were married and George would sit with that little tart. An innocent, wild animal, I would call her."

On another occasion George was making *The Light Touch* with newcomer Pier Angeli, who had just arrived from Italy, and in describing her to his wife praised her beauty in glowing terms. Zsa Zsa seethed quietly until that evening at a party given by George's California psychiatrist, where she took George outside by the pool and began berating him at great length and in strong language. Without warning, he exploded, seized her neck in both hands, and said "I'm going to kill you." A moment later he came to his senses, burst into tears, and apologized. Zsa Zsa was not afraid because she believed he was only "play acting."

George's Academy Award for his role in *All About Eve* was not a surprise or a fluke: a *Daily Variety* poll had accurately predicted the film's Oscars for best picture, direction, screen-play, and supporting actor. Nonetheless, the night of the award ceremonies was for him "an occasion filled with such painful suspense that I never rose above a state of frozen stupefaction." Zsa Zsa, he added, was "filled with delight at attending this top-flight Beano." George was presented his Oscar by Merce-des McCambridge, who had won the Best Supporting Actress award the year before. When his name was announced he rose without looking at Zsa Zsa, walked to the stage, accepted the statuette with a bow to the audience, and disappeared behind the curtain. He did not return to get his wife for the backstage celebration afterwards, and Zsa Zsa remembers waiting for him in the auditorium until it was empty and being cleaned, certain that George had simply forgotten about her. The fact was that he had been emotionally drained by the experience. Once behind the curtain and backstage, he began to weep uncontrol-lably. "I can't help it," he sobbed. "This has unnerved me."

His next picture would have a different and even more unnerving consequence. In the summer of 1951 he was leaving for England and his role in *Ivanhoe*; Zsa Zsa begged to accompany him. "You stay home," he told her. "You would just be bored and would make it impossible for me to work." She was despondent. "I cannot live without him," she cried to her mother. "I will kill myself." Less than a week later her life changed so suddenly and dramatically that she, and her marriage, would never be the same. "I was handed a career on a silver platter," as she later put it. George's brother Tom, a regular panelist on a new television show called "Bachelor's Haven," called to ask a favor. An actress scheduled to be on the guest panel had canceled at the last minute, and the producers were looking for "the wife of a celebrity" to fill in. Would she do it? Still smarting and insecure from George's rejections, Zsa Zsa reluctantly agreed. She appeared on the show liberally sprinkled with diamonds and wearing a 21-carat solitaire ring, which prompted the host to comment admiringly on her jewelry. She responded with a remark that brought down the house: "Darling," she said offhandedly, "these are just my working diamonds." Ad-libbing her way in similar fashion through the rest of the show, she became, in the words of *Daily Variety* a week later, an "instant star" and a regular on the program. Within four months she had a manager, a dramatic coach, a public relations organization, offers for ten motion pictures, and a cover on *Life* magazine. It was her face on this October 13, 1951 cover that smiled at George from an airport newsstand when, the filming of *Ivanhoe* completed, he got off a plane from London. She would in subsequent months smile from the covers of *Look*, *Collier's*, and *Paris Match*.

"Now there were two stars sitting by the same hearth," she later remarked. It was this radically altered phase of their life together that George would remember with undisguised resentment: "My presence in the house was regarded by Zsa Zsa's press photographers, dressmakers, the household staff, and sundry visitors and friends with tolerant amusement. From time to time, as more space was needed to store her ever-mounting stacks of press clippings and photographs . . . I would empty drawers in my room and make them available for the more vital function of housing Zsa Zsa's memorabilia." He saw himself living in her shadow at home, a peripheral figure "standing at the bar under the large portrait of Zsa Zsa, fixing drinks for her newspaper interviewers and photographers. They were most appreciative and would nod to me quite affably as I tended to their needs."

His resentment is more apparent to her today than it was then. In 1960 she still believed George had been "genuinely excited by my success," but by 1972 she saw in deeper retrospect that "our marriage could never survive" the threat to George presented by that success, and more recently, she has acknowledged that "he resented it. He really didn't want me to be an actress." George did recommend her, however, for Tallulah Bankhead's Sunday night radio program, "The Big Show," on which he had himself appeared several times. His motives may not have been the best, for it was a show based on a scripted "comedy of insult" format (*Tallulah*: "I've decided to grow old gracefully." *George*: "And have you?" *Tallulah*: "Whenever I'm in Hollywood I turn down dozens of offers." *George*: "Any for pictures?"). This pattern was unanticipated and unappreciated by Zsa Zsa. She walked out on the show when asked to feed George straight lines for responses she thought demeaning to her, to wives, and to women generally. "The lines were so insulting," she recalls. "I still remember some of them. He says, 'I never see my wife—only when she washes my socks.' I didn't like it." George was angered because he had got her the job, and they had one of their fights that ended with his moving out to the apartment. On this occasion he stayed away for five days.

The new context for their relationship—Zsa Zsa's growing success and independence—deepened George's long-standing insecurity. Some time before, he had moved his piano into the Bel Air house, and "every time he'd become angry after my career started, he'd move the piano out, back to his apartment," Zsa Zsa remembers. "I'd be at the studio and my maid would call, saying, 'Miss Gabor, Mr. Sanders has the mover here moving his piano out.' When his mood would change, he'd move the piano back in." It was during this difficult period that George was offered an opportunity to change the direction of his own career.

To this point the public was largely unaware that George Sanders, the arrogant, silken-tongued cad on-screen, was a trained singer. "I've used my singing voice principally for singing little songs of a scurrilous nature for my friends," he told an interviewer during this period. Zsa Zsa relates with pride that when he felt like it, George could be "a gay, delightful host who sat at the piano and entertained us for hours with hilarious, off-color songs." Many of his costars remember those impromptu performances: "Sometimes at parties he would play the piano and sing bawdy songs—very well," recalled Cornel Wilde; Ella Raines thought his voice "elegant, quite natural and well trained"; and Anthony Quinn was struck by his "wonderful singing voice . . . a wonderful baritone." Joan Fontaine, not surprisingly, holds a contrary opinion: George often "sang for his supper," she says, by playing the piano and singing "ribald ditties in a constipated voice."

An independent opinion may be formed by listening to any of several albums George recorded in the mid-fifties: *The George Sanders Touch*, for example, an anthology of twelve nostalgic pieces—among them "September Song," "As Time Goes By," "More Than You Know," and a song of his own composition, "Such Is My Love." By any reasonable standard, it must be said that George possessed a rich baritone voice. When he sang an aria from *Simon Boccanegra* in one of his appearances for Tallulah Bankhead, many in the the audience did not believe the voice they heard was his and left convinced he had been mouthing a recorded selection from the opera. Brian Aherne always insisted that George could have had a career as an operatic baritone and tells of an incident at the studio of Maestro Cepparo, George's voice coach. Without his knowledge, the maestro had planted the manager of the San Francisco Opera Company outside an open door while George sang several arias. According to Aherne, who was present, this gentleman immediately offered George the role of Scarpia in *Tosca* for the upcoming opera season. To their astonishment, George "said he did not want to become an opera singer" and politely but firmly declined.

When it became known that Ezio Pinza was leaving the cast of the Broadway production of *South Pacific* and the producers were looking for a replacement, George saw an opportunity to move outside the shadow of his successful wife and perhaps embark on a new career himself. Deciding "it was high time I stopped hiding my light under a bushel," he worked with unaccustomed vigor for several weeks getting his voice into condition. After practicing "Some Enchanted Evening" day after day until even little Francie knew all the words to the song, he made a recording and sent it off to Rodgers and Hammerstein. Surprised and impressed, they flew him to New York for a personal audition and then quickly signed him to a fifteen-month contract.

When the replacement was announced, many in the movie colony regarded it as a publicity plant until George sang two numbers from the musical on Hedda Hopper's Sunday night radio show, convincing doubters that he had the voice to play the role. He had the voice but, as it turned out, not the confidence. A week later he telephoned Brian Aherne and asked anxiously, "Do you think I can do it?" Despite Aherne's reassurances and similar encouragement from others, the day the final contract arrived in the mail George became quite agitated and within a few hours developed a backache so severe he couldn't walk. Doctors could find no physical cause for the pain; nevertheless, he called Rodgers and Hammerstein in New York and got them to release him from his contract. "No sooner had I been freed from my commitment than the backache vanished," he confessed. To Zsa Zsa he simply said, "I can't explain it, but I can't face a live audience. It appalls me."

He had reacted the same way before in a similar situation: when Robert Morley quit the stage play *Edward, My Son* at the peak of its run, the producer persuaded George to take over the role; on the eve of rehearsals he "succumbed to funk," convinced he could not match Morley's characterization, and begged off. It would be fifteen years after the *South Pacific* fiasco before he would again consider a stage performance; that too would end badly, but owing to personal tragedy rather than insecurity. Hollywood, not Broadway, finally showcased the Sanders voice, for George was comfortable and confident singing only for the camera in *Call Me Madam* (1953). His costar Ethel Merman remembered him as "sweet and believable and warm as toast" in the part of Cosmo Constantine.

George's failure to achieve a career move with *South Pacific* was in striking contrast to Zsa Zsa's continuing success. In two years, she appeared in four films: *Lovely to Look At, Lili, The Story of Three Loves,* and most importantly, John Huston's *Moulin Rouge.* When she was offered the role of Jane Avril in that production, George warned her that it was a major part in a very distinguished picture, one that would become a classic; he didn't think she could do it, or should even try. When she did and received excellent reviews for her performance—her slow and sensuous descent of a staircase, singing the famous "Song From the Moulin Rouge," is one of the high points in the film—he was not pleased. "He still wanted me just as his wife, a housewife who cooked his meals, made him hot sandwiches and brought him a glass of milk before bedtime."

As they arrived for the Hollywood premiere of the picture, "the kids rushed after me for autographs. They all knew me. One turned to George with 'You look familiar; what's your name?' " Zsa Zsa sensed then that the marriage might not survive. The situation was made even more precarious as their work kept them apart for extended periods during 1952 and 1953: Zsa Zsa was in Paris and London for the filming of other pictures and George in Italy to appear with Ingrid Bergman in Roberto Rossellini's *The Lonely Woman*. It was during these lengthy separations that Zsa Zsa began a love affair which would create an international scandal, cripple her career, and deal the final blow to her marriage.

"Diplomat Extraordinary, His Excellency Don Porfirio Rubirosa, Dominican Ambassador to the Republic of France," as George referred to him some years later, started his climb to notoriety by marrying the daughter of Dominican dictator Rafael Trujillo, eventually to be divorced by her on grounds of desertion. French film star Danielle Darrieux became his next wife, followed in two years by tobacco heiress Doris Duke, whose subsequent divorce settlement provided "Rubi" with a generous income for life. Not a man of extraordinary abilities, his talents were reputed to be mainly athletic and limited to the polo field and the boudoir. It was this primitive masculinity which attracted Zsa Zsa when they met during the New York premier of *Moulin Rouge*. She was especially vulnerable at that time. George had left her to make his picture in Italy with the words, "Don't come to Rome, you will just spoil my work—and my fun." Rubirosa was attentive, flattering, and insistent. "On the one hand there was my husband—indifferent, supercilious, and hurting me far more than anyone knew," she rationalized. "Then there was Rubi . . . Because I was overexcited and overmiserable, because I was lonely, I said yes to him." She later explained this and other "amorous entanglements," as George would kindly call them, with the simple statement, "It is my fate."

The affair was played out across America and Europe, continuing on and off for some three years. Although she first became involved with Rubirosa to satisfy emotional needs, the physical attraction proved to be what bound her to him for so long, despite the risk to reputation, career, and marriage. Zsa Zsa found Rubirosa's sexual prowess "so wonderful that he was addictive" and confessed to her mother that "Rubi is for me like a disease," unconsciously paraphrasing one of George's lines from *The Moon and Sixpence*. Although Rubirosa proclaimed undying love for Zsa Zsa, he was soon mounting a campaign to woo and wed yet another heiress, Barbara Hutton, at that time probably the second richest woman in the world after Doris Duke. This came to involve a good deal of commuting for both: Rubirosa would jet between continents to see Zsa Zsa and Barbara, Zsa Zsa dashed back and forth between Rubi and George. She spent a week with her husband at Ravello, Italy, where location shooting of Rossellini's project was in progress.

George was unhappy with the production. He had accepted the offer because of his admiration for the director and also because he wished to work with Ingrid Bergman again. But on his arrival in Naples he learned that the Maestro, as he came to call Rossellini disdainfully, intended to shoot the picture without a script. This and other of the director's eccentricities—aimless shooting, jumbled dialogue, non-existent plot—eventually reduced George to tears of frustration, and he told Bergman, "I can't go on inventing dialogue or getting the lines at the last minute." When he asked to be released from the picture, he was told that Rossellini, whose reputation was at low ebb, had been able to raise money for the production only by getting a "name" actor to costar with Bergman and that backing had been secured on the basis of his being in the film. He felt ill-used, and Zsa Zsa's visit did little to cheer him.

As her successes steadily mounted, she no longer seemed the woman he had married. At a cast party in Ravello, she and Bergman met for the first time when Ingrid walked over to the renowned Zsa Zsa Gabor and said, "I want to meet George's wife." Zsa Zsa bristled, but managed a smile and replied, "And I would like to meet Mrs. Rossellini." As she later explained, "I resented Ingrid calling me 'George's wife.'" In fact, she objected to the term "wife" itself. "I don't like to be called that. It is bourgeois and unglamorous," she had complained to a reporter interviewing George. "Call her my married mistress," George said to the journalist. "Or perhaps a lady pirate."

Her sporadic visits to Italy were tense and uncomfortable for him because he had known for some time of her indiscretions with Rubirosa, having received letters and cablegrams from friends about the affair. But there was no blow-up, no direct confrontation. George showed his anger and resentment in small, indirect ways. At a gathering of the combined casts of Rossellini's picture and John Huston's *Beat the Devil,* which happened to be shooting on location in Ravello at the same time, Humphrey Bogart mentioned to George that Zsa Zsa should have sandals for the rough streets of the town. "I can't afford it," he snapped. "You cheap bastard," Bogart muttered angrily, then walked across the street and bought her a pair. Two years before, lunching with her and Stewart Granger in the MGM studio commissary during the filming of *The Light Touch*, George was sulking over another, less devastating domestic crisis with Zsa Zsa and refused to give her a cigarette, saying he "couldn't afford" to. Granger got up and bought her a pack.

When the filming of *The Lonely Woman* was at last completed, George flew to Cannes to meet Zsa Zsa, who had come down from Paris, where she was Rubirosa's house guest. Still, there were no accusations; they spent a placid two weeks going to parties and casinos. From there George left for Hollywood, and she returned to Paris "to assist in the promotion of good will between the Dominican Republic and France," as George put it. On his return he spent a week or so relaxing in solitude at the Bel Air mansion. Then, having sold his apartment building, he moved all of his belongings into a rented house in Pacific Palisades. Zsa Zsa's liaison with Rubirosa continued. Publicly, George feigned indifference: Rubirosa? "I'm too discreet to inquire." Zsa Zsa? "I had a card from her this morning. I don't remember what it said."

In the autumn of 1953 Zsa Zsa went to New York to do a television show and was joined there by her lover. This particular assignation was widely reported in the newspapers, and two days later George, in a surprise move, filed for divorce. The suit complained that his wife had subjected him to inhuman treatment, had humiliated him in front of the entire world, and had caused his health to deteriorate (Zsa Zsa thought this last charge was "tongue-in-cheek"). She filed a cross-complaint for separate maintenance, charging mental cruelty. In order to obtain concrete evidence of Zsa Zsa's infidelity, George retained a firm of private detectives. This produced the long-deferred confrontation in what would prove the final and most bizarre chapter of their marriage.

It was a traditional Gabor family gathering on Christmas Eve of 1953, with one notable difference: joining Mama Jolie, Magda, and Eva at Zsa Zsa's Bel Air home was her illicit lover, Porfirio Rubirosa. None of the other assembled Gabors wanted him there. Jolie warned Zsa Zsa that she was courting disaster by continuing to see him, and the two sisters unsuccessfully tried to ignore him. When all the presents had been opened and the after-dinner brandy drunk, the group dispersed with relief all around, Mama and her two daughters to their automobiles in the driveway, Zsa Zsa and Rubirosa to her bedroom upstairs.

Outside in a rented car parked down the street sat George and two detectives. They had arrived several hours before but were waiting until the visiting Gabor family departed. George was apprehensive enough about facing Zsa Zsa; to break into the house with all the Gabors present, he remarked, would be like "confronting the Spanish Armada in a rowboat." Waiting a discreet half-hour after the cars pulled out of the drive, the three men put their plan into action. Silently crossing the lawn, they assembled an expandable metal ladder and leaned it up against the house under Zsa Zsa's bedroom. While the two detectives steadied it, George mounted the shaky steps until he was standing on the top rung, eye-level with the middle of the windows. As he leaned forward to peer in, there was a small cracking sound, followed immediately by a loud crash as the glass gave way and shattered, pitching him forward and into the darkened room. Zsa Zsa screamed and quickly pulled on a robe; Rubirosa fled noiselessly into a dressing closet. George, momentarily disoriented, found the light switch and flipped it on, then strode to her desk where a photograph of himself was displayed and angrily tore it to pieces.

Zsa Zsa had not seen him in several months. Despite the circumstances, she stared at him admiringly: "He had grown a beard for a new film," she remembers. "He wore a blue turtleneck sweater, faded blue jeans, and he looked so beautiful—a big, bronzed, bearded, blue-eyed man, so much more beautiful, I thought, than Rubi could ever be." She noticed that he was breathing with difficulty and seemed unsteady. Rushing to his side, she asked if he was ill.

"No, my dear," George replied. "I'm an old man. I've absolutely no business climbing ladders." He was calm now, almost subdued. They went downstairs and had a drink together, neither of them mentioning Rubirosa. As he was leaving, Zsa Zsa gave him the Christmas package she had planned to send him. Remembering what had brought him there,

George said with a wicked laugh, "This visit is my Christmas present to you" and departed. When the door closed she burst into tears. Rubirosa, now fully dressed, materialized from the top of the stairway. "You don't know it, but you're still in love with him," he told her. "You are crying like a little idiot because you love that man."

Life would not be the same for the lovers after that evening. Brian Aherne observed them at a dinner party some time afterward and noted that Rubirosa drank heavily and was quarrelsome with her. (He mentioned this to George, who was amused. "You see," he said, "even a Dominican worm will turn"). Yet their affair continued sporadically for more than a year, punctuated by incidents that furnished more fodder for the tabloids: Zsa Zsa showed up for a Las Vegas premiere wearing a velvet patch to cover the black eye given her by Rubirosa, whom she described to reporters as "a beater of women, a blackguard, a coward." She soon forgave him, and their antics resumed, accompanied by increased attention from the press after Ruirosa wed Barbara Hutton. "Zsa Zsa was ruining her career by courting such scandalous publicity," Mama Jolie fretted. Her agent dropped her, and Paramount notified her new representative that the "unhealthy publicity must end." It did end, finally, as one of the most publicized romances of the decade, by weary mutual consent. Zsa Zsa realized the price she had paid for this "amorous entanglement": "On account of Rubi I have lost George, who I really love," she told her mother tearfully. "I'll always love George."

The divorce hearing was held on April 2, 1954, one day after what would have been their fifth wedding anniversary, in a Los Angeles courtroom crowded with reporters and photographers. George was not present. In Spain making a picture, he had instructed his attorney by overseas telephone not to contest Zsa Zsa's countersuit or restrain her testimony. "She seems to need some kind of passion play to restore her life," he said. The divorce was granted to Zsa Zsa on her petition.

"After our divorce, Zsa Zsa and I enjoyed a much more harmonious relationship," George later reflected. "We got along infinitely better than we did as marriage partners." Zsa Zsa happily agrees: "George was right. Our divorce made us good friends." They would be friends, and occasionally lovers, until the end of his life. During the filming of *Death of a Scoundrel* (1956), in which they appeared together, she "very often went home with him" after a day's shooting. After George married Benita Hume Colman in 1959, Zsa Zsa remained his close friend. "I always saw George, even Benita and George. They always said they wanted to adopt me." Benita often invited her to their home, saying on one occasion "come over, our husband is not feeling well at all . . . You make the old boy laugh and keep him happy." After Benita died in 1967 and George returned from Majorca, lonely and unhappy, Zsa Zsa relates that he "stayed at my house for quite a while." When in 1969 Zsa Zsa replaced Julie Harris on Broadway in "Forty Carats," George came to New York, moved into an adjoining apartment in the Waldorf Towers, and stayed the entire four months of her engagement: "We were always together," she says of this period. After George and her sister Magda were married in 1970, Zsa Zsa went to their home in Palm Springs to show her how to prepare the foods he liked. She and George were "always in touch," almost to the end: they were together at a dinner party in England a few days before his death.

"We had really never been out of each other's lives entirely from the day we first met," Zsa Zsa said when he died. "He was part of my life—like my child, my father, my family . . . He was the love of my life." To this George would likely have replied, still in character twenty-five years after that first meeting, "How well I understand, my dear."

11 "Ripe for the Headshrinkers"

Sixteen years old when she costarred with George in *The Moon and Sixpence* and enabled by the intuitive perceptions of youth to glimpse behind his off-screen mask of cynicism and aloofness, Elena Verdugo remembers thinking at the time that "though he *looked* 'superior,' I don't think he *felt* so." The year was 1942, four years before George would begin the round of psychiatrists and analysis that continued for the rest of his life and upon which he became increasingly dependent. "He was always in therapy," Zsa Zsa recalls sadly today. "Always." George himself maintained that his experience with psychiatry began in 1951 after the *South Pacific* debacle. "It was then that I decided I ought to see a psychiatrist," he later wrote about the episode. "I had just thrown up an opportunity I would probably never have again; for weeks I had worked and plotted and schemed to get that part and then when I had got it, I didn't want it. I was ripe for the headshrinkers." In fact, he had been in analysis since Susan left him in 1946 and was in New York when he first met Zsa Zsa in 1947 only because his psychoanalyst was there.

Before as well as during the periods he was in therapy, George dealt with his insecurity by constructing various mechanisms of escape. As his backache had been a means of escaping the commitment of live public performance, so his personal "eccentricities" were to the same end: avoidance and escape by withdrawal. He withdrew both directly and indirectly, the first by his reclusive lifestyle and distancing stance with people; the other with what may be termed the sleeper motif, an extraordinary ability to cat-nap, to drop quickly into sleep whenever he wished to avoid either confrontation or contact of any kind with those around him.

Certainly, throughout his film career his relations with other actors were characterized by withdrawal and aloofness. Gene Tierney, a costar in three films in the forties and with whom he was on intimate terms, nonetheless describes George as "reserved." Anthony Quinn, with him in a 1942 picture, found him "a very private person. We did not socialize very much." Ella Raines, his costar in 1945, remembers "he didn't mix with the cast or crew and stayed in his trailer alone unless called for camera," adding that "he was very withdrawn." Cornel Wilde, with him in a 1947 production, thought him "very lonely and perhaps unhappy," and during a 1949 filming, Victor Mature remembers George as "a recluse" on the set. Robert Douglas, in 1952 and 1955 pictures with him, recalls that George "preferred his own company to associations with other actors." "He was a private person," according to Patric Knowles who costarred with him in a 1958 film, "and hard to know well." Elke Sommer, who worked with him in 1964, is more specific. "He was asocial, very aloof during the filming, and rarely joined the cast at meals," she recalls. "Between takes he usually went off by himself and read a book. When the day's work was ended he left the studio instantly." Even George's director on that film, Blake Edwards, describes their relationship as "never close, never personal," adding cryptically that "the one or two anecdotes I can recall would not be appropriate" to relate. Juliet Colman, who became George's stepdaughter when he married Ronald Colman's widow Benita in 1959, worked for George on the sets of pictures in 1964 and 1965 and confirms that "when not on camera, he was alone in his dressing room reading, thinking, snoozing, occasionally on the phone. He did not socialize on the set."

The ability to withdraw quickly into sleep was one of George's most widely known—because well-publicized—"eccentricities." Early in his Hollywood career some mention of his predeliction for sleep was a hallmark of magazine articles and interviews. "His big ambition is to snaffle 20 hours sleep a day," one interviewer wrote in 1938, "but failing that, he snaffles as much as he can." Another in 1942 refers to "the local Rip Van Winkle legend about George Sanders. On the set he cat-naps between takes and even dozes in the face of people talking to him." The piece goes on, however, to quote a perceptive friend, who theorized that "George pulls the sleep act mostly to avoid boring small talk and cheap conversation. It's a defense." Another interviewer came to the same determination: after observing that "on the set between scenes Sanders could be mistaken for an abandoned body. He can sleep anywhere at any time," he concludes that "he uses sleep as a kind of fender against press agents, visitors, and other pests." When his brother Tom gave an interview about himself and George, he mentioned an episode in England before George came to Hollywood which involved his sleeping and felt obliged to explain, "oh yes, he liked to sleep even then." By 1944 the legend had become so familiar that an article purporting to be about some of George's worries was entitled "Things That Keep Sanders Awake" and began with the observation, "Mr. Sanders' lust for sleep has become a part of Hollywood folklore." Zsa Zsa points out, however, that George's acting was never affected by his between-takes napping, even as late as 1956 during the film she made with him: "He went into the dressing room, laid down on a flat, and when they called him for a take, he just came out and could act wonderfully."

These modes of withdrawal and escape were successful in keeping others at a distance when George was required to be among them in the course of his work. Off the set, his reclusive lifestyle kept at bay those with whom he was uncomfortable associating. As the courses of his on-screen and private lives converged, he increasingly put to his own uses the screen persona of disdain, cynicism, and rudeness. The cold, aloof, haughty Cad insinuated himself into George's own personality at the expense of his emotional and psychological well-being.

Unaware of the sources of his problems, he could nonetheless see the consequences of their symptoms, and he sought help. His most extensive experience with psychiatry, during the early 1950s, involved a half-dozen analysts on both coasts. He saw the first, in New York, on a daily basis for three months. "He was a very friendly, chatty sort of psychiatrist," George recalled, "and he would frequently spend a large amount of my fifty-dollar hour telling me funny stories about his other patients." George left him and began seeing a Jungian analyst. "He seemed almost exclusively concerned with my dreams. I had always been a rather modest dreamer, but by the time I got through with this man my dreams had become Cecil B. De-Mille productions. It was the least I could do for him." He found no help in dream interpretation. "None of this explained why I had developed a backache at the thought of having to appear for fifteen months in *South Pacific*."

His next choice was a hypnotherapist. "When you wake up," he was told, "you will feel much happier, your anxieties will have diminished. You will have more confidence in yourself. You will be able to use your great natural talents to the full. Your performances on the screen will become even more brilliant." But George had, of course, been feigning the light trance his therapist thought had been induced. "I was thinking that it would have been a pity to have been asleep and have missed such delightful eulogies," he joked about the session. He then tried a more unconventional therapist, one who did not subscribe to the theories of Freud, Jung, or hypnotism. "He didn't even believe in aspirins." This time he was told that he was "suffering from the sickness of our age: cynicism." The treatment prescribed was to "return to the basic rhythms of life, to simplicity" and to renounce all material possessions. When this therapist's hourly charge was revealed to be seventy-five dollars instead of fifty, George asked the reason and was told it was part of the treatment: "It will help you to attach less importance to money and material things."

Clearly, George did not take seriously these ministrations and reported them with tongue in cheek. Yet he had his own insights about his problems: "One of the difficulties about being cured of anything by a psychiatrist is that, since basically one does not want to be cured, one seeks out those practitioners who are least likely to cure you," adding in any case that "most people in distress are more interested in being comforted than being cured." It was not until he took Zsa Zsa's advice to see her own analyst that he began to think he was making progress and acquiring some insight into the workings of his mind. "Zsa Zsa's taste in psychiatrists, as in other spheres, turned out to be exemplary. He was one of the best." The treatment involved injections of sodium pentathol, and for a period of several months George seriously immersed himself in the therapy. He was diagnosed as obsessive-compulsive owing to "a profound need on my part for self-punishment." He came to the realization, "in the light of the psychological knowledge I was acquiring," that "my rejection of the Rodgers and Hammerstein offer made sense. And so did my marriage to Zsa Zsa." At this point George believed he was cured of his obsessional implulses and periodic backaches. He also thought himself "cured" of Zsa Zsa.

Having made these "discoveries," he was able to report in 1960 that "nowadays, I am on much better terms with myself and am learning to view my failings with infinite compassion," adding that if he had at times taken psychiatrists lightly, he nonetheless regarded many of them as "brilliant and dedicated men and their discoveries about the human mind of supreme importance." But at that point he had another twelve years of living to endure, a period that would bring considerably more anguish and tragedy than he had yet experienced or could accommodate and which would eventually destroy what faith in psychiatry he had managed to build. In April 1972, only days before he left London for Barcelona, where he ended his life, Zsa Zsa visited him and, realizing how mentally distressed he was, insisted on taking him to an English psychiatrist she was certain could help him. When they walked into the the analyst's office, George immediately announced, "All right, here I am. And now, as there is no point in wasting your time, I might as well leave." Seventy-two hours later he was dead by his own hand.

12 "This Is My Mask"

"On the screen I am usually suave and cynical. This is my mask, and it has served me faithfully," George acknowledged well past the mid-point in his career and not long after his extensive experience with therapy and analysis in the 1950s. "Fortunately, my mask has not only protected me but provided me with a living." The high point in his on-screen use of this mask, the apotheosis of the Cad, was reached during the period 1947-1956 and is illuminated by four film roles in particular: *The Private Affairs of Bel Ami* (1947), *The Ghost and Mrs. Muir* (1947), *All About Eve* (1950), and *Death of a Scoundrel* (1956). Two of these were supporting performances, the others lead roles. Each demonstrates the culmination in final form of what had been developing for nearly twenty years.

George, as Duroy (Bel Ami) in *The Private Affairs of Bel Ami*, an adaptation of the Guy de Maupassant novel, heartlessly uses women and coldly betrays friends to further his career as a newspaper journalist. When the friend (John Carradine) who got him his start dies, Duroy marries his influential widow (Ann Dvorak), after casting aside his mistress Clotilde ("you've behaved toward me like a cad ever since I've known you," she reproaches him bitterly). He subsequently persuades his bride to encourage the romantic overtures of his publisher in order to get inside information useful to him. When she does, he has them spied on and sues for divorce, for by this time he intends to marry a wealthy banker's daughter (Susan Douglas), whose middle-aged mother (Katherine Emery) he had earlier seduced ("I have lighted a fire in an old, soot-filled chimney," he muses). All very complicated and nasty. The denouement has Duroy killed in a duel with the recently discovered heir to a title Duroy had appropriated in order to make himself a count.

Scattering epigrams in much the same manner as his Lord Henry Wotton in *The Picture of Dorian Gray,* George plays the part of Bel Ami with the detachment of a blasé boulevardier. "Marriage and love are two entirely different subjects," he tells his assembled dinner guests. And, "Human society could hardly exist without deception" to a man he has cheated. He accounts for his success as a society columnist by explaining that "people are so full of malice they are always ready to believe gossip." The film was not a critical success ("Blame the whole mess on Albert Lewin, who not only directed but wrote the screenplay," advised Bosley Crowther in his relentlessly negative New York *Times* review), but for George it was a portrayal of the sociopathic cad that had its genesis in *The Moon and Sixpence* and would find further and more subtle development in another picture released the same year.

"A perfumed parlor snake," the ghost of Captain Daniel Gregg (Rex Harrison) accurately characterizes Miles Fairley (George) for Mrs. Muir (Gene Tierney) in the romantic fantasy *The Ghost and Mrs. Muir.* His warning is of course to no avail. The widow needs companionship and love, and when Miles proposes marriage she acknowledges that he is "conceited, erratic, and childish" but is unaware that he is also married. They first meet in a publisher's office where Miles condescendingly asks if her manuscript is "a cookbook? I hope not another life of Byron?" He himself is a writer of children's books under the pseudonym "Uncle Neddy." Then "all your cynicism must be nothing but a pose," Lucy Muir suggests, to which Miles replies, "Uncle Neddy is a pose, but deep in my heart I loath all the little monsters." When the inevitable confrontation between Mrs. Muir and Mrs. Fairley (Anna Lee) takes place, the wife informs her, "It isn't the first time something like this has happened." George plays the now familiar role of the suave, ingratiatingly self-indulgent bounder with a fatuous honesty ("I am not only irresponsible but unreasonable") which charms Mrs. Muir, the audience, and reviewers (the New York *Times* took note of how George's "acting skill" carries off the role of Miles).

But it is his Academy Award-winning performance as Addison DeWitt in *All About Eve* which remains George's consummate and most finely etched portrait of the elegantly mannered, cynical, venom-tongued Cad. More menacing than the lordly fop of *Lloyd's of London,* more urbane than the arrogant, monocled Germans of *Lancer Spy* and *Man Hunt,* more refined than the heartless, woman-hating artist of *The Moon and Sixpence,* more malevolent than the blasé, epigrammatic Lord Henry Wotton of *The Picture of Dorian Gray,* George's Addison DeWitt both incorporates and transcends all of them in a masterful synthesis which is more than the sum of its parts.

The script of *All About Eve* calls for the voice of narrator Addison to be "crisp, cultured, precise" and the character himself "not young, not unattractive, a fastidious dresser, sharp of eye and merciless of tongue." Writer-director Joseph Mankiewicz did not have George in mind for the part of Addison when he wrote the script, but by general accord of both audiences and critics George matched the role as if it had in fact been written for him. "To those of you who do not read or know anything of the world in which you live," Addison intones in the opening scene, "it is perhaps necessary to introduce myself. I am Addison DeWitt. My native habitat is the theatre—in it I toil not, neither do I spin. I am a critic and commentator. I am essential to the theatre as ants to a picnic, as the boll weevil to a cotton field."

From the first scene at the Siddons Award banquet the story unfolds in flashback, a saga of theatrical ambition and conceit, pride, deception and hypocrisy. Young Eve Harrington (Anne Baxter), who wants to become the brightest star on Broadway, employs a calculated image of shy helplessness to insinuate herself into the confidence of one of the leading ladies of the stage, Margo Channing (Bette Davis), and becomes her understudy. By playing on Margo's fear of aging, Eve creates conflict between the star and her fiance, director Bill Sampson (Gary Merrill), tricks Margo into getting stranded out of town so, as understudy, she can go on the night that top New York critics will be in the audience, and breaks up the marriage of playwright Lloyd Richards (Hugh Marlowe) and his wife Karen (Celeste Holm). She deceives all but Addison, who has seen everything and is suprised by nothing in the theatre; he recognizes at once Eve's pretense and calculating designs. It is he who confronts her with her real past and then uses her for his own purposes. She becomes trapped in her own web and must accede to him in order to achieve the success she aspires to. The end of the film comes full circle out of flashback to the sham of the awards dinner, where Eve accepts her trophy as Actress of the Year with affected humility. After the ceremony, in an ironic commentary, a young and aspiring actress (Barbara Bates) attaches herself to Eve in much the same manner as Eve had to Margo.

"George Sanders is walking wormwood, neatly wrapped in a mahogany veneer, as a vicious and powerful drama critic who has a licentious list toward pretty girls," wrote Bosley Crowther in his enthusiastic New York *Times* review. One of those pretty girls and his protege of the moment is, of course,

Marilyn Monroe in her bit part as Miss Caswell, whom Addison sneeringly introduces to Margo as "an actress . . . a graduate of the Copacabana School of Dramatic Arts." By and large it is Addison's commentary both as narrator and character which sustains the level of withering satire at the heart of the film: "We are a breed apart from the rest of humanity, we theatre folk. We are the original displaced personalities, concentrated gatherings of neurotics, egomaniacs, emotional misfits, and precocious children." And in the scene in which he traps Eve with the facts of her deception, Addison carries the thematic burden of the picture. "That I should want you at all suddenly strikes me as the height of improbability," he tells her as she finally submits. "But that, in itself, is probably the reason. You're an improbable person, Eve, and so am I. We have that in common. Also a contempt for humanity, an inability to love and be loved, insatiable ambition, and talent. We deserve each other."

Nominated for a record 13 Academy Awards, *All About Eve* was voted Best Picture, and Oscars went to Mankiewicz for both his screenplay and direction, as well as to costume designers Edith Head and Charles LeMaire. Both Bette Davis and Anne Baxter were nominated but neither was honored; Baxter insisted upon campaigning for Best Actress rather than in the supporting actress category and split the Academy vote with Davis, enabling Judy Holliday to win for *Born Yesterday*. George's Oscar as Best Supporting Actor for his role surprised no one in Hollywood, for he was the pre-ceremony favorite over nominees Erich von Stroheim, Edmund Gwenn, Sam Jaffe, and Jeff Chandler. It was a performance all but impossible to top, and in fact George never did. His next role as full-blown cad was in a far weaker vehicle, *Death of a Scoundrel*.

"George Sanders, who appears to have made a profession out of portraying a variety of heels, clicks effectively in the title role," wrote one reviewer of *Death of a Scoundrel*. "He is

thoroughly at home in the role: urbane, elegant, and deft."
Aside from this effective portrayal, the picture is of interest
because George is joined in the cast by his brother Tom (again
playing his screen brother) and ex-wife Zsa Zsa. It was the only
film in which she and George appeared together. Essentially a
rake's progress incorporating theft, betrayal, seduction, murder
and suicide, the story follows the career of suave and callous
Clementi Sabourin (George), whose personal history is reminiscent of the life of notorious financier and gallant Serge
Rubenstein. In the course of rising to the top of the financial
heap, Sabourin betrays his brother (Tom), who is killed as a
consequence, and takes advantage of a succession of lovely
women, played by Yvonne DeCarlo, Nancy Gates, Coleen
Gray, and Zsa Zsa. George gives a smooth performance in this
"king-sized cad's vehicle," but the picture is absorbing only as
melodrama rather than the dissection of a complex character it
was apparently intended.

At this point, the "curious sorcery" of George's life had
fashioned a protective mask compounded of the memorable
cads he had played on the screen: the haughty Lord Everett
Stacy, the unfeeling Prussian von Tranisch, the woman-hating
Charles Strickland, the blasé Lord Henry Wotton, the careerist
Bel Ami, the conceited seducer Miles Fairley, the manipulative
Sabourin, and perhaps most of all, the elegant, urbane, and
cynical Addison DeWitt. This carefully cultivated, almost
seamless mask was the face George presented to the world.
Were there none who were permitted to glimpse behind it?
Despite the assimilation of aloofness and rudeness of his screen
personalities into his personal life, George did on rare occasions
reveal to "safe" friends and acquaintances enough of his inner
self to validate in part his facetious remark later in life that
"whereas on the screen I am invariably a sonofabitch, in life I
am a dear, dear boy." Fewer than a half-dozen co-players and
only two personal friends were aware of the kindness and

compassion that lay dormant behind his facade of cynicism and detachment.

"There were sides to him the public and many of his co-workers never knew; he was a man about whom volumes could be written." This observation comes not from Stuart Hall or Brian Aherne, the two men who were generally thought to be George's only "close" friends (although as Douglas Fairbanks Jr. comments, "he had many companions; I don't know what *close* friends he had"), but from Mike Mazurki. However unlikely it might appear on the surface, ex-professional wrestler and typecast heavy Mazurki shared some common ground with George—age, physical size, foreign background, for a start—and they became good friends while working together on *Samson and Delilah* (1949) and *The Light Touch* (1951). Mazurki was born in Austria, of Ukranian descent, before emigrating to America as a boy, and he and George "enjoyed showing off to cast and crew by chatting away in a kind of Russian/Ukranian," he recalls, and they spent a good deal of time together "discussing the world in general and sports in particular. George was interested in one-to-one sports, especially wrestling." When Mazurki was in London filming *Night and the City* (1950), George was in England and visited Mike on the set, where they "hung around to rap with Stanislalu Zbyszko, former international wrestling champion."

From those few with whom he felt affinity or kinship, George neither withdrew nor escaped into sleep. "He had a sensitivity to other people's moods and needs," Mazurki remembers, "and when he talked with you he really concentrated—you felt you were the only other person in the world." Another actor George felt close to and whose company he enjoyed was Robert Douglas, who appeared with him in *Ivanhoe* (1952) and *The Scarlet Coat* (1955). "My friendship with George was very good," Douglas says, "starting out with an ability to compete well with him at the game of croquet" (at which

George was also an accomplished player, having once won the Goldwyn Cup—a competition among the Hollywood British colony). "We had adjoining rooms during *Ivanhoe*, and he preferred to dine with my wife and me in his robe rather than dress and go out. I liked him so much."

Clearly, George could be sincere and pleasant to those he believed genuinely liked him or who did not pose a threat to him. "He was one of the most warm and friendly actors I've ever worked with," Elena Verdugo acknowledges. "I was an ignorant sixteen-year-old, and when he corrected my speech ('Elena, the word is height, not heighth'), it was as a friendly teacher." Three decades later on the set of *Dark Purpose* (1964), costar Shirley Jones recalls, George "who claimed to dislike children" sat beside her four-year-old son Shaun every day on the set and "ended up reading him comic books in French. They became best friends." And despite his reputation for tight-fistedness, George is remembered otherwise by some co-players. Victor Mature thinks of him as "a very generous man." When George learned that Mature had recommended him to De Mille for the part in *Samson and Delilah*, he bought twenty-six television sets from an appliance store Mature owned and sent them to various friends. "And enemies," Mature adds. During the filming of *A Shot in the Dark*, as Elke Sommer remembers, the cast continually broke up in laughter at Peter Sellers' pronunciation of a word. George suggested that each person who broke up during the scene should contribute five English pounds to a kitty. Before they finally had a usable take there was more than two hundred pounds in the kitty, and because it was his idea George was asked what ought to be done with the money. "He had noticed a run-down horse farm near the studio where many old horses were put to pasture until they died and suggested we give the owners of the farm the money," she recalls. "That was the first time I was aware of George's humanity and generosity."

George's real friends numbered only two: one was an Englishman of the "old school," Stuart Hall, a dress extra, George's stand-in on the set and a companion off, whom he affectionately called "Stewpot." "George adored him," Zsa Zsa recalled in 1986. "In the evenings he always had his tuxedo and came to the most elegant parties. He was one of the most elegant men ever. He died not long ago." Asked why he was a friend to George, a man thought to be incapable of real friendship, Hall answered "because the son of a bitch never bores me, and frankly most people do." The other close friend was presumably Brian Aherne although Zsa Zsa asserts, "I personally don't think that Brian knew much about George's private life at all." George once remarked to her that "Brian puts on a big act, but I always hear a little bit of the cockney." As for herself, Zsa Zsa allows that "Brian, Eleanor, and George and I were very close friends" but after he wrote *A Dreadful Man* , "I really didn't care for him at all any more. The book is so nasty." Moreover, Aherne's autobiography, a work of some 350 pages fulsomely treating his life from birth to 1959 and discussing his English and Hollywood friendships, even listing people at parties as well as members of the "British Colony," unaccountably makes not one mention of George Sanders. In any case, Aherne later wrote that after 1941 he "saw little of him for some years," until George married Zsa Zsa—in fact a period of eight years—and that "our friendship chilled" in 1956 after Aherne lost the money he invested in one of George's business schemes. Aherne's closest relations with George appear to have been during the period 1959 to 1967, the years George and Benita were married, a friendship maintained largely by means of correspondence.

Glimpses behind George's protective mask, then, were permitted only to the few friends and co-players with whom he felt relatively comfortable and who in his view would not or could not probe further. By this time, the full flowering of the consummate cad on-screen, he had indeed withdrawn inviolate, fully and securely carapaced from the world by that mask.

13 "Ostentation's Favorite Cad"

"CAD (kæd). Apparently an abbreviation of CADDEE, CADDIE, CADET, the senses of which show the development of meaning. The modern sense appears to have arisen at Oxford in the early nineteenth century as an application to anyone whose manners or conduct were in question. **1839**: HOOD: *Kilmansegg* 230: 'Not to forget that saucy lad, Ostentation's favourite cad, the page who looks so splendidly clad' " (*Oxford English Dictionary*).

"I was beastly, but I was never coarse," was the way George characterized his screen portrayal of the cultured Cad. "I was a high-class sort of heel." And indeed it was this special "high-class" element of villainy, this aura of patrician hauteur, which his audiences found compelling. No other actor could match his "air of insouciant meanness," as one film historian has put it, or "ability to deliver disdainful dialogue in an elegant, cello-like voice." If Basil Rathbone was occasionally more cruel, Vincent Price more arrogant, or Clifton Webb more waspish, George blended all of these qualities with others in his unique fashioning of what would ultimately be termed "the consummate Cad."

"When I began my career in films," George once wrote,

"I found it rather frustrating not to be cast in romantic parts, since it seemed to me that I was just as handsome, dashing, and heroic as any of my contemporaries. But I soon became adjusted to the idea that I would always be cast as the villain, and I have found many compensations for this state of affairs."

One of the principal compensations, he speculated, was psychological. "Perhaps the greatest fulfillment in acting is not just the satisfaction involved in the opportunity for the extrovert to exhibit himself, but more the opportunity to act out that part of himself for which he has the imagination and the capacity but not the heart or the courage. One thinks of Basil Rathbone, master of the curled lip and patronizing glance, but in life warm, cozy, and a pushover for a laugh. Vincent Price, another consummate villain, is an uproarious host, warm-hearted and kind and full of love for his fellow men. Charles Laughton, an unprincipled sadist on the screen and stage, in life is interested in the gentle arts, paintings, porcelain, people, and poetry."

These and other screen villains were able to to break the mold of studio typecasting and develop new dramatic personae in career shifts which George could not effect much less seriously attempt, so deeply was the single persona of the Cad ingrained in both his public and private lives. The extent to which he had assimilated his screen image into his own life infused his portrayals with a subtle cogency, a credibility which other actors with contrasting and discrete off-screen personalities could not fully convey. The media-conditioned perception of moviegoers and fans, their unspoken assumption, was that George Sanders not only played the Cad, he was a Cad—haughty, cynical, imperious and, most significantly, condescendingly amused by or contemptuous of women—who was simply playing himself. It is this which accounts in large measure for the uncommon appeal his screen portrayals have exercised upon audiences and which forms the core of his most enduring characterizations.

Basil Rathbone, "in life warm and cozy," was a middle-class, old-school-tie Edwardian Englishman born in South Africa. In England he played juvenile leads in a variety of Shakespeare productions and later joined the Stratford Festival Company, where he had leads in several productions. Rathbone came to America in 1922, got into films playing supporting roles, and in 1935 was cast by David Selznick in *David Copperfield* as Murdstone, Copperfield's coldhearted and vicious stepfather. In *Anna Karenina* (1935) he played arrogant, ruthless Karenin. His role as Levasseur, the treacherous French buccaneer opposite Errol Flynn in *Captain Blood* (1935), opened up a series of parts as a rapier-flashing costume cad—notably the Marquis d'Evremonde in *A Tale of Two Cities* (1936), a character created by Dickens to illustrate the cruelty and arrogance of the French aristocracy; the ruthless and ambitious Sir Guy of Gisbourne in *The Adventures of Robin Hood* (1938); the callous Louis XI opposite Ronald Colman in *If I Were King* (1938), for which Rathbone received an Academy nomination; and as the murderous Richard III in *Tower of London* (1939). But at this point Rathbone shifted type and shed his villainous image, beginning a long tenure in the part for which he is best remembered, Sherlock Holmes in *The Hound of the Baskervilles* (1939), a role he would reprise in thirteen subsequent films. Today Basil Rathbone is remembered not as a lip-curling, saturnine villain but as the cerebral consulting detective of Baker Street.

Vincent Price was born to a well-to-do family and took his college degree in art history at Yale and master's degree in fine arts at University of London. He made his stage debut in London in 1935 and later played the lead opposite Helen Hayes in *Victoria Regina*. Price was an established stage actor before coming to Hollywood in 1938. After playing a few romantic roles, he became typed in character parts as a smooth villain because of a memorable stage role—the suave and sinister villain in *Angel Street*. Twentieth Century-Fox then put him in *The Song of Bernadette* (1943) as the heartless prosecutor, following which Price, "warmhearted and kind" off the screen, began specializing in elegant villains: a lawyer spurned by Jennifer Jones in *Leave Her to Heaven* (1945), spitefully trying to convict her of murder; in *Shock* (1946) a psychiatrist and a murderer who commits to an insane asylum the woman who witnessed him kill his wife; a fuedal landowner in *Dragonwyck* (1946) who murders his first wife and tries to do the same to his second; Cardinal Richlieu, the villain of *The Three Musketeers* (1948); a treacherous pasha commanding a band of murderous tribesmen in *Bagdad* (1949). Then in 1952 his career took a significant turn when he played the role of the mad sculptor in the chilling *House of Wax*, and he went on to become one of Hollywood's best known horror actors, most notably in Roger Corman's adaptations of Poe—*House of Usher* (1960), *The Pit and the Pendulum* (1961), and *The Masque of the Red Death* (1964). Today Vincent Price is remembered not for his suave villains but as the past master of the macabre.

Clifton Webb, born Webb Parmallee Hollenbeck, came to screen villainy late in his career. Trained as a dancer and actor from an early age, he appeared in musical comedies in the early twenties and then played straight dramatic parts on the London stage and on Broadway. In 1944 he was cast as the elegant and duplicitous Waldo Lydecker in Otto Preminger's chic murder mystery *Laura* and received an Academy nomination for the role. As a result he was typecast as a series of threatening if somewhat prissy villains. Webb broke out of that mold by taking the role of the male babysitter Mr. Belvedere in *Sitting Pretty* (1948) and its two sequels, as well as sympathetic leads in *Cheaper By the Dozen* (1950) and *Stars and Stripes Forever* (1952). Today Clifton Webb is remembered not as a sinister murderer but as the effete, fastidious Mr. Belvedere.

140

Basil Rathbone, Vincent Price, Clifton Webb, and other villains of Hollywood's Golden Age could make career moves by stepping away from their types on the screen, for audiences perceived them as actors playing parts, parts often wildly divergent from their personal imaginations and capacities. George Sanders, however, was perceived as eminently the Cad both on screen and off and as such tapped wellspring responses from culturally conditioned audiences of the thirties, forties, and fifties.

Much has been made of and a great deal written about the influence of American films and film-star role models in shaping American cultural attitudes and values, including those relating to women. Such analysis addresses primarily the dominant heroic male as a type. As every culture has norms defining "masculine" and "feminine," the popular arts and films in particular have served to perpetuate specific images and ideals of manliness. Among these are suspicion, disdain, and domination of women.

Throughout a good part of its history Hollywood seems to have demanded that audiences admire and imitate males who in one way or other dominate others. Male stars are fashioned from the raw material of humanity to seem superior beings who overcome women and lesser men by experience, ability, or charm. In the past there have been dominant screen males who appealed primarily to women, such as Rudolph Valentino, or who were men's men intended for a male audience, such as John Wayne. A compilation of such dominating "big bad wolves" in one study of the phenomenon, for example, lists William S. Hart, Tom Mix, Douglas Fairbanks Sr., Gary Cooper, Errol Flynn, Henry Fonda, Alan Ladd, and Marlon Brando as "self-controlled, invulnerable, stoical heroes who justify the image of unfeeling masculinity as a means of winning in a world that pounces on any sign of weakness." However, the influence of the screen villain—rather than the hero—on men's

141

perception of women as well as women's perception of themselves has been little attended and largely undervalued.

The woman-hating Cad as a fully dimensional character type in films was essentially a product of the thirties. Hollywood's response to the Depression, for example, showed that hardheartedness was both successful and an acceptable route to survival. The economic collapse provoked in American men a fear of inadequacy and failure, a fear that also generated suspicion of the female, contempt for women who might unman them. To see their collective suspicion and contempt acted out on the screen in the persona of the Cad was reassuring of manhood and protective of the fragile male ego. The male in the films of the thirties and forties was often the man who is happiest without women or, if he does want them, despises them. Moreover, some women find irresistible the men who ignore them or who, if they have softer feelings, conceal them behind a mask of disdain and indifference.

The magazine and newspaper advertising campaign for *The Private Affairs of Bel Ami*, for example, had as its centerpiece a photograph of Angela Lansbury on her knees looking up plaintively at George while grasping his leg with both hands. "All women take to men who have the appearance of wickedness," ran the copy splashed in large print across the ad, and in the film she tells her lover, "Your cruelty is dearer to me than the love of others."

In a recent television interview Zsa Zsa Gabor validated from personal experience the attraction of indifferent, disdainful men. In response to the question, "Have you ever fallen in love with a man who's been kind to you?" Zsa Zsa responded:

"A very rich man from New York. I hated him because he was so good. He wouldn't fight with me. I couldn't stand it. He gave me diamonds. I cried every day. I don't need a man who just loves me. I have to love him, and then he doesn't have to love me."

"Why do you only love him if he's difficult?"

"Since I was a little girl, when I went to school in Switzerland. There were twelve boys, and I was with the other girls, and all the eleven boys paid attention to me and one boy didn't look at me. I fell madly in love with the one who didn't look at me. I am like that."

A woman strongly attracted to men who act superior and cold toward her rather than to men who treat her well lacks self-esteem, and a woman's low self-esteem is at least partly the result of the traditional "feminine" stereotype—that women are not presumed to be strong intellectually, physically, or emotionally. This stereotype leads her to endure unhappiness in order to win approval and acceptance. The traditional masculine stereotype provides a corollary to women's unhappiness insofar as it encourages the male's right to use and abuse physical, economic, and emotional power.

If the portrayal in films of male superiority had its genesis in the thirties and carried forward through the forties and fifties, it is today manifested in a significantly altered form, which adds brutalization and sexual violence to simple disdain and contempt. The suave Cad-villain of the early Hollywood years has given way to the violent loner employing physical intimidation or abuse to subjugate women. The Cad of the golden age dominated by means of the operative cultural imperatives at the time: intellectual, sexual, and emotional control.

George's characters—Lord Everett Stacy in *Lloyd's of London*, Lord Henry Wotton in *The Picture of Dorian Gray*, George Duroy in *The Private Affairs of Bel Ami*, Addison DeWitt in *All About Eve*, and Clementi Sabourin in *Death of a Scoundrel*—controlled women by virtue of position, money, sexual presence, contempt, and emotional isolation. These were also the means by which George attempted to control relationships in his private life.

George was involved with many women during the thirties

and forties and engaged in a number of love affairs—many, as was seemingly the Hollywood pattern, with his leading ladies: principal among them were Dolores Del Rio, Gene Tierney, Hedy Lamarr, and Lucille Ball.

George's love afffair with Mexican-born Dolores Del Rio, his costar in *Lancer Spy* (1937) and *International Settlement* (1938) and a former silent film star (*The Loves of Carmen, Ramona*), was carried on while she was still married to her second husband, art director Cedric Gibbons. The affair lasted two years until George met Susan Larson and abandoned Dolores. She later became involved with Orson Welles, who directed her in *Journey Into Fear* (1942).

George costarred with Gene Tierney in *Sundown* (1941), *Son of Fury* (1942), and *The Ghost and Mrs. Muir* (1947), all made during the time he was married to Susan and while Gene was legally the wife of designer Oleg Cassini. Although she today remembers George as only "a nice, reserved friend," Gene Tierney was one of the women whom Zsa Zsa listed as "after him" when she first started seeing George. His sister confirms that Gene and George "were involved" at one time, very likely in early 1947 when George was staying at Gene's home in Los Angeles after his marriage to Susan ended.

One of the few memorable moments in the otherwise forgettable *The Strange Woman* (1946) takes place between George and costar Hedy Lamarr, a surprisingly erotic dark-and-stormy-night love scene in a deserted hut. The couple had their off-screen moments as well. "When I first met Hedy Lamarr," George recalled later in life, "she was so beautiful that everybody would stop talking when she came into a room. Wherever she went she was the cynosure of all eyes. I don't think anyone concerned himself very much about whether or not there was anything behind her beauty. Of her conversation I can remember nothing: when she spoke one did not listen, one just watched her mouth moving and marveled at the exquisite shapes made by her lips." That they were involved in a love affair at the time was apparently no secret. Both Zsa Zsa and George's sister knew of it, and George's friend Tyrone Power wrote his wife in a letter that year, "You've heard about George and Hedy?" The affair ended before George and Zsa Zsa met in 1947.

"A delightful gentleman," Lucille Ball once said of George, and then added, "He loved beautiful women." To the list of beautiful women he loved and who loved him during this period can be added Lucy herself, who co-starred with George in *Lured* (1947). Before Zsa Zsa and George were married but while they were living together in George's apartment in 1948, Zsa Zsa accidentally discovered that Lucy was still pursuing him. "Once I heard on the telephone—I picked up the phone and he was downstairs in his workshop and I was upstairs, and she said to him 'What are you doing with that Hilton woman? You know that I love you.'" Lucille Ball had married Desi Arnaz in 1941 and was still his wife when she knew George.

George's marriage to Zsa Zsa in 1949 did not put an end to his amorous inclinations. "George Sanders was always un-faithful," Zsa Zsa has recently remarked. "Once he didn't come home, and I said, 'What happened?' He said, 'I saw a Spanish woman on the street, so I wanted to know how a Spanish woman is in bed.' Next day he came home and I forgave him. George couldn't do wrong. He was torturing me, but I just—you know, when you love somebody. I forgave him because I really adored him."

Forty years before the occassion on which this remark was made, Zsa Zsa had offered essentially the same observation about being drawn to the type of man who could control and ultimately dominate her: "I was always attracted to indifferent, unapproachable men," she said when she and George married. "They were the great challenge of my life." Like Dolores Del Rio, Gene Tierney, Hedy Lamarr, and Lucille Ball before her, as well as thousands of female moviegoers in the golden age of American films, she had come under the spell of this lordly, disdainful, condescending "high-class sort of heel"—Hollywood's favorite Cad.

14 "Rulers, Kings, Noblemen"

"**B**y nature I'm a frustrated ruler," George declared in a mid-career interview. "I love to sit on thrones and play kings who possess a great deal of luxury and power," he explained. "I've played a lot of royal roles, and I think it's a very good line." It was a line he had begun developing in 1947 and continued to exploit with a succession of kings, lordly nobles, and ancient rulers until 1959. Recalls Virginia Mayo, his costar in one of these chain mail and toga epics, "There were none better than he in certain types of roles: rulers, kings, noblemen."

"No, no, my dear. Never lead from the ace-queen," George in the role of King Charles II admonishes his mistress as they play a game of piquet in *Forever Amber* (1947). "Because, you see, the king always takes the trick." The trick in this instance is his having sent the lady's would-be lover on a lengthy and dangerous sea voyage. This was George's first portrayal of Charles II of England, who was said never to have spoken a foolish word nor listened to a wise one. It is one of his best performances in a type of role which he made especially convincing. Although costumed as Charles in foppish cavalier attire, long black wig, large feathered hat, and accompanied by a half dozen small dogs on leashes, George plays the king as a much wiser and more contemplative monarch than previously film renderings had credited him for.

Realizing that Amber St. Clare (Linda Darnell), "a slave to ambition, a stranger to virtue," has betrayed him for love of Bruce Carlton (Cornel Wilde), he muses that "perhaps, granted the moral level I've permitted this court to sink to, even a king should expect to be used as a pawn in a dirty game." Moreover, his is a reflective nature: "If I hadn't been king I might have managed sometime in my life to fall in love myself. But instead I've had to create an illusion of happiness, to pretend to love, pretend to be loved." His interpretation of the role is more than simply an amusingly blasé King Charles. Darryl Zanuck's sumptuous if bowdlerized production of Kathleen Winsor's bestselling novel was successful in its presentation of the Restoration age "with all the lush theatricality that the author originally employed." Although he delivered an affecting performance as the king, George was not particularly interested in the production and escaped the tedium of its details by sleeping at odd moments. Cornel Wilde, who was fascinated by George's voice and delivery and had practiced imitating him, played a joke on one such occasion. "George and I were sitting at a table, and the cameraman was lighting us," he recalls. "George fell sound asleep. When the lighting was ready and the director called for a rehearsal, I said my first line and then switched to my imitation of George and said his first speech. He awoke to hear himself acting." The crew roared with laughter; George, wrapped in monarchial dignity, was not amused.

His next role as a lordly ruler was as the Saran of Gaza in Cecil B. De Mille's flamboyant but inflated biblical epic, *Samson and Delilah* (1949), a part he once facetiously termed "the role I liked best. I was a supporting player rather than a principal," he explained. "Therefore I didn't have to work so hard. Then, too, I didn't have to wear my own clothes, which not only saved me money but put me more at ease." In a more serious vein he added that "I had a wonderful director in Cecil B. DeMille, and Victor Mature and Hedy Lamarr were easy to work with." George is able to convey in this portrayal once again the sensibility of the lordly and powerful ruler all too aware that he is feared rather than loved and will ultimately be betrayed. When the spurned and vindictive Delilah (Lamarr) reviles Samson (Mature) to the Saran, he tells her, "I am jealous of your hatred. Don't share even that with someone else;" when she proposes going to Samson to learn the secret of his strength and make him captive, the Saran senses her real feelings: "As a king I have no choice; as a man, I'm letting you go because you want to." Later, when he fully realizes that she loves the blinded and chained Samson, he acknowledges to himself that "there can be only one master of a kingdom or a woman's heart." Despite George's thoughtful performance and Academy nominations for cinematography and music, the picture was ravaged by the critics, although it was a box-office smash.

Better received by both public and reviewers was *Ivanhoe* (1952), the adaptation of Sir Walter Scott's tale of thirteenth-century Norman-Saxon Britain, in which George plays the role of feudal Norman Lord De Bois-Guilbert, deadly enemy to Ivanhoe (Robert Taylor). The cast is a solidly professional ensemble, in particular Felix Aylmer, Robert Douglas, and Joan Fontaine (as Rowena). The picture, which was Academy nominated for Best Picture, Cinematography, and Musical Score, is notable for the integrity and candor with which it treats the theme of anti-Semitism in medieval England and the implications of the injustice of social bigotry.

"A motion picture that does Scott and English history proud," reported the New York *Times*. "A remarkable forcefulness is achieved not customary in spectacle films. It brings to the screen almost as fine a panorama of medievalism as Laurence Olivier gave us in *Henry V*." George's performance as the emotionally torn De Bois-Guilbert is praised as "intriguingly fluid." Once again he loses his heart—and the girl (Elizabeth Taylor as the Jewess Rebecca)—with an affectingly shaded portrayal.

Disastrously directed, poorly edited, and lacking production values, *King Richard and the Crusaders* (1954) is a crude and inept adaptation of another of Scott's classic novels, *The Talisman,* and features an obviously embarrassed and unenthusiastic George in the title role. The story follows Richard Lion-Heart, "languidly played by Mr. Sanders," his adventures in the Holy Land on the Third Crusade, the attempt on his life by traitors, his rescue by Sir Kenneth (Laurence Harvey) as the only knight truly loyal to Richard, a romance between Kenneth and Lady Edith (Virginia Mayo), and the machinations of the Sultan Saladin (Rex Harrison). George passed the time during filming by composing limericks about the foibles of other cast members. Laurence Harvey, for example: "Hark to the tale of young know-it-all Larry/A cross between Shakespeare and Madame DuBarry/With the vices of both and the virtues of neither/He says to the world, 'You may have me as either.' " A "droning, static, conversation piece," the picture was a critical and commercial failure, closed three weeks after its Hollywood premier, and eventually lost Warners nearly a million dollars.

The King's Thief (1955) gave George the opportunity to again assay the role of King Charles II, but because the script called for a standard portrayal of the monarch as incompetent and foppish, he could do little with the part. Manipulated by his trusted but disloyal counselor, the Duke of Brampton (David Niven), Charles is persuaded to arrest and execute members of the artistocracy, who in fact fought for the restoration of the monarchy, and to confiscate their wealth, most of which goes into the pockets of Brampton. "You're doing such a splendid job," the naive Charles tells him, petting a lap dog. "I am truly in your debt." The scheme is uncovered and foiled by Capt. Michael Dermott (Edmund Purdom), who had fought "to restore the royal bottom to the throne" but went ignored and unpaid, like thousands of others when the war ended, and became a highwayman. Dermott is aided by Lord Ovendon's daughter (Ann Blyth), who seeks revenge for her father's death caused by Brampton's plot. After many sword fights, Dermott finally makes the bumbling monarch aware of Brampton's treachery and all ends well. Despite a veteran production crew which included director Robert Z. Leonard, cinematographer Robert Planck, and art director Cedric Gibbons, *The King's Thief* remains a dismal and disappointing costume piece.

"You and your Sheban slut have defiled the fair name of Israel," George screams at Yul Brynner in *Solomon and Sheba* (1959). The dialogue given him for his role as Adonijah, the wicked brother of Solomon (Brynner), rarely rises above this banal level. A fabricated sand-and-sequins fable of romance between the Israelite king and the Arabic queen Sheba (Gina Lollobrigida) in tenth century B.C., the picture was shot on location in Spain on a $6-million budget and grossed $15 million, which ranked it as a commercial success. Reviewers, however, thought it a "solemn, slow, and ponderous" vehicle of the jewel-in-the-navel school of Hollywood films. In the story, wise and upright King Solomon becomes enamoured of the ravishing Sheba, sent by the Pharoah of Egypt to charm him, and so becomes vulnerable to the schemes of brother Adonijah to usurp the throne. George later said of his part that "all I had to do was to look heroic and not fall out of my chariot. I was hard put to it to do either." But the filming of *Solomon and Sheba* proved significant for George personally if not professionally, for during the production he lost an old friend and acquired a new wife.

Tyrone Power, George's co-player in several films early in their careers, had been signed for the part of Solomon, went to

Spain for the shoot, and played the role through two-thirds of the production. On November 15, 1958 the cast was in Madrid to film interior scenes, one of which was a sword duel between Power and George. Power did all of his own fencing; George, who was not skilled with a sword, used a double for rear or reverse shots and appeared with the sword only when the camera was on his face. This required additional work for Power, who had to move between the two camera setups. One take which required both players' faces to appear had to be reshot several times, and it was during these retakes that Power suddenly clutched his shoulder and staggered backwards. He lighted a cigarette and said, "I've got to stop. I don't feel well." He was taken to his dressing room where a few minutes later George visited him, noticed that his face had "a sort of bluish color," and asked how he felt. "Oh, it'll go away," Power replied. "It's this damned bursitis." Reassured, George left. A few minutes later Power lapsed into unconsciousness, was rushed to a car bound for a hospital, but died of heart failure three minutes into the trip. He was forty-five years old. Yul Brynner would later be called in as his replacement, with filming started again from the beginning.

"During the days that followed I had ample time to reflect upon the extraordinary enigma of death," George recalled. "I am not irreligious, atheistic or irreverent. I am not a champion of apostasy nor even an agnostic. I am just plain bewildered." He was "deeply affected" by Power's death, his sister Margaret remembers even today. A burial mass was said at the Church of San Francisco el Grande in Madrid, where cards in both English and Spanish were passed out which read: "One of the greatest tributes to Tyrone Power was by a friend of many years standing. Mrs. Power expressed a wish that the many individuals involved in the production of *Solomon and Sheba* and Mr. Power's friends be given an opportunity to read the following

tribute to the actor by Mr. George Sanders." The brief eulogy
was as follows:

I shall always remember Tyrone Power as a bountiful man.
A man who gave freely of himself. It mattered not to
whom he gave. His concern was in the giving. I shall
always remember his wonderful smile, a smile that would
light up the darkest hour of the day like a sunburst. I shall
always remember Tyrone Power as a man who gave more
of himself than it was wise for him to give. Until in the
end he gave his life.

At the memorial service later in Hollywood, Cesar Romero
delivered a eulogy and concluded by paraphrasing George's
tribute.

Because the exterior filming of *Solomon and Sheba* was done
in Zaragoza, only a few miles from an American Air Force
base, the cast were invited to give a concert for the troops one
Saturday evening in October 1958, near the end of their stay.
For his part, George played the piano and sang one or two
songs. A woman reporter for the London *Daily Express* sent to
cover the event used the occasion to interview George, who
gave out his views at the time on the subject of marriage: "A
marriage must be something of mutual gain—which it is if you
both add a new dimension to each other's personality," he told
her. "Marriage is like taking your first job as an actor. You do
it, but then they say, 'Come back when you've had more
experience.' Well, I've had that experience you need in marriage
and now I think I have a pretty good chance of happiness."

The year 1958 saw the passing of another well-known
screen actor, Ronald Colman. Some weeks after his death, his
widow, Benita Hume Colman, was visited at her home in Kent,
England by old friends Brian and Eleanor Aherne. At afternoon
tea Benita turned suddenly to Brian and said, "I want to ask

you something." Aherne, who had come to comfort Benita in her time of loss, nodded sympathetically but was stunned by the question which followed. "What would you think," she asked, "if I were to marry George Sanders?"

Hollywood and Europe: 1958–1967

15 "She Remains Incontrovertibly English"

"**B**enita's experiences parallel mine," George wrote Zsa Zsa from Spain, informing her of his impending marriage. "I find we think alike on all subjects and our values are the same," he explained. "After twenty-two years of uninterrupted residence in America, she remains incontrovertibly English. I think we have a good chance to be happy." George had known Benita on and off for almost twenty years, having first met before her marriage to Ronald Colman. He saw her from time to time afterwards at social functions, although according to Brian Aherne, "Ronnie had not approved of Sanders, who was rarely invited to the house." But in fact, as late as 1957 George attended weekend gatherings at the Colmans' ranch in San Ysidro. "The weekenders included chums from radio and television," daughter Juliet Colman remembered, "as well as film friends: the Carl Esmonds, the Brian Ahernes, the Joseph Cottens, the Boyers, Patricia Medina, George Sanders, the Ronald Reagans."

George and Benita were married at the British Consulate in Madrid on February 10, 1959. "George is the kind of man who makes it a joy to wake up in the morning and find he is there," she wrote the Ahernes. "I haven't laughed so much since I was a little girl. I don't think he is 'dreadful' at all." Brian had responded to Benita's question that autumn afternoon in Kent by tactlessly exclaiming, "Oh, darling. He's a dreadful man!" and, further, that George was "not the kind of man to make any woman happy." Her letter was the first she had written him in the several months since the wedding, and only after Aherne had sent her "a groveling letter of apology" for his outburst. To another friend she wrote, "George has been the kindest and most gentle man who brought me out of the depths of despair and helped me to start living again." Aherne could not have been more wrong. George would make Benita very happy, and she him, until her death in 1967.

Benita Hume was born in London in 1906, the year of George's birth in St. Petersburg. An actress from age seventeen, she made her British screen debut at nineteen and went on to play leads and supporting roles in both British and Hollywood films ranging in quality from Alexander Korda's *The Private Life of Don Juan* (1934) opposite Douglas Fairbanks Sr. (in his last film) and Merle Oberon to *Tarzan Escapes* (1936). Following her marriage to Colman in 1938, she retired from acting. During their twenty-year marriage they were one of Hollywood's closest couples. "All our love and life together lies now inviolate, in a pocket of the past," she wrote not long after his death. "It was full of joy and it is over."

Joan Fontaine, between whom and George little love was lost and who has always characterized him as miserly, offers as an example of his heartless penny-pinching during this period this story: When Benita was contacted in Spain about Colman's wish to have his ashes scattered over the hills of Montecito, George advised her that "the cost was too much," and she refused to authorize the expense. Fontaine gives film director Robert Sinclair as her source for this incident. Sinclair died in 1970, and his widow, Heather Angel, has "no recollection of this episode." She does state, however, "I do not know what Ronald Colman's wishes were, and I do not believe my late husband did either." Moreover, Juliet Colman writes that her father's remains are in the Santa Barbara cemetery, "surrounded by the countryside he loved," but makes no mention of any desire or request on his part to have his ashes scattered.

After the initial shock of what seemed a precipitant marriage ("I was very surprised when he married Ronald Colman's widow," Douglas Fairbanks Jr. recalls) their friends accepted the new situation, and their life together was pleasant and mutually rewarding. "She was the best thing that ever happened to him," his sister Margaret believes. "It was a combination of many things. They were both English, so they had a great deal in common, ideas and things. They made each other laugh. She used to call him 'my king.' It was a nice relationship." Margaret adds that "Ronald Colman was sort of on the boring side. And George, whatever else he was, was never boring." Benita thought him also "cozy and enchanting and generally down my alley. When he staggers in from the studio I am so overwhelmingly pleased to see him."

In late 1959 they set off on a leisurely Continental and Mediterrean trip, ending in London, from where they motored down to Weeks Farm in Kent, Benita's English home. They had been looking for a place to establish a permanent residence and had considered various locations: Le Toquet, "the obvious place if one wishes to be near London without putting one's neck into the British tax-gatherer's noose;" the Bahamas, with "plenty of servants and a reasonable tax structure;" Soto Grande, near Gibraltar, "which has an airport providing direct service to London." They finally chose Lausanne in Switzerland, a country with relatively lenient tax regulations, where they leased a flat on Chemin de Montolivet. "We now refer to ourselves as The Alpine Set," Benita wrote the Ahernes, a set apparently at the center of a celebrity social swirl. "We see the Van Johnsons a lot, and Noel of course, and the Rubensteins are arriving for a concert shortly, and Niven is about to show up too. Larry [Olivier] and Viv [Leigh] are gradually getting back together again. Betty Bacall I talked to yesterday. My God, it's getting to be like the Flight from Egypt. Anyhow we feel no end central and gay."

For his part, George felt "liberated from the American rat-race and able to contemplate it from the proper side of the Atlantic," wishing to know of Hollywood only "who won the Sam Goldwyn Croquet Cup." He was busy professionally and making good money, his new-found happiness having provided a release for his energy. He traveled from one film location to another: London, Rome, Paris, Madrid, Monte Carlo, Beirut, Budapest, Cairo, Tel Aviv, and between pictures he flew to New York or Hollywood for television engagements. None of these was a significant role or, for that matter, picture. On auto-pilot at this stage of his career, he was accepting almost any project offered him as simply the source of a paycheck. "We go back to England at the end of the month for some horrible picture about Landru," Benita wrote of George's upcoming part in the eminently forgettable *Bluebeard's Ten Honeymoons* (1960).

When not working on a film, George spent his time contentedly at home fixing up their flat in Lausanne. "We have four servants and a secretary," he wrote in 1960, "all of whom, plus ourselves, are dedicated to the task of making our little nest comfortable." He was happy "under the therapeutic influence of Benita and Switzerland" and wished only to live a "normal, unhurried, carefree existence." Benita's feelings for George "after all this time with him," she wrote the Ahernes, were "of such unmixed delight and admiration" that she had

The birth of the Cad. As Lord Everett Stacy in *Lloyds of London,* 1936,
Twentieth Century-Fox.

George's first starring role, as Baron von Rohbach in *Lancer Spy,* with Lionel
Atwill, 1937, Twentieth Century-Fox.

Lovers on screen and off. With Dolores Del Rio in *International Settlement,*
1938, Twentieth Century-Fox.

"The nadir of my career." As the Saint, 1939–41, RKO.

As Jack Favell in Hitchcock's *Rebecca* (Selznick), with (from left) Laurence Olivier, C. Aubrey Smith, and Reginald Denny, 1940.

In *Rage in Heaven,* with Robert Montgomery and Ingrid Bergman, 1941, MGM.

"Women are strange little beasts." As Charles Strickland in *The Moon and Sixpence,* 1942, United Artists.

 nasty bit of goods." As double agent in *They Came to Blow Up America,*
 ith Anna Sten and Dennis Hoey, 1943, Twentieth Century-Fox.

"Rulers, kings, noblemen." As Charles II in *Forever Amber,* 1947, Twentieth Century-Fox.

The sociopathic Cad. As George Duroy in *The Private Affairs of Bel Ami,* 1947, United Artists.

The consummate Cad. His performance as Addison DeWitt in *All About Eve*, 1950, Twentieth Century-Fox, won him an Academy Award. Shown here is a scene with Bette Davis, Gary Merrill, and Anne Baxter.

As Lord De Bois-Guilbert in *Ivanhoe,* with Elizabeth Taylor, 1952, MGM.

As Emperor of Rome in *Jupiter's Darling*, 1955, MGM.

In *Death of a Scoundrel,* with Zsa Zsa, their only film appearance together, 1956, RKO.

As the wicked Adonijah, with Laurence Naismith (center) and Yul Brynner, in
Solomon and Sheba, 1959, United Artists.

On location for the filming of *Cairo,* 1963, MGM.

The last time on stage. As Sheridan Whiteside in *Sherry*, 1967, musical-comedy remake of *The Man Who Came to Dinner*.

"become violently attached to him." Even Brian, on the occasion of his and Eleanor's long-delayed holiday to Lausanne to visit them, could see "their evident mutual happiness" and had to admit that the marriage was a success. "Each had brought to the other the qualities which at that time of their lives they needed and appreciated. George was no longer irascible but very amiable, while she in turn was captivated by his eccentricity. She knew what she wanted, she had miraculously found it in George, and she was fiercely loyal to him."

George's good fortune in his personal life was complemented by the film offers which continued to come his way. His unique personality and presence in a picture made him valuable, even in small parts which would have otherwise been ineffective. Characteristically, he still took no interest in these productions except for the salary each brought him, and he continued to accept roles indiscriminately. "I am glad I shall never have such a problem," he replied when Aherne mentioned having turned down a role in a bad picture. "I have got to the point where the lousier the part the better I like it. I would find it quite embarrassing to get a really good part nowadays, for it would call forth the feeble flames of inner fires long since banked." Another time, asked about the nature of the role in a picture he had just signed for, George responded with mock astonishment, "Oh! I am much too discreet to ask questions like that." When he went to Budapest for a part in *The Golden Head* (1964), Benita could only say to friends, "I don't know what the picture is that George is doing, and he of course would not consider apprising himself of this superfluous information."

Taken in all, the years 1959 to 1964 were for George the most consistently peaceful and contented period of his adult life. He was collecting decent wages if not artistic credits for his eclectic roles in pictures, and his marriage was a solid and satisfying one, a relationship founded and sustained more by companionship than passion and the better for it in the long

161

term. He had also established a warmly paternal relationship with Benita's daughter, Juliet, which much gratified her mother. "George has been tearing around the country on his motor bike with Juliet on the back," Benita wrote in 1964. "Juliet told me she had to get off and push every time they encountered a slight incline, and George goes so slowly that the machine balks at the least hazard. He really is the best natured creature." Juliet grew so close to George that he eventually seemed more a father to her than a stepfather: "I not only knew him as long as my own father," she reflects today, "but I knew him better and loved (and miss) him as much." She still refers to him as her "tresh," short for "treasure."

This was also the period of high hopes and great expectations for George in a financial venture, the "CADCO" scheme, that began with extraordinary promise but would come crashing about his ears in November 1964, putting an end to the five-year idyll and to his peace of mind forever. A yet more sinister eventuality showed its first signs in 1964 as well. "I haven't answered your lovely letters," Benita wrote the Ahernes early that year, "because I have been laid supine for five weeks by lumbago. It was agony. I could hardly turn over in bed. Anyhow, it's better now." Not long afterward, George took her to the Bahamas because she was "suffering from mysterious pains which had been diagnosed as acute arthritis" and the doctors had recommended that she spend time in a hot climate. A Harley Street specialist in London whom they then consulted confirmed that diagnosis and advised a course of irradiated hot mud baths at Abano in Italy, which she undertook in December 1964.

On January 16, 1965, George wrote Aherne from Lausanne, "Yesterday morning at 9 o'clock Benita underwent an emergency operation for cancer of the chest. She survived it well, and is making normal progress towards recovery." The cancer had been detected during a routine checkup, and the physician informed her that both breasts would have to be removed without delay. She returned home stunned and incoherent, much to George's alarm. When she was finally able to tell him of the diagnosis and the recommended mastectomy, the "dreadful man" gave a relieved sigh and said softy, "Is that all? Well, who needs them?" Had it been accurately diagnosed, the disease might have been arrested in its early stages, but it was even then spreading throughout her body and would eventually destroy her. "I'm sure I'm going to die," she wrote from her hospital bed, "but George says this is not so. He's a remarkable man all right, and never more so than now."

As a consequence of George's now tangled CADCO financial scheme, he and Benita left Switzerland in November 1965, bound for New York and then on to Los Angeles, where they moved into a friend's house in Brentwood. George managed to get some television work—a panel game show and an episode of *The Rogues*—and more followed on the strength of that. They purchased a small house on Medio Drive in Brentwood and stayed there a year as Benita's condition steadily worsened. Then late in 1966 George received out of the blue a remarkable offer to play the lead in a musical comedy based on the Kaufman and Hart play, *The Man Who Came to Dinner*. The show was to be called *Sherry!* after the nickname of the lead character Sheridan Whiteside, played in the first 1939 production by Monty Woolley. The handsome salary offered him for the role was persuasion enough for George to put aside his long-standing fear of live performance. There was considerable money invested in the project, and a feature article with a photo of George in costume appeared in *Life* magazine, announcing that "Broadway is about to see a musical version of *The Man Who Came to Dinner.*"

"All my hopes are riding on this play," George wrote Aherne from New York just before beginning rehearsals. "It has a very good chance, and I will never again be given such an

163

opportunity. Or, even if I were, I would never again have the fortitude to take advantage of it." Five weeks of rehearsal began in December, after which the show was scheduled to open in Boston for a three-week engagement and play Philadelphia before going on to New York. "George's voice is really lovely and floats out like yards of blue velvet," Benita proudly wrote to the Ahernes. Brian had apparently remarked gloomily on George's irascibility under pressure, for she added, "such an angel he is—you're quite wrong you know Brian, in point of fact we have never had a cross word." She accompanied George to Boston for dress rehearsals and finally the opening, which proved to be an unqualified disaster. The Boston press ravaged the production and singled out George for their most barbed criticism.

It was in the midst of all this that Benita, in great pain, was rushed by ambulance to the hospital where it was discovered that her cancer had spread throughout her body. Surgeons operated immediately but could only postpone the inevitable, and George was told she had but a few months to live. "I think it was the darkest moment of his life," Aherne reflected years later. With Benita lying critically ill in hospital, George had no recourse but to resign his part in the show but courageously played out the remaining three weeks of the Boston engagement. Clive Revill took over the role in Philadelphia, but once the show reached Broadway it closed almost immediately.

As soon as Benita could be safely and comfortably moved, George brought her to New York and shortly thereafter to California, where he had opportunities for work and where they both had friends. As Benita was fading, George decided to go to Majorca and buy a house for them to move to. "We have to go somewhere," Benita explained in June of 1967, "and all other considerations aside, Majorca is the cheapest, as well as having a mild climate and being within reach of London." George did find a house there, and Benita planned to fly with

Juliet to London and then drive to Weeks Farm, which was up for sale, while George completed arrangements for the house in Palma. "This new Majorca venture I do believe could be made quite heavenly," she wrote a few days later, "but I seem to be so awfully ill it's hard to imagine I shall be able to put it together or even get there at all." Benita did not in fact live to see Majorca. Juliet took her by ambulance to the airport in Los Angeles and then in a bed on a flight over the Pole to England and by ambulance again to the hospital. A few days later she was allowed to go home to George at Weeks Farm, where she died.

It was not an easy death, rather one which added to George's grief a nearly paralyzing emotional trauma. "They had made some sort of pact, the two of them," Margaret confides, "that if either of them got seriously ill the other would administer a drug. Poor Benita was so terribly sick; the things were there by her bedside and he felt he wanted to end her suffering, but she couldn't keep anything down, she was vomiting all the time. She had cancer everywhere." George was deeply scarred by the experience yet able to mask his feelings save on rare occasions when he was unexpectedly confronted by them. In the spring of 1968, several months after Benita's death, he was enroute to Mexico to make a picture and stopped in London to visit the Ahernes. "He was his old original and amusing self," Brian remembered, "playing the piano, seeming relaxed and contented." At the end of his stay Aherne took him to the airport and as they drove asked George a question about Benita's death. "Suddenly, to my dismay, he burst into uncontrollable sobs. I said no more, and we drove on in silence. By the time we arrived at the airport his reserve was fully restored." Shortly after arriving in Mexico George met a lovely woman who would subsequently become his close companion over the next several years. On their first evening together, she relates, "he cried over dinner, remembering the recent death of his wife Benita."

The manner of his wife's passing, coupled with the circumstances of his mother's death little more than a year later, would set him on a course carefully designed to preclude a similar fate for himself. The debilitating physical blow which would trigger that final step had yet to strike him, but it was gathering force and would be the direct result, as he himself came to realize, of "grief and financial disaster." The story of that financial disaster is the tangled and humiliating history of George's most elaborate and ultimately most devastating get-rich scheme, the CADCO fiasco.

16 "A Rip-Snorting Scandal"

"I am not interested in money," George declared to an interviewer in 1943, then qualified the remark by adding "what I mean, of course, is vast pyramids of money. Dollar-chasing is what I particularly object to." What, he was asked, would interest him more than money? "Risk," he answered. "A gamble." In 1961 he combined risk with unabashed dollar-chasing in a venture to accumulate vast pyramids of money which ended three years later in what his friend Noel Coward called a "rip-snorting scandal." George, he reported, "who has always been one for grandiose ideas and splendid pipe-dreams about making vast amounts of money for nothing, dreamed up a scheme for making sausages in Scotland!" Observing that "the whole thing went sky high" and that George and Benita lost £150,000 (about $360,000 at that time) with a full inquiry pending, Coward went on to say, "I am sorry for Benita. I am not at all sorry for George because he has behaved like a perfect ass."

This was George's disastrous CADCO Ltd. enterprise, the final though not the first attempt to "get out of the ridiculous acting profession" and become a business tycoon. An earlier fiasco was the creation in 1956 of HUSAN Ltd. to finance, develop, and market inventions. Having discovered an Italian engineer with an idea for making lighter and more durable phonograph records, George formed a partnership, rented a small factory, and hired workers. As Managing Director of the company, he outfitted a plush office for himself complete with a huge semicircular desk, an intercom with rows of shiny buttons, and a pretty secretary. His duties were confined largely to signing checks, since he was providing the basic finance for the operation.

When the company began issuing stock, George prevailed upon friends to invest. One such investor was Brian Aherne who, having received no accounting whatever from the company after a year's time, took it upon himself to visit the plant in California. To his dismay he found the factory deserted, hundreds of phonograph records lying about in heaps, and the furniture, carpeting, and pretty secretary gone from the Managing Director's office. The business had failed, and George lost all of his and his investors' money. Creditors put liens on his personal bank accounts; the sheriff seized both his house and his car. He left the country to make a picture, the "ridiculous acting profession" having come to his rescue with a handsome salary for a role in *Solomon and Sheba*.

In 1960 he turned his financial affairs over to Thomas Roe, an international lawyer with offices in Lausanne, where George and Benita had by then taken up residence. Roe represented a number of Hollywood celebrities, who had moved to Switzerland to benefit from the lenient Swiss tax regulations, and had contrived elaborate schemes for avoiding taxes. In George's case this involved laundering money through Curacao and Lichtenstein and eventually into a Swiss company they formed called ROTURMAN, S.A., of which the two were co-directors and which was financed by George's earnings from films. They planned investments in Swiss real estate and Canadian oil, and

George began talking again of quitting the acting profession to become a tycoon.

At this point Roe introduced him to one Denis Loraine, a glib, opportunistic, and irresponsible Englishman who told them a fascinating story: In Brighton he and his wife had bought some remarkably fine sausages from a local butcher and, on persistent inquiry, learned that they were made from an old and closely-guarded secret recipe, once the favorite of none other than King Edward VII, which the butcher had discovered in the basement of his shop. The king, according to the tale, could tolerate no other sausages on his breakfast table than those produced under this recipe. Loraine had talked himself into a partnership with the butcher and, on the strength of "the royal recipe" story, also talked the Register of Companies into listing the operation under the grand name of Royal Victoria Sausages Ltd. As would later be revealed, "Royal" referred to a brand of seasoning used in the recipe and "Victoria" came from the street address of the shop—11 Victoria Terrace—in Brighton. The recipe was dated 1919; the fact that King Edward had died in 1910 apparently went unremarked by all principals subsequently involved. Loraine was looking for backers to develop the enterprise, and Roe suggested it to George as an investment for ROTURMAN, S.A. In August of 1961 a subsidiary company was formed under the name CADCO Ltd., and George became a director of Royal Victoria Sausages. "Isn't CADCO terrific," Benita wrote to Brian and Eleanor Aherne, "Everyone keeps making dark remarks and offering the gloomiest wishes for its success . . . but we think it madly exciting and feel very proud." (Four years later she would say of Thomas Roe, "He has been like a terrible disease in our lives.") With more enthusiasm than planning, CADCO opened a large factory at Partridge Green, near Horsham in Sussex, and immediately experienced major production and logistical problems.

By spring of 1963 Royal Victoria was $400,000 in the red, but Loraine came up with a plan not only to recoup the losses but expand the operation even further. He persuaded the British Board of Trade to subsidize the company with funds from the government-administered Glenrothes Development Corporation on condition that CADCO establish a new factory in the distressed mining area of Glenrothes in Scotland, where closing of the coal pits had resulted in widespread unemployment. CADCO was required to match the subsidy and also guarantee a loan of $1.3 million from the Royal Bank of Scotland. Because neither Roe nor Loraine had any money beyond what they drew from the company, George alone signed the notes. The development corporation funding eventually totaled $2.5 million; private investors provided an additional $750,000. Construction began on a Glenrothes factory site with facilities for some 20,000 pigs and employment for 2,000 Scottish workers.

Exuberantly, George and Loraine made plans to expand far beyond the Glenrothes project by constructing a huge fruit and vegetable processing plant in Italy. "I shall become 'CADCO's Man in Rome,' " George wrote expansively to Aherne. "If we are successful in this venture, then Rome will become our permanent base." Lavish parties were given to attract investors, directors' meetings were held in the Bahamas, and a $30,000 "contribution" to the Christian Democratic Party of Italy was given "in order to establish good relations." CADCO money found its way into various other projects, including the financing of *The Death Rays of Dr. Mabuse*, a film made in Germany. There was also the purchase of a twin-jet aircraft in which Loraine and his accountant flew to Rome for weekend parties with Italian starlets.

Seemingly a tycoon at last, George lived in a state of constant euphoria. "He already has people looking for the most gilded palazzo in Rome where we can entertain villainous Italian businessmen and shifty ministers in marbled splendor," Benita wrote to the Ahernes. George urged Brian to join him in a "sensible, dignified business career" instead of pursuing "the puerile follies of an adolescent thespian." Aherne, mindful of his losses in the HUSAN affair, ignored the invitation. In any case, and unknown to them all, CADCO was rapidly heading for disaster: in a matter of weeks the Sussex factory was forced to close owing to inefficiency and lack of management; construction of the plant at Glenrothes, poorly planned and executed, came to a halt for lack of money; the German film could not find a distributor and proved a total loss. In September, 1964 CADCO Ltd. ceased making payments to Glenrothes Development and collapsed. The British Board of Trade moved in and commissioned an investigation.

During its brief, costly life, from April 1961 to November 1964, Royal Victoria Sausages lost $1.9 million through "gross inefficiency, mismanagement, gross extravagance, and the abuse, misuse, and loss of capital money," as the Board of Trade report put it. In a bizarre turn of events, Roe was arrested in Bern for trying to pass $371,000 worth of counterfeit U.S. currency and was subsequently brought to trial and sentenced to six years in prison. Loraine disappeared for a time, then turned up in Las Vegas, where he was arrested on charges of acting as front man for a group of counterfeiters. It was he, apparently, who had shipped the counterfeit bills to Roe in Switzerland. All this left George in a desperately vulnerable position: the Royal Bank of Scotland demanded that he honor his personal guarantee immediately; panicked investors threatened lawsuits. "The press were chasing them," his sister Margaret recalls. "Benita said to me, 'You don't know what it's like to dread the postman every day.' They got all sorts of horrible letters." On the advice of his lawyer he fled Europe for California and in October 1966 filed a petition in bankruptcy, listing assets of $57,657 and liabilities of almost $1 million. He described himself as the "victim of an international swindle" and of unfortunate circumstances. "I was completely taken in," he told reporters. "Believe me, I am dumbfounded."

The Board of Trade investigation of CADCO Developments Ltd. and Royal Victoria Sausages was meticulously conducted by a team of government lawyers and accountants and included dozens of interviews with persons in Scotland, London, Lausanne, Paris, and Rome. Its findings strongly suggested that George had been neither a simple victim nor an innocent tool of Roe and Loraine, even if his direct responsibility had been less than theirs. The commission found that the entire Glenrothes project was "a device by which its originators could recoup the very substantial sums of money which they had lost in Royal Victoria Sausages. Sanders was a party to this device, and must be held materially responsible for launching the disastrous venture at Glenrothes." Furthermore, "It was Sanders who first suggested the Italian venture." Moreover, the investigators believed that "his behaviour was . . . indifferent to the point of recklessness to the truth or untruth of statements in which he acquiesced," basing this opinion on press handouts, "which Sanders took no steps to have altered" that described him as a trained engineer and a highly successful businessman. Another press release put together by George and Loraine contained "greater falsehoods" which even Roe felt necessary to alter, for it claimed that Robert Mitchum, William Holden, Charlie Chaplin, and Graham Greene were connected with CADCO. The report concluded with a frightening recommendation: "The whole matter of the deception played upon the Development Corporation to induce it to enter into these contracts should be referred to the Director of Public Prosecutions in England and to the Lord Advocate in Scotland for them to consider prosecutions against Roe, Loraine, and Sanders."

"My husband is ruined financially," Benita complained bitterly to reporters. "And now these terrible things are being said by the Board of Trade to add to the misery. George is completely innocent of these terrible charges." It was true at least that George had not been milking CADCO as had Roe and Loraine; the fact of his bankruptcy would seem to indicate this. The Board's recommendation for prosecution was never acted upon; according to the Lord Advocate, no proceedings were warranted in Scotland, and in England the Director of Public Prosecutions decided that no action could be taken. It may be that the Royal Bank of Scotland and the British Board of Trade wished to avoid the publicity which their staggering losses would have precipitated had action been taken in the matter. The Board's report, for whatever reasons, was not made public until some sixteen months after its completion.

The fact that he escaped criminal prosecution did little to lift George's spirits, for he had begun to despair of the future. "The thought of having to rebuild my whole situation from scratch weighs heavily upon me, and I wonder if it is worth it, whether there is any point in it," he wrote in 1966. "I have no confidence in any of my decisions, since my life seems to have been characterized by one piece of foolishness after another, and there is no reason to suppose that it won't go on this way." It was at this point that George first gave expression, if not in realistic form, to thoughts of suicide: "I am almost ready to give up entirely and do what the French builder did at Frejus, when his business was washed away in the dam-burst. He put twenty-five pounds of dynamite in his car, took his wife with him for a drive to the top of the hill, and then blew himself up in a tremendous explosion."

More than financial ruin, George had suffered a cruel loss of dignity which the mask of disdain and indifference could not entirely conceal. He would soon suffer other losses, more shattering and with more tragic consequences, but for the present he withdrew into himself, contemptuous of everything that had been given him or which he had so ardently sought: "When you're in Florida," he wrote to Aherne the same year, "you must drive across the peninsula to Tampa and St. Petersburg and watch the oldsters playing shuffleboard. They seem to be quite happy. They have no problems. They have no choice. They are not cursed with money or talent."

17 "Like Any Factory Worker"

"I am a businessman actor," George candidly remarked at the high point in his film career, not long after he won his Oscar for *All About Eve*. "I do my job, pick up my paycheck, and go home like any factory worker." It was a view of himself he never had occasion to modify, and there is no better example of the consequence of that attitude than the pictures he made during the period 1960–1967. Film historians are in general accord about his performances during this decade, a typical commentary noting that "he just walked through the parts in his tired fashion and picked up his wages." George never bothered to see any of the pictures after they were completed, and in any case few could be considered distinguished productions.

Some indication of the uneven production quality and care devoted to the making of *Bluebeard's Ten Honeymoons* (1960) may be gathered from the fact that two actresses prominently listed in the credits and in the synopsis of the film do not even appear in the finished picture. George has the lead as Henri Landru, a famed French mass murderer who seduced and then poisoned his female victims with montonous regularity. Corinne Calvet costars as Odette, and they are supported by Jean Kent, Patricia Roc, and other veterans whom George rather uncharitably described collectively as "a number of professionally moribund actresses," all of whom he was to murder during the course of the picture. Called to start rehearsing the first scene of the first day's shooting, George "took a quick glance at the first two pages of the script" and made his way to the set. This cavalier attitude is reflected in his performance; in the words of one reviewer, "George Sanders half-heartedly tries to inject an occasional note of jocularity into this heavy business but soon surrenders to occupational fatigue." The filming took only three weeks.

A far better production but of no more interest to George than any other during this time was *The Last Voyage*, also released in 1960. Because the picture was filmed in Japan, George took Benita with him on location as a belated honeymoon trip. He plays the captain of a luxury liner which explodes, catches fire, and then sinks. A bizarre aspect of the project was the use the old French liner *Ile de France* just before it was scheduled to be scrapped. The script called for the ship to be flooded and sunk for the climactic scene in the picture, but devious Japanese junkyard tycoons employed delays, blackmail, extortion, and even death threats to producer Andrew Stone in an effort to stall production and keep their salvage rights. The cast was in a state of constant agitation and anxiety. "One member of the group seemed oblivious to it all," lead actor Robert Stack remembers. "Although I was nominally the star, George Sanders did not waste time with protocol. He arrived on board the *Ile de France* in his captain's uniform and installed himself at the captain's table where the crew brought him his choice of food and wine for the rest of the picture." Stack and George had known each other since the early fifties when they worked together on a television remake of the classic mystery film, *Laura*. Stack and Dana Wynter were cast in the Dana Andrews and Gene Tierney roles; George of course was given Clifton Webb's role as the malicious Waldo Lydecker. The show, shot for Fox in fourteen days, was a hash and never released.

George had the lead in another 1960 release, *Village of the Damned*, a British horror film adapted from John Wyndham's novel *The Midwich Cuckoos*. Here George and Barbara Shelley play the parents of a child whose strange manner and supernatural intelligence are shared by other children born at the same moment. George manages a respectable if uninspired performance, and there are some affecting scenes between him and Shelley. *Trouble in the Sky* (1961), a well-made British aviation drama, finds George in a supporting role amid a strong cast including Peter Cushing, Elizabeth Seal, and Bernard Lee, whose performances show him to some disadvantage. "Only George Sanders, smirking familiarly as a vindictive prosecuting attorney, seems out of place in this fast company," comments one reviewer. The role calls for little more than what had become an almost automatic rendering of type, and he is content to leave it at that.

In *Five Golden Hours* (1961) George supports Ernie Kovacs and Cyd Charisse in a comedy about a professional pallbearer who fleeces lonely widows. He is "perfectly at ease" in his role as a suave con man comfortably hiding out in a sanitarium and, in the light of the coming CADCO disaster, delivers several ironically prophetic lines: "One draws a curtain between oneself and one's creditors," he tells Kovacs. "You weave it yourself. If you don't, they'd see you for what you really are—a stark naked fraud." From this, a series of films followed in which George supported English slapstick comics Tony Hancock, Terry-Thomas, and Charlie Drake in routine, low comedy vehicles. *Call Me Genius* (1961) is a tasteless project in which Tony Hancock stumbles about in a futile attempt to be funny and in which "the presence of such accomplished people as George Sanders, Dennis Price and Mervyn Johns in modest support of the likes of Mr. Hancock is as depressing as the stab at comedy." In *Operation Snatch* (1962) Terry-Thomas pops his eyes and hisses words through cleft teeth in his usual frantic, bumbling characterization, this time as a clumsy army officer in charge of the Barbary apes on Gibraltar during World War II. "Caught up in this trap," the New York *Times* laments, "are George Sanders and Jackie Lane, who have little more to do than draw their salaries." And in *The Cracksman* (1963) George, with Dennis Price again, supports the diminuitive English comic Charlie Drake, whose role as a locksmith duped by a gang of safecrackers gives the picture some bright moments until it ultimately collapses under its own weight.

"We never saw any of these pictures," Brian and Eleanor Aherne confessed, adding "nor, I am sure, did George. But he got handsomely paid for them." George's next film was to be shot in Egypt, and he took Benita on location for *Cairo* (1963), a lackluster remake of John Huston's *The Asphalt Jungle* (1950). "We can't distinguish this place from Osaka, Japan," Benita wrote from the Nile Hilton in Cairo. "All cities look alike nowadays, and awful is what they look. I didn't want to leave Lausanne." George plays the lead role as an international thief known only as The Major, who masterminds a robbery of King Tut's treasures from the Cairo Museum. He is assisted by Faten Hamama, as an exotic belly dancer, and Richard Johnson. Benita was afforded another opportunity to complain about foreign locales when she accompanied George to Budapest for the filming of *The Golden Head* (1964) with Buddy Hackett and Robert Coote, a thinly plotted and slow moving caper story involving the theft of the golden head of St. Laszlo. "We have just come back from a perfectly ghastly meal of stuffed cabbage, so divine in California and absolutely lethal in its home town," she wrote the Ahernes. "O dear me, the dismal trials of the

Socialist experiments. No room for the gifted, the colourful or the indigenous talents."

Returning to England for the making of *A Shot in the Dark* (1964) with Peter Sellers, was a much-appreciated change. "George is always going on about 'contrast,' " Benita wrote from London. "Maybe he's right, for after eight weeks in Budapest this seems like paradise, pure paradise." The contrast here was for George simply another illustration of his theory about the proportions of life's tragedy and joy, formed during his days in the Argentine and variously expressed throughout his life. "As Montaigne says," he paraphrased in a 1960 letter, "the insights of suffering are essential ingredients of a well-rounded person."

The Amorous Adventures of Moll Flanders was the only of George's pictures released in 1965, for the CADCO bubble had burst in late 1964 and he was constantly occupied in fending off creditors, lawsuits, and possible indictments. Based on the Daniel Defoe book but attempting to emulate the bawdy costume humor of *Tom Jones* (1963), the film stars Kim Novak as a fully endowed but confused tart in a light, fast-paced, and ultimately shallow story. In the role of William, a lecherous banker who marries Moll and then conveniently dies of a heart attack, George and such other veteran supporting players as Angela Lansbury and Vittorio De Sica "have a rough time sledding through this pat, labored charade of sex by one-dimensional players," according to one reviewer. George is "a convincing albeit weary roue" in his part, according to another.

Trunk to Cairo (1966), a routine mystery-action story in which George languidly performs in support of Audie Murphy and Marianne Koch, is of interest here only for having opened Christmas week of 1966 in New York City on the bottom half of a double feature top-billing *Arrivederci, Baby*, in which a substantial supporting role is played by Zsa Zsa Gabor. The *Times* took on both pictures in the same review, dismissing

Trunk to Cairo as "a dismal little clinker" and complimenting Zsa Zsa, who "radiantly clanking jewels, for once fits perfectly into a movie as a Hungarian chatterbox."

In both *The Quiller Memorandum* (1966), an international spy thriller, and *Warning Shot* (1967), a private-eye melodrama, George has little more than cameo appearances in distant support of George Segal and Senta Berger in the former and David Janssen and Stephanie Powers in the latter. His roles were so neglible that some co-players never saw him during the production. "George Sanders and I never met," Senta Berger reports. And Max von Sydow laments that although he and George both appeared in *The Quiller Memorandum*, "I never had the privilege of working *with* him." George Grizzard, who had a strong supporting role in *Warning Shot*, "never met George Sanders." George collected his last paycheck during this period for a performance in *Good Times* (1967), a Sonny and Cher music and comedy vehicle in which they play themselves. Although his is a supporting role, George is billed as costar, evidence that his name was still viewed as a draw of sorts. In the light of his recent personal history, the part was not without some irony: he plays an international financier in a plush office complete with huge semicircular desk, rows of shiny buttons, and pretty secretaries: a tycoon at last. And at one point during a long-winded spiel by another player, George's character nods off to sleep in a chair.

"We will make the picture. We will make money. And that, my boy, is what it's all about." While this line of George's is from the film, it could well serve as a commentary on the state of his career at this point and a depressingly appropriate conclusion to nearly a decade of performing like a factory worker in whatever roles in whatever pictures came his way. Sadly, the worst was yet to come.

Hollywood and Europe:
1968–1972

18 "It's the Ash Heap for Him"

Mexican actress Lorraine Chanel, who was George's companion as well as romantic interest for several years near the end of his life, met him in the spring of 1968 in Mexico City while he was there for his role in *The Candy Man* (1969), a film she calls "a dreadful piece" which she hopes "everyone has forgotten." Indeed one of George's least memorable pictures, it is also representative of the work he undertook the last four years of his career. Some fifteen years earlier he had confided to Zsa Zsa his conviction that "other professionals command more respect and higher fees as they grow older, but the aging actor—it's the ash heap for him."

The Candy Man was written, produced, and directed by Herbert J. Leder and filmed at Studios Churubusco in Mexico City. In it George plays a drug dealer known as "the candy man" ("everybody needs some candy of one kind or another," as he tells a confederate) who kidnaps the small daughter of a touring American movie star (Leslie Parrish) and gets his comeuppance by tumbling to his death down a stairwell at picture's end. George plays the part with a stilted nastiness, scowling and looking vaguely sinister, a standard villain devoid of the subtle shadings he once brought to such roles. Moreover, he appears

183

tired and stoop-shouldered, his voice is thick and muted, and he moves about with some difficulty. The supporting players are weak and look to have been recruited from the cast of a high school play.

In a 1969 interview George was asked to discuss a recent film he had made. "I don't know what it was about," he responded. "I never see any of my films. All I know is there were some planes going over and parachutes fell out and there was a big mystery of some sort because there were no bodies attached." And his role? "I played a general or something, because I remember looking through binoclulars and saying 'Good God!' and a lot of rubbish like that." The picture was *The Body Stealers* (1969), made in England and costarring Maurice Evans and Patrick Allen. Both George's description and attitude stand as a fair estimate of its quality.

By far the most professional production he would be involved in during this final stage of his career was *The Kremlin Letter* (1970), which nonetheless had him in a role which moviegoers and critics thought of questionable taste at best and demeaning at worst. He plays an American espionage agent with a homosexual bent assigned to seduce a top Russian spy of similar leanings. He is required to play the character in drag with blond wig, black satin sheath dress slit up the thigh, and long feather boa draped about his neck. "I feel rather silly," he admitted in an on-set interview, "but acting queer seems to be the trend these days." Yet he wrote soon after to Lorraine, "although I am now so old that it doesn't matter what I am or used to be, the fact is I am not now nor have I ever been a queer." In another interview after the picture was completed, George confessed, "I really don't understand the film. It's too modern for me. I just do what I'm told." Director Huston thought George did it well and recalls that in the transvestite scenes "he was exactly right in voice and gesture." Even so, it proved an embarrassment, and George refused to discuss the role any further.

Doomwatch, made in England in 1971 but not released until 1976, is an unambitious and consequently ineffective horror story about a toxic chemical dumping ground and the gruesome disease it inflicts on the inhabitants of a nearby village. George virtually walks through his role in support of Ian Bannen and Judy Geeson, but veteran character actor Simon Oates shows him to disadvantage by delivering a solid supporting performance. *Endless Night* (1971, a British thriller adapted from the bestselling novel by Agatha Christie, is a more polished production. George does a pleasant if bland turn as an avuncular family lawyer trying unsuccessfully to avert the tragedy overtaking costars Hayley Mills and Hywel Bennett on the Devon coast. As a young girl Mills had worked with George in the engaging and popular *In Search of the Castaways* (1962), but in this production it was apparent to her that "he was very tired and very lonely."

Now undeniably the aging actor he had feared becoming, George found himself firmly mired in the ash heap with *Psychomania* (1972), his last picture. Also released under the title *The Death Wheelers*, this inane tale of the supernatural casts him as Shadwell, butler to Mrs. Latham (veteran British character actress Beryl Reid), a spiritualist and medium whose son, leather-jacketed biker Tom (Nicky Henson), presses her to reveal to him "the secret of how the dead come back." When she does, he promptly kills himself in order to return to life along with other members of his gang, who have undertaken mass suicide for the same reason. George spends most of the film in butler's black tie and tails running errands for his mistress or bowing with a tray and solicitously inquiring, "Sherry?" Keeping a straight face while intoning such lines as "anyone taking a *Maximus Leopardi* from a graveyard is either foolhardy or ignorant" (the specious Latin refers to a lumpy brown toad) was a matter not of control but rather ennui. When her dead son's girlfriend (Mary Larkin) seeks permission to bury the young man sitting upright on his motocycle, Mrs. Latham asks Shadwell what he thinks of the idea. "Well, it *is* a little unusual," George replies solemnly, "but I think it's what Tom would have wanted."

A decade earlier his eyes and the curl of his mouth would have revealed a bemused disdain for playing such transparent inanity, but now he was too old, too tired. And for the first time since his early childhood, he was seriously ill. In several scenes his speech is slurred, his movements are lethargic, and he has difficulty with his balance. It is profoundly disturbing to watch him in this role when one remembers his performances as Charles Strickland in *The Moon and Sixpence*, Lord Henry Wotton in *The Picture of Dorian Gray*, and Addison DeWitt in *All About Eve*.

When George agreed to an interview by Rex Reed in the summer of 1969, Reed was warned by a press agent, "you may find him difficult. He has vertigo, he's convinced he's going to die." During the interview, Reed tactlessly asked what was ailing him. "Maybe it's pernicious anemia," George dissembled. "The doctors will have to tell me what it is." What he was unwilling to reveal was the fact he had suffered a stroke only weeks before and was on his way to a hospital in Boston for consultation and physical therapy. The interview went badly, for Reed was largely ignorant of George's personal history and specific details of his film career. Including *Uncle Harry* and *Solomon and Sheba* among George's "very impressive films," Reed asked if he had fond memories of any of his pictures. "No," George replied curtly. "Not even *All About Eve*? It certainly holds fond memories for most moviegoers." "You may have fond memories of it, but it was just another picture to me." Does he remember his first film? "Yes, I was the wicked husband of Madeleine Carroll in *Lloyds of London* and I've played nothing but wicked bastards ever since." George was of course referring to his first American film, but in the published piece Reed added parenthetically and mistakenly that "actually his first film was *Strange Cargo* in 1929. He doesn't remember it."

The most revealing part of the interview shows the extent to which George had by this time emotionally insulated himself from painful memories and from the "extraordinary enigma" of death. "I understand you were a great friend of Tyrone Power," Reed probed. "Who told you that?" George shot back defensively, "he died on the set of *Solomon and Sheba*, but he was just someone I knew. One knew lots of people." The interview concluded with Reed perfunctorily wishing George luck. "Don't bother," was the gruff reply. "I shan't need it. I have no friends, I have no interests, I have no plans. I just want to be left alone." As Reed took his leave, George reached for a cane he needed in order to maintain his balance. It was the one Benita had used during the last months of her illness. Now it was his.

19 "This Sweet Cesspool"

"Who is Rex Reed?" George asked Lorraine in a letter two weeks after the publication of the interview, "and to what article are you referring?" When he went to Boston for treatment of his first stroke, she had joined him; she then returned to her home in Mexico City and he to his in Majorca. They had become quickly and closely involved during their time together in Mexico in 1968, and afterward George wrote to Aherne in high spirits, "think only this of me—that in some corner of a crummy foreign village there lives that old shit-heel from St. Petersburg—Sanders. I had a glorious time in Mexico." He had a photograph taken of himself in full Mexican regalia—sombrero, serape, even a guitar and false moustache. "It was his favourite photograph," Lorraine says. "He longed to be Latin looking." In October of that year George wrote her, "I pray you decide that you could do a lot worse than me as a partner, even though I am getting to be kind of a broken-down, crotchety old fart who loves you." In Boston he asked her to marry him. "I have to think about it," was her answer. She had been married twice and was then in the midst of an unpleasant divorce settlement.

"They had a lot in common," Margaret believes. "She

spoke Spanish, he spoke Spanish. They were both musical. It was a long-standing friendship. She's a very sweet person." Lorraine also understood George's moods and eccentricities. On their first evening together at her apartment in Mexico City "he stormed into my living room and boomed 'WHERE'S THE PIANO?' I didn't have a piano and felt terrible," she remembers. "Later I realized that playing the piano was his way of not having to talk with people." Three years later at his home in Majorca, after his health had seriously deteriorated, he ordered servants to drag his mahogany grand piano out into the garden where he chopped it to pieces with an axe because he could no longer play it. At about this time he also decided to gather all of the family records and Russian documents in a heap and set fire to them, perhaps the one thing Margaret "never forgave George for."

"I was good for George, really," Lorraine is convinced. "I might have married him if Margaret had encouraged me, but she told me one night, 'Lorraine, we would love having you in the family, but think about it, please, because George can be terribly difficult sometimes.' She liked me and didn't want me to get hurt." Looking back on it today, she believes "we could have given it a go, George and I in marriage, if I had taken him less seriously." In any case, it was she who made his years of failing health tolerable, often joyful. "Queen of my heart, object of my desires, and my passion," he began one letter in Spanish, as was his custom with her, or in a different mood and in English, "my most delectable Mexican piece." When apart, they corresponded regularly, exchanging chatty news of Majorca and Mexico, although often the subjects were serious and revealed George's most abiding concerns.

"Mother is in worse condition," he wrote during the last year of her life. "She has gone around the bend entirely. It is a terrible thing to lose your brain. Poor Margaret is having a very rough time taking care of her." Their mother had suffered a massive stroke and was completely bedridden. Margaret had to use a mechanical lift to get her in and out of bed. "My mother is still alive and a vegetable," George wrote several months later. "Poor Margaret has a terrible life now." He saw in his mother's terminal condition the same pain and helpless dependence on others he had witnessed during Benita's final days, a loss of dignity and control he had resolved he would not himself endure. He confided to Margaret that his greatest fear was "being helpless, having someone wipe my bum for me." In August 1969 he wrote that "Margaret and I have just come back from Mother's funeral. She died last Saturday."

During one of several visits Lorraine made to Majorca, he startled her by exclaiming, "Euthanasia, that's the answer!" The answer to what, she asked. "I don't want to become gaga like my mother did before she died," he replied, "and I'm damned if I want to be a helpless old man. So I shall do myself in when the time comes." On another occasion he couldn't manage to park his small automobile in Palma. "He tried and tried and finally screamed at me, 'PLEASE! Help me. I can't park it and I want to cry like a little boy.' He had very little patience with anything or anyone," she says. "He simply didn't want to grow feeble and useless, and he was frightened. Something was creeping up on him." During this period Lorraine believes "he was afraid to be happy. He could be very sweet, and when he was nearing the point of being tender, he would catch himself and revert to His Imperial Highness."

George's letters at this time were often taken up with matters relating to his health, sometimes encouraging and other times not. "My own news is good," he wrote in June of 1969. "My blood pressure is on the way down. Everybody tells me that I look ten years younger, and I am walking better even though I still need the stick some of the time." He was on a strict diet and had given up "everything including coffee, tea, and butter in addition to all forms of alcohol and tobacco."

Even so, vertigo rendered his balance still precarious, and on one occasion he fell and cut his head badly. "Had a bit of bad luck yesterday," he wrote Aherne in July. "I pitched forward on my face and cut open my head requiring eleven stitches, which they cheerfully put in without an anaesthetic." Two weeks later he wrote Lorraine, "all the stitches have been taken out of my head and I am looking quite normal nowadays." He suffered several more small strokes during the next year. "After the first one," Margaret recalls, "he telephoned me from Spain and said he couldn't move his right arm and was very upset about it. He couldn't get himself up out of a chair, and he couldn't quite control his speech." The vertigo remained, and he developed partial deafness in one ear.

"George wanted so much to work, but it wasn't coming his way," Lorraine recalls of that period. "If he had had more work and projects he would not have dwelled upon so bleak a future. He was to have done a few movies but because of his weakness—falling—the production companies didn't want to take a chance." That summer George wrote hopefully that "I have just returned from London where I went for an interview with Billy Wilder, who wants me for a picture called *The Private Life of Sherlock Holmes*—he wants me to play the older brother of Sherlock Holmes." But George was worried about his physical condition. "I don't know if I will be well enough in time. I would not want to attempt this part unless I'm in top shape. I would rather do some crummy guest spot in a second-rate movie and take my time to get well." Later the same month in another letter he had to report, "I'm afraid that I lost the Billy Wilder picture. Was not able to get well quick enough." The film was released in 1970, with the part of Holmes' older brother Mycroft played by Christopher Lee, whom George later saw in London. "He says it was very much of a mixed blessing since the cast was required to speak every word as written as though it was the Bible. They all got pretty jittery towards the end of the picture—it's a good thing I didn't do it in my condition."

Yet he felt that "this goddam stroke is proving very expensive," as he complained to Lorraine. "Have had to give up three movies already. By the time I'm ready to work again they will have forgotten who I am." Six weeks later he wrote from England, "I have written a television series for myself and will have a conference with television people in London. I will only work two days a week and spend every weekend in Majorca. I hope they buy it." This too was not to be. "My television series has run into trouble," he wrote in early 1970, "on account of a government levy on TV profits that the Labour government has just dreamed up." He was able to report, however, that "my health has improved quite a bit although I still have difficulty walking a straight line."

That summer Lorraine came to Majorca to visit him for several weeks. "I had never seen him so happy," she remembers. "We had a great time. He was relaxed and working about the house. We saw very few friends of his there, and he didn't care for museums or churches." One day while shopping they saw a lovely ring at a local jewelers and George remarked that "maybe I should give it to you as an engagement ring" since he still wanted to marry her. "You'll be the only woman in the world I have ever given a piece of jewelry to," he told her. Eventually she had to leave, and their idyll ended in August 1970. "Lorraine is leaving to go back to San Antonio," George wrote Aherne. "It was W.H. Auden who said that life is a process whereby one is gradually divested of everything that makes it worth living, except the gallantry to go on. Well, screw the gallantry."

"The last time I saw George was at the airport in Palma when I left to return to Texas and then Mexico," Lorraine reflects. "I said, 'George, just give me time and then we'll talk, and in the meantime let's keep writing and let's keep seeing each other.' " He wrote her a few days afterward to say "I hope you had a smooth flight" and tell her that "my condition seems about the same." It was the last word she would have from him for over fifteen months. It was during this period he suffered the additional strokes and also married for the fourth time. His bride was Magda Gabor, Zsa Zsa's older sister.

"What do you say to George's news?" Margaret wrote Lorraine at Christmas of 1970. "He didn't tell a soul. He phoned me the day after, by which time I knew already." Lorraine's reaction was understandable: "I was shocked to hear he had married Magda." Others were equally shocked. "He had given us many surprises over the years, but none greater than this," said Aherne when to his astonishment he heard on the radio that George and Magda had been married the afternoon before, December 4, 1970, in Indio, California. He later telephoned to offer congratulations and was stunned when George burst out, "It wasn't my idea! It was all Zsa Zsa's doing." And so it was. "George told me that Zsa Zsa was responsible for the marriage," Margaret relates. Zsa Zsa confirms this. "He was completely miserable," she recalls. "He lived in Majorca after Benita died, then he came back and stayed at my house for quite a while. One day he came to me and said he wanted to marry me again. I was sort of afraid of it, I don't know why. Then I talked him into marrying my sister."

In 1966, Magda Gabor had suffered a massive stroke which paralyzed her right arm and severely impaired her speech. Her usable vocabulary consisted of no more than thirty words. After her husband Tony Gallucci died in 1967, she became a wealthy woman and moved to Palm Springs. When George asked Zsa Zsa to marry him she knew that his strokes had left him physically limited and emotionally depressed. "George," she told him, "you are lonely and so is Magda. She is also rich. So why don't you marry her?" What followed is perhaps best recounted by Margaret, to whom George later gave a complete account of the doings that December afternoon. "It was a very impetuous and hilarious affair," she relates, "with Zsa Zsa planning to drive down with George on a Saturday, then having to cancel at the last minute so that he went down alone." George went first to Jolie's home and told her of his intention to marry Magda. "Jolie was quite understandably taken aback and suggested he should first of all move down and stay with them for a while and think things over.

"But the idea had taken a firm hold in his head—and when he got an idea he went after it without another thought. He charged straight down to Magda's house and confronted her with the announcement that they were getting married that afternoon! And that is what they did, believe it or not." Magda's personal secretary was recalled from her free weekend to arrange special licenses and find a judge. After the wedding a reception was held at the Palm Springs Racquet Club. "I wanted to keep George in the family," Zsa Zsa said later. "We all loved him. And I was doing it for him also because he was very lonely." Mama Jolie was pleased, observing that "it's always nice when you recapture a son-in-law."

Margaret was staying at George's house in Majorca at the time and remembers "getting quite hysterical with the Charles Boyers next door over all these goings on." After about six weeks, George returned home "ostensibly for a change of wardrobe, but obviously a bit worried, or chastened by his impetuosity. After much discussion on the phone there was a mutual agreement to terminate the marriage on a very friendly basis." An annulment was granted by the Indio Municipal Court in mid-January 1971. They remained friends, for George had known Magda for many years and in fact told Margaret "of an affair they had had years before Zsa Zsa ever came into the picture." After the annulment he wrote Aherne, "age is a ghastly phenomenon. I am now an irascible old fart, deaf and intractable. It seems, as I look around me, that all my friends are either dead or dying. It really *is* the last mile for all of us."

In December 1971 Lorraine received a brief letter from George in response to a Christmas card she had sent him. "I have not been in touch with you for more than a year now because I thought that my life was over," he explained. "This was also my reason for my marriage to Magda Gabor, who also had a stroke several years ago which left her with partial paralysis and total aphasia. I thought that my time had come and that one might as well settle down and face the facts in company." That was his last letter to her. Today Lorraine Chanel spends her time between residences in Mexico City and San Antonio, devotes her energies to animal shelters and animal rights, and has "no plans for another marriage. After knowing a man like George, other men frankly bore me."

There was to be one other woman in George's life, however, and she would in the end bring him as much grief as Lorraine had brought him happiness. It was the compounding of life's experience of joy and tragedy George had believed the "essential ingredients of a well-rounded person" and which he would characterize in his last statement to the world as "this sweet cesspool" of life. "In November 1971 I dined with George in London at the apartment of a lady friend of his, hitherto unknown to me," Brian Aherne wrote. "She had taken him in while he was making a picture and was cooking his meals and looking after him." The picture was *Psychomania,* and the friend was a woman named Helga Moray. She was a writer and had been briefly connected with the film industry, but her career had been only tangentially related to George's. One of her books, a bestseller based on her grandmother's emigration to South Africa during the Irish potato famine, was made into a Boer War film called *The Untamed* (1955) starring Tyrone Power and directed by Henry King, star and director of *Lloyd's of London* some twenty years earlier. Helga had been married to talented British director Jack Clayton (*Room at the Top*, *The Innocents*), who had been associate producer of *Moulin Rouge*.

She lived in London, and from late 1970 to early 1972 was involved with George and stayed with him in Majorca on extended visits during that period. According to Margaret, who was living there with George most of that time, "it was obvious she hoped to marry him." Juliet Colman wrote to Lorraine about "Sanders and Savage Helga, whom we now all think he is going to marry. She's rotund and dear and a marvelous giggly, tolerant companion, the only trouble being that she drinks just too much to be good for him, in other words he follows suit a bit too much, which is worrying." Margaret relates that when George was told after his strokes not to have any drink at all, "he religiously kept to that for two years. He didn't touch a drop of vodka, which was his favorite tipple. And then it was this Helga, I'm afraid, who started him off on drinking more heavily. She would start about four o'clock in the afternoon, saying to George, 'Well, what about a drinkee?' " While this can only have had a detrimental effect on his health, it was his emotional well-being that her influence most disastrously affected.

"Why did I do it?" George asked Margaret on overseas telephone from Los Angeles in late 1971. "You should have me committed. I must be losing my mind." He had been persuaded to sell his Majorca house and bitterly regretted it. "It was his roots," Margaret reflects sadly, "the only roots he had anywhere after Benita died. He built the house, he furnished it, it was his baby. It was Helga who persuaded him to sell it." Margaret had earlier met with George and Helga in London to discuss the matter, and she managed to convince him not to sell. "Then Helga took him to Los Angeles with her, talked him into selling the house, and he had a breakdown. He really had a serious breakdown there, and it was because he'd lost the house. He felt he didn't belong anywhere anymore. The house was a stable base for him. He loved it." Eighteen months earlier in Majorca, Lorraine had told George, "you are a typical Cancer. You must live near the water, and you love your home. If you ever get rid of it you will be sorry and heartbroken." She was making lighthearted conversation about astrology over a late supper. "He thought it was a lot of bunk," she recalls.

"Was that wise?" Aherne had asked him at that dinner in London. "I knew that Benita had planned it as a haven for him for the rest of his life, and in her last days had done her utmost to help him with it." Aherne saw George for the last time in March 1972 in Los Angeles. Helga invited him to a Sunday lunch, where he observed that George "was drinking large glasses of straight vodka, looking dreadfully ill, and hardly made any sense." He and Helga were planning to fly to Biarritz soon to look for a home, and as Aherne spoke to him about it, George suddenly exclaimed, "I never should have sold the Majorca house! That was my great mistake. Why did I do it? Everything I do is wrong. I can't do right. I must be crazy." Helga interrupted them to say cheerfully that George would "be fine when they got to Biarritz, found a house and started the fun of fixing it up." As it developed, her plans would come to nothing: she and George would not go to Biarritz, they would not buy a house there or anywhere, she and George would not marry.

Shortly after his death Helga wrote a series of sensational-ized articles about her relationship with George and sold them to a London tabloid. The pieces were, in Margaret's words, "quite scurrilous and vengeful, bringing up all kinds of detri-mental things from his past life, calculated to extract as much money as possible from the scandal sheet." Margaret later was obliged to send clippings of the articles to the executor of George's will, from whom Helga was claiming money for "expenses" owing her. It was in all a nasty business.

In late April, Aherne telephoned George and spoke to him

one last time, inviting him to come to Italy for a small house party on the occasion of Brian's seventieth birthday. George declined, saying "I am on my way to Barcelona." Aherne was puzzled. "Barcelona?" he asked. "Whatever for?"

20 "Anticipating the Inevitable"

"Nembutal" is a pharmaceutical brand name for the chemical compound sodium phenobarbital, a central nervous system depressant affecting especially the respiratory system. As a sedative, the normal dose is one 30-milligram capsule. A hypnotic dose consists of approximately 100 milligrams, a toxic dose 1000 milligrams, and a fatal dose any amount over 2000 milligrams. The symptoms of an acute overdose are central nervous system and respiratory depression, areflexia, paralytic dilation of the pupils, tachycardia, lowered body temperature, and coma. Concomitant use of alcohol produces added central nervous system effects. The onset of symptoms occurs from twenty to sixty minutes after ingestion.

Still planning to remove to Biarritz and live there with Helga, George left California for Europe but went first to England to visit Margaret at her home in Horsham.

"I was completely shocked at the change in him. He had had some sort of serious emotional collapse—too many pills, and too much vodka, with much talk of suicide, in a state of deep emotional agony. He stayed here with me, during which time there was such a marked improvement that I was quite fooled by it. Majorca was still on his mind most of the time, plus a tendency to list all the mistakes of his

lifetime, but gradually things came into a better proportion, and he began to show signs of interest, if not enthusiasm, in new plans. We decided to share in a fourteen-acre place not far from here, with real seclusion, surrounded by pretty woodland, and lots of outbuildings to convert into workshops. He said that this plan would make life 'worth living' again and wanted to find a small beach villa near Barcelona in which to spend the colder months. This is why he went down there. When I think that I actually helped him make the reservations there and drove him to the airport myself, it is just too terrible."

At a dinner party in London on April 20th, two days before he embarked for Barcelona, George saw Zsa Zsa, who had just recently arrived in England, and spoke with her and her escort.

"I came with a doctor, a very famous doctor. I asked him 'what should we do about George?' He said George was having a nervous breakdown. I always thought that if someone always tells people 'I'm going to kill myself' they never do. When he died, killed himself, I asked a psychiatrist, who said that a man who says it all the time, that he's going to kill himself, usually does. Then he went to Barcelona. It broke my heart because George and I were on our honeymoon there. Terrible, terrible. I can't get over it yet."

The weather in Barcelona was unpleasant, cold and raining. George had hoped to arrive unnoticed, but a group of reporters awaited him at the airport.

"He would have done it sooner or later," Juliet wrote to Lorraine, "because he adamantly refused to become old and decrepit or ill and incapacitated. The last time I saw him was at Christmas. He was knocking back a bit too much with Helga as usual, but otherwise all seemed well. He then went to the States with her on what according to Margaret was a boozy trip and a nerve-wracking one, for having finally un-rooted himself from everything and being homeless, he was very unhappy. He returned rather a wreck and stayed with Margaret."

After answering the usual questions from reporters at the airport, George made his way to the seaside resort hotel Rey Don Jaime in Castelldefels, some ten miles south of Barcelona.

"He sold his house here in January, completely furnished and with all his records and everything," one of George's neighbors told Lorraine. "Since then he had been living in hotels and in Helga Moray's flat in London, and he had been constantly phoning to say how much he regretted selling up. It would seem that a series of things accumulated and must have built up in his mind, and he must have realized that Helga was absolutely unsuitable for him."

George checked into a suite at the hotel on April 23rd. Assistant hotel manager Juan Carbonell said later that George had been drinking heavily during his stay. He went to bed the night of the 24th and asked to be awakened early. He did not answer his call the next morning, and the manager went to investigate.

"Dear World. I am leaving because I am bored. I feel I have lived long enough. I am leaving you with your worries in this sweet cesspool. Good luck."

In addition to this note, police reported that five empty tubes of Nembutal were found beside his body. Twelve 30-milligram capsules per tube, sixty in all, amounted to almost two grams. Combined with the vodka he had washed them down with, it was a fatal overdose.

"He phoned us only a couple of hours before taking the lethal dose," another of George's neighbors reported. "He would be alive today had he not sold his house. He was lost without it. He walked out with only the clothes he stood up in."

George left a second note, written in Spanish, asking the finder to telephone Margaret in London.

"I am filled with all manner of self-recriminations, mainly because I feel that I failed him through not having the sense to realize how seriously disturbed and unstable he had become. Unknown to me, he had been to a psychiatrist in Los Angeles more than a year ago, who had diagnosed then an emotional or mental disorder and tried to persuade him to enter a sanitorium for treatment. Brian Aherne's wife,

who shares the same doctor, now says he told her that George should never, ever be left alone."

The press and the public uncritically accepted "boredom" as the reason for George's suicide, for his farewell note seemed perfectly consistent with the image of the world-weary cynic he had so carefully cultivated both on the screen and off.

"Off camera, Sanders maintained a reputation that dove-tailed with his screen image"; "His suicide note was totally in character"; "His note matched his screen image"; "Read the note he left behind: short and sad and, in the final hours of his desperation, still in the public's image of George Sanders." Even Brian Aherne, seemingly unaware of or insensitive to the nature of his friend's problems and the state of his mind, would write seven years later that George had "tamely succumbed to the ignominy of boredom."

A Barcelona newsmagazine published a tasteless and inaccurate article on George's death, consisting largely of interviews with his two servants in Majorca—cook Mary Canellas and valet-houseboy Dadou Conhey—in an apparent effort to unearth details of a sensational or scandalous nature. The piece, which among other lapses misidentifies Juliet as Benita in a photograph, labels Van Johnson "also dead" in another, and refers to Magda Gabor as George's "widow" and Lorraine Chanel as a "Mexican singer," offers the servants' statement that their employer "had no illness. On the contrary, he was in perfect health."

What press and public did not know was that in addition to the two notes George left to be found, he had the same night written and posted another to Margaret confirming what she already knew in her heart, why he could not face the prospect of continuing his life.

"Dearest Margoolinka. Don't be sad. I have only anticipated the inevitable by a few years."

Homeless and without roots, overwhelmed by loss of loved ones, by financial disasters, by humiliating errors of judgment in his personal life, in failing health, and horrified moreover by the long drawn and painful deaths of Benita and his mother, George recognized as inevitable the continuing and relentless attacks of illness and age that had ravaged his last years and that would ultimately present him with an intolerable loss of dignity and control against which the mask of disdain and indifference would prove hopelessly inadequate. He had not exhausted life; life was slowly exhausting him. The soul which sought escape from an inevitably cruel and protracted final exhaustion by slipping gently into death April 25, 1972 was not that of the bored and cynical cad but of the bewildered and despondent prince who in this instance chose to fly to the undiscovered country rather than make calamity of so long life.

More than a decade earlier, in perfect health, before the financial tangles and the painful personal losses, with the world before him and everything to live for, he thought on the death of Tyrone Power in his forty-fifth year and wrote, "he died in possession of all his faculties and in the full bloom of his manhood. It would not be incongruous to say that he died bursting with health. Those of us who must look forward to advancing decrepitude may think of him at times with a certain degree of envy. For while ours was the loss, who knows but what his was the gain." He ended by quoting in full this sonnet:

Whom the gods love die young; that man is blest
Who having viewed at ease this solemn show
Of sun, stars, ocean, fire, doth quickly go
Back to his home with calm uninjured breast.
Be life or short or long, 'tis manifest
Thou ne'er wilt see things goodlier, Parmeno,
Than these; then take thy sojourn here as though
Thou wert some playgoer or wedding-guest
The sooner sped the safelier to thy rest,
Well-furnished, foe to none, with strength at need

Shalt thou return; while he who tarries late
Faints on the road wornout, with age oppressed,
Harrassed by foes whom life's dull tumults breed;
Thus ill dies he for whom death long doth wait.

Notes

Abbreviated forms refer to sources cited fully in the Bibliography.

Chapter 1: "My Father Came in the Mail"

Page

3   "It came to": Margaret Sanders Bloecker, interview with author, Sept. 6, 1986.

3   "it was from": *Memoirs of a Professional Cad*, p. 10.

4   "a prince of": Charles Kidd, Debrett's Peerage Ltd., interview with author; preliminary genealogical outline, Sept. 9, 1986.

4   "Only in recent": Correspondence with author, April 1986.

4   "a world of": *Memoirs*, p. 10.

5   "a strong, healthy": Margaret Kolbe Sanders, manuscript memoirs, p. 2-A.

5   "When I look": *Memoirs*, p. 12.

5   "the famous Henry": Manuscript memoirs, p. 9-B.

6   "He never had": Interview with author, Sept. 6, 1986.

7   "during tea the": Manuscript memoirs, p. 6-A.

7   "I'd be a": "If I Weren't An Actor," p. 33.

7   "It might not": Martin, "He Sneered His Way to Stardom," p. 53.

Page

7   "from his great": *Memoirs*, p. 15.
7   "until the position": Manuscript memoirs, p. 29-B.
8   "the appropriation of": *Memoirs*, p. 14.
8   "saying that there": Manuscript memoirs, p. 41-B.
9   "never did much:" Interview with author, June 10, 1986.
9   "I wouldn't have": "The Strangely Fascinating Mr. Sanders," p. 57.

Chapter 2: "A Sense of Utter Worthlessness"

Page

11   "the vulnerability of": Conway, "My Brother George and I," p. 66.
11   "my parents sent": *Memoirs*, p. 19.
11   "Everything is so": Letters to Margaret Kolbe Sanders, 1917–1919.
12   "an institution": *Memoirs*, p. 21.
13   "I was top": Letters to Margaret Kolbe Sanders, 1919–1922.
13   "won the French": M.D.W Jones, Archivist, Brighton College, correspondence with author, May 1986.
14   "George had grown": Conway, p. 66.
15   "an austere and": *Memoirs*, p. 21.
16   "especially in our": Letter to Henry Sanders, Aug. 28, 1921.
17   "pretty well fed": Letter to Henry Sanders, Mar. 8, 1924.
17   "for which, even": *Memoirs*, p. 22.

Chapter 3: "We Men of Steel"

Page

19   "It is extraordinary": Letter to Henry Sanders, June 12, 1926.
19   "He spoke Spanish ": Anthony Quinn to author.

Page

.19 "It's impossible to": Baskette, "The Strange Case of George Sanders," p. 83.

19 "He learned to": Correspondence with author, April 1986.

20 "I miss the": *Memoirs*, p. 29.

20 "I should really": Letter to Henry Sanders, June 12, 1926.

21 "into the wilds": *Memoirs*, p. 23.

22 "In Patagonia they": Dillon, "He's Allergic to Skirts," p. 62.

22 "a primitive existence": *Memoirs*, p. 24.

25 "George had changed": Conway, p. 66.

Chapter 4: "And Never Looked Forward Since"

Page

27 "in disgrace": *Memoirs*, p. 37.

28 "a fairly deafening": Hall, "Things That Keep Sanders Awake," p. 80.

28 "I promptly accepted": *Memoirs*, p. 38.

29 "He was one": Douglas Fairbanks Jr. to author.

30 "The part of": Clipping scrapbook, 1934–1949.

30 "a really good": *Memoirs*, p. 47.

30 "very well acted": Clipping scrapbook, 1934–1949.

30 "I was the": *Memoirs*, p. 39.

31 "indifferent, remote, and": Guerin, "The End of a Love Affair," p.38.

31 "In the movies": *Memoirs*, pp. 47–48.

32 "a major movie": Thomas, *Cads and Cavaliers*, p. 63.

32 "oddly compounded of": *Memoirs*, pp. 41–42.

Chapter 5: "A Profound Sense of Unreality"

Page

35 "I find it": Ruddy, "Film Pictorial Book," n.p.

37 "the job George": New York *Times*, Nov. 26, 1936.

Page

37 "especially effective as": *Film Weekly,* Apr. 10, 1937.
37 "a newcomer, George": London Sunday *Express,* Apr. 11, 1937.
37 "There is a": London Sunday *Times,* Apr. 11, 1937.
37 "George Sanders plays": London Daily *Telegraph,* Apr. 12, 1937.
38 "I have told": Letter to George Sanders, Aug. 20, 1936.
38 "I had had": *Memoirs,* p. 39.
39 "I don't like": Baskette, "The Strange Case of George Sanders," p. 82.
39 "He used to": Interview with author.
39 "Why should I": Ruddy, "Film Pictorial Book," n.p.
39 "I suppose one": Deere, "Blood and Sanders," p. 79.
40 "the nadir of": Martin, p. 55.
40 "his sophisticated": Zinman, *Saturday Afternoon at the Bijou,* p. 221.
41 "almost as famous": Wilson, "Do Ordinary Looking Girls Have the Deepest Passion?" p. 79.
41 "I appeared in": Martin, p. 55.
42 "they gave George": quoted in Zinman, pp. 221–22.
42 "In the midst": *Crime on My Hands* (condensation), *Photoplay,* p. 50.
43 "is signed by": Beatrice Hurwitz, Simon & Schuster, Inc. Correspondence with author, May 20, 1986.
43 "know for a fact": Correspondence with author, Feb. 17, 1987.

Chapter 6: "In the Strictest Confidence"

Page

45 "To Dad, in": Dedication, manuscript journal, 1937–1938. Subsequent quotations are from the text, pp. 1–270, *passim.*

210

Chapter 7: "Women Are Strange Little Beasts"

Page

65   "it's a pity": Dodd, "Ten Ways to Avoid Matrimony," p. 47.

65   "George kept his": Conway, p. 66.

66   "The reason I'm": Baskette, "Hollywood's Most Baffling Bachelor," p. 100.

66   "in the background": Eaton, "Too Well Remembered," p. 35.

67   "a quiet, timid": Aherne, *A Dreadful Man* p. 21.

67   "he never took": Joan Fontaine to author.

67   "placid and calm": Conway, p. 66.

67   "The story is": Hall, "George Sanders Puts Women in Their Place, " p. 73.

68   "If people wish": Hall, "I Can't Make Anyone Understand Me," p. 30.

68   "his semi-mythical": Manners, "Love Is a Disease," p. 36.

68   "unbelievable that a": Eaton, p. 70.

68   "George lives very": Riley, "Sneers for Mr. Sanders," p. 45.

68   "nonsense. We lived": Eaton, p. 72.

68   "Hollywood has done": Dillon, p. 41.

69   "months of tireless": Foster, "The Strictly Private Life of George Sanders," p. 53.

69   "His marriage is": Hall, "I Can't Make Anyone Understand Me," p. 31.

69   "Her mental trouble": Correspondence with author, August 1986; interview with author, Sept. 6, 1986.

69   "he had a": Zsa Zsa Gabor to author.

69   "He was deeply": Correspondence with author.

70   "I didn't give": Quoted in Eaton, p. 35.

71   "You only have": Eaton, p. 72.

Chapter 8: "Schweinehund"

Page

73   "For a long": *Memoirs*, p. 60.

73   "one of the": Dooley, *From Scarface to Scarlett*, p. 103.

Page

74 "only right that": Nov. 4, 1937.
74 "subtle inclusion of": Oct. 6, 1937.
74 "the only actor": Mar. 28, 1960.
75 "a deeply affecting": Sept. 22, 1939.
75 "shrillness of tone": Rubenstein, *The Great Spy Films*, p. 114.
76 "George Sanders plays": Nov. 22, 1940.
76 "just a routine": Dec. 5, 1940.
76 "keen and vivid": New York *Times*, June 14, 1941.
77 "plays the Nazi": *Photoplay*, Sept. 1941, p. 98.
77 "his usual grace": New York *Times*, May 15, 1943.
77 "By this time": *Memoirs*, p. 60.

Chapter 9: "Circumstances Beyond My Control"

Page

79 "If I have": *Memoirs*, p. 59.
79 "Film acting is": *Memoirs*, p. 58.
79 "I am not": Thomas, p. 69.
79 "Acting is for": Zsa Zsa Gabor, *My Story*, p. 191.
79 "He didn't seem": Elena Verdugo to author.
80 "He didn't take": Anthony Quinn to author.
80 "never really cared": Lucille Ball to author.
80 "he was ashamed": Zsa Zsa Gabor to author.
80 "at that time": Margaret Sanders Bloecker to author, April 1986.
80 "I wonder which": Aherne, p. 58.
80 "It would make": Aherne, p. 189.
80 "I can only": *Memoirs*, p. 58.
81 "an excellent actor": Douglas Fairbanks Jr. to author.
81 "a natural actor": Vincent Price to author.
81 "vulgar and unpleasant": Laraine Day to author.
81 "a fine actor": Marguerite Chapman to author; Gene Tierney to author.
81 "Absolutely one of": Lucille Ball to author.

Page

81   "unique in giving": Ella Raines to author.
81   "He was consistently": Cornel Wilde to author.
81   "truly a great": Victor Mature to author.
81   "He was born": Mike Mazurki to author.
81   "a lot alike": Gary Merrill to author.
81   "slightly intimidating": Virginia Mayo to author.

82   "as an actor": Robert Douglas to author.
82   "He didn't consider": Zsa Zsa Gabor to author.
82   "admired him greatly": Eva Gabor to author.
82   "an actor with": Shirley Jones to author.
82   "He was an": Elke Sommer to author.
82   "admired his professionalism": Herbert Lom to author.
82   "He understood his": Lila Kedrova to author.
82   "George Sanders was": Max von Sydow to author.
82   "George Sanders possessed": John Huston to author.

84   "splendidly in character": New York *Times*, Mar. 29, 1940.
84   "how well George": Dame Daphne du Maurier to author.
84   "external enamel": Joan Fontaine to author.
84   "You know that": Spoto, *The Dark Side of Genius*, p. 226.

85   "damned winning heavies": Martin, p. 55.
85   "made his cads": Thomas, p. 64.

86   "Mr. Sanders continuously": Laraine Day to author.

87   "Had I become": *Memoirs*, p. 56.

89   "once in love": Baskette, "Hollywood's Most Baffling Bachelor," p. 45.

91   "George was called": Holland, "Actors Are Lousy Lovers," p. 72.

91   "It was a": *Memoirs*, p. 114.

92   "supreme satisfaction": Cook, "A Spade's a Spade," p. 70.

93   "A whole mass": *Memoirs*, pp. 114–15.
93   "Mr. Sanders, what": *Memoirs*, p. 115.
93   "A woman's place": "The Strangely Fascinating Mr. Sanders," p. 57.
93   "A woman's highest": Dillon, p. 41.

Page

93 "The most attractive": Manners, p. 74.
94 "The entire relationship": Hall, "George Sanders Puts Women in Their Place," pp. 72–73.
94 "Well, perhaps not": Martin, p. 32.
94 "Women don't really": "There's a Lot to Like About Women," p. 84.
95 "Working as I": Hall, "I Can't Make Anyone Understand Me," p. 70.
95 "I find I": *Memoirs*, p. 67.
96 "There is my": Zsa Zsa Gabor, "Exactly What I Wanted," p. 48; *My Story*, p. 169 ; Jolie Gabor, *Jolie*, p. 190.

Chapter 10: "Cokiline"

Page

99 "I always adored": "Exactly What I Wanted," p. 48.
99 "like a disdainful": *My Story*, p. 169.
99 "I'm a fatalist": "Exactly What I Wanted," p. 49.
99 "like a pasha": *My Story*, p. 171.
99 "Mr. Sanders, I'm": "Goodbye, My Love," p. 48.
100 "I wouldn't have": "The Strangely Fascinating Mr. Sanders," p. 57.
100 "And by the": *My Story*, p. 174.
100 "We always lived": Guerin, p. 41.
100 "I just adored": Zsa Zsa Gabor to author.
101 "Zsa Zsa is perhaps": *Memoirs*, p. 110.
101 "walking on clouds": "Exactly What I Wanted," pp. 58–59.
101 "we were able": *Memoirs*, p. 110.
101 "Mostly I called": "Exactly What I Wanted," p. 59.
102 "It can't last": *Jolie*, p. 191.
102 "I'm marrying George": *My Story*, p. 186.
103 "You had better": Brown, *Such Devoted Sisters*, p. 103.
103 "I am dying": *Jolie*, p. 230.

Page

103   "Finally in Las Vegas": *Memoirs*, p. 109.
103   "neither of us": Aherne, p. 22.
103   "George never wanted": "Goodbye, My Love," p. 48.
103   "I'm a very": *My Story*, p. 193.
103   "They went nowhere": *Jolie*, p. 229.

104   "Cokiline, I don't": Brown, p. 105.
104   "allotted a small": *Memoirs*, p. 119.
104   "commuting between my": "Goodbye, My Love," p. 54.
104   "If you bring": *My Story* , p. 215.
104   "a sort of": *Memoirs*, p. 88.
104   "You know how": *My Story*, p. 189.

105   "I don't know": "Goodbye, My Love," p. 54.
105   "I was doomed": *Memoirs*, p. 91.
105   "Whatever else could": *Memoirs*, p. 93.

106   "sick with jealousy": *My Story,* p. 196.
106   "I lunched with": *Memoirs*, p. 70.
106   "He kept coming": Zsa Zsa Gabor to author.

107   "I'm going to": "Goodbye, My Love," p. 54.
107   "an occasion filled": *Memoirs*, p. 70.
107   "I can't help": Wiley and Bona, *Inside Oscar*, p. 209.

108   "You stay home": Brown, p. 109.
108   "I cannot live": *Jolie*, p. 233.
108   "I was handed": *My Story*, p. 202.
108   "Now there were": Brown, p. 113.
108   "My presence in": *Memoirs*, pp. 119–20.

109   "genuinely excited by": *My Story*, p. 207.
109   "our marriage could": "Goodbye, My Love," p. 54.
109   "he resented it": Zsa Zsa Gabor to author.
109   "I've decided to": Israel, *Miss Tallulah Bankhead*, p. 289.
109   "The lines were": Zsa Zsa Gabor to author.

110   "every time he'd": "Goodbye, My Love," p. 54.
110   "I've used my": Martin, p. 55.
110   "a gay, delightful": *My Story*, p. 191.
110   "Sometimes at parties": Cornel Wilde to author.
110   "elegant, quite natural": Ella Raines to author.

Page

110   "wonderful singing voice:" Anthony Quinn to author.
110   "sang for his": Joan Fontaine to author.

111   "said he did": Aherne, p. 14.
111   "it was high": *Memoirs*, p. 74.
111   "do you think": Aherne, p. 24.

112   "No sooner had": *Memoirs*, p. 76.
112   "I can't explain": *My Story*, p. 192.
112   "succumbed to funk": Maney, *Fanfare*, p. 306.
112   "sweet and believable": Merman, *Merman*, p. 188.
112   "He still wanted": "Goodbye, My Love," p. 48.

113   "Diplomat Extraordinary": *Memoirs*, p. 128.
113   "Don't come to": Brown, p. 132.

114   "It is my": *My Story*, p. 240.
114   "So wonderful that": Brown, p. 239.
114   "Rubi for me": *Jolie*, p. 236.
114   "I can't go": Leamer, *As Time Goes By*, p. 230.

115   "I want to": *My Story*, p. 238; Leamer, p. 231.
115   "It is bourgeois": Martin, p. 51.
115   "I can't afford": *My Story*, p. 239.

116   "to assist in": *Memoirs*, p. 128.
116   "I'm too discreet": "Zsa Zsa vs. George," p. 50.

117   "confronting the Spanish": Brown, p. 135.
117   "He had grown": *My Story* , p. 252.

118   "You see, even": Aherne, p. 26.
118   "a beater of": Brown, p. 141.
118   "On account of": *Jolie* , p. 236.
118   "She seems to": Brown, p. 155.

119   "After our divorce": *Memoirs*, p. 110.
119   "George was right": *My Story*, p. 274.
119   "very often went": Zsa Zsa Gabor to author.
119   "We were always": "Goodbye, My Love," p. 48.
119   "He was part": Guerin, p. 41.

Chapter 11: "Ripe for the Headshrinkers"

Page

121   "though he looked": Elena Verdugo to author.
121   "He was always": Zsa Zsa Gabor to author.
121   "It was then": *Memoirs*, p. 76.

122   "reserved": Gene Tierney to author.
122   "a very private": Anthony Quinn to author.
122   "he didn't mix": Ella Raines to author.
122   "very lonely and": Cornel Wilde to author.
122   "a recluse": Victor Mature to author.
122   "preferred his own": Robert Douglas to author.
122   "He was a": Patric Knowles to author.
122   "He was asocial": Elke Sommer to author.
122   "never close, never": Blake Edwards to author.

123   "when not on": Juliet Colman Toland to author.
123   "His big ambition": Dodd, p. 15.
123   "a local Rip": Baskette, "The Strange Case of George San-
        ders," p. 83.
123   "On the set": Riley, p. 44.
123   "oh, yes he": Conway, p. 65.
123   "Mr. Sanders' lust": Hall, p. 28.
123   "He went into": Zsa Zsa Gabor to author.

124   "He was a": *Memoirs*, p. 77.

126   "All right, here": quoted in Aherne, p. 223.

Chapter 12: "This Is My Mask"

Page

127   "On the screen": *Memoirs*, pp. 71–72.

128   "Blame the whole": June 16, 1947.

130   "George Sanders is": Oct. 14, 1950.

131   "George Sanders, who": New York *Times*, Nov. 6, 1956.

132   "whereas on the": *Memoirs*, p. 73.

133   "There were many": Mike Mazurki to author.

Page

133 "He had many": Douglas Fairbanks Jr. to author.
133 "My friendship with": Robert Douglas to author.
134 "He was one": Elena Verdugo to author.
134 "who claimed to": Shirley Jones to author.
134 "a very generous": Victor Mature to author.
134 "He had noticed": Elke Sommer to author.
135 "George adored him": Zsa Zsa Gabor to author.
135 "because the son": quoted in Aherne, p. 8.
135 "I personally don't": Zsa Zsa Gabor to author.
135 "saw little of": Aherne, p. 22.

Chapter 13: "Ostentation's Favorite Cad"

Page

137 "I was beastly": *Memoirs*, p. 96.
137 "his air of": Thomas, p. 60.
137 "the consummate Cad": New York *Times*, Apr. 26, 1972.
137 "When I began": *Memoirs*, p. 40.
141 "big bad wolves": Joan Mellen, *Big Bad Wolves*, pp. 4–5.
142 "Have you ever": Sally Jesse Raphael Show, transcript 229, July 20, 1989.
144 "a nice, reserved": Gene Tierney to author.
144 "after him": Zsa Zsa Gabor to author.
144 "were involved": Interview with author.
144 "When I first": *Memoirs*, p. 116.
145 "You've heard about": Guiles, *Tyrone Power: The Last Idol*, p. 112.
145 "A delightful gentleman": Lucille Ball to author.
145 "Once I heard": Zsa Zsa Gabor to author.
145 "George Sanders was": Sally Jesse Raphael transcript.
145 "I always adored": "Exactly What I Wanted," p. 48.

Chapter 14: "Rulers, Kings, Noblemen"

Page

147 "By nature I'm": "The Role I Liked Best," p. 57.
147 "There were none": Virginia Mayo to author.

Page

148 "with all the": New York *Times*, Oct. 27, 1947.
148 "the role I": "The Role I Liked Best," p. 57.

149 "a motion picture": Aug. 1, 1952.

150 "languidly played by": New York *Times*, Aug. 23, 1954.
150 "Hark to the": Quoted in Aherne, p. 183.

151 "solemn, slow, and": New York *Times*, Dec. 26, 1959.
151 "all I had": *Memoirs*, p. 148.

152 "I've got to": Guiles, p. 248.
152 "a sort of": *Memoirs*, p. 162.
152 "deeply affected": Interview with author.

153 "A marriage must": Lewis, "I'm in Sunny Spain Listening to Sanders on Love," Oct. 3, 1958.
153 "I want to": Aherne, p. 71.

Chapter 15: "She Remains Incontrovertibly English"

Page

157 "Benita's experiences parallel": quoted in *My Story*, p. 303.
157 "Ronnie had not": Aherne, p. 71.
157 "The weekenders included": Juliet Colman, *Ronald Colman*, p. 272.

158 "George is the": Aherne, p. 75.
158 "the cost was": Joan Fontaine to author.

159 "no recollection of": Heather Angel to author.
159 "surrounded by the": Colman, pp. 277–78.
159 "I was very": Douglas Fairbanks Jr. to author.
159 "She was the": Interview with author.
159 "the obvious place": Aherne, pp. 82 *ff.*

162 "I not only": Juliet Colman Toland to author.
162 "tresh": quoted in Lorraine Chanel to author.
162 "I haven't answered": Aherne, pp. 146 *ff.*

163 "Broadway is about": Prideaux, "Happy Encore for Kaufman's Classics," Nov. 26, 1966.

163 "All my hopes": Aherne, p. 190.
165 "They had made": Interview with author.
165 "He was his": Aherne, p. 206.
166 "he cried over": Lorraine Chanel to author.

Chapter 16: "A Rip-Snorting Scandal"

Page

167 "I am not": "I Can't Make Anyone Understand Me," p. 79.
167 "rip-snorting scandal": *The Noel Coward Diaries,* entry for Nov. 18, 1964.
167 "get out of": Aherne, p. 27.
169 "The royal recipe": Lee, "They Bought $4 Million Pig in Poke," p. 18.
169 "Isn't CADCO terrific": Aherne, p. 106.
170 "in order to": Lee, p. 19.
170 "He already has": Aherne, p. 139.
171 "gross inefficiency": Lee, p. 19.
171 "The press were": interview with author.
173 "The thought of": Aherne, pp. 180–82.

Chapter 17: "Like Any Factory Worker"

Page

175 "I am a": Martin, p. 53.
175 "he just walked": Thomas, p. 75.
176 "a number of": *Memoirs*, p. 188.
176 "George Sanders half": New York *Times*, Nov. 8, 1960.
176 "one member of": Stack, *Straight Shooting*, p. 233.
177 "Only George Sanders": New York *Times*, July 13, 1961.
177 "perfectly at ease": New York *Times*, Oct. 17, 1961.

Page

178 "the presence of": New York *Times*, Oct. 19, 1961.
178 "Caught up in": Sept. 26, 1962.
178 "We never saw": Aherne, pp. 119 *ff.*
179 "have a rough": New York *Times*, May 27, 1965.
179 "a convincing albeit": Thomas, p. 75.
180 "a dismal little": Dec. 29, 1966.
180 "George Sanders and": Senta Berger to author.
180 "I never had": Max von Sydow to author.
180 "never met George": George Grizzard to author.

Chapter 18: "It's the Ash Heap for Him"

Page

183 "a dreadful piece": Lorraine Chanel to author.
183 "other professionals command": quoted in *My Story*, p. 191.
184 "I don't know": Reed, "Hey There, Georgy Girl," p. 11 D.
184 "I feel rather": *Time*, Apr. 11, 1968, p. 42.
184 "although I am": Apr. 22, 1969.
184 "I really don't": Reed, p. 11 D.
184 "he was exactly": John Huston to author.
185 "he was very": Hayley Mills to author.
186 "you may find": Reed, p. 11 D.

Chapter 19: "This Sweet Cesspool"

Page

189 "Who is Rex": Jul. 21, 1969.
189 "think only this": Aherne, p. 210.
189 "It was his": Lorraine Chanel to author.
189 "I pray you": Oct. 16, 1968.
189 "I have to": Lorraine Chanel to author.
189 "They had a": Interview with author.

Chapter 20: "Anticipating the Inevitable"

Page

180   "I never had": Max Von Sydow to author.

180   "never met George": George Grizzard to author.

Chapter 18: "It's the Ash Heap for Him"

Page

183   "a dreadful piece": Lorraine Chanel to author.

183   "other professionals command": quoted in *My Story*, p. 191.

184   "I don't know": Reed, "Hey There, Georgy Girl," p. 11 D.

184   "I feel rather": *Time*, April 11, 1968, p. 42.

184   "although I am": Apr. 22, 1969.

184   "I really don't": Reed, p. 11 D.

184   "he was exactly": John Huston to author.

185   "he was very": Hayley Mills to author.

186   "you may find": Reed, p. 11 D.

Chapter 19: "This Sweet Cesspool"

Page

189   "Who is Rex": Jul. 21, 1969.

189   "think only this": Aherne, p. 210.

189   "It was his": Lorraine Chanel to author.

189   "I pray you": Oct. 16, 1968.

189   "I have to": Lorraine Chanel to author.

189   "They had a": Interview with author.

190   "he stormed into": Lorraine Chanel to author.

190   "Queen of my": Dec. 3, 1968.

The Films of George Sanders

George Sanders, whose film career spanned 1936 to 1972, appeared in 111 pictures, with title or lead roles in thirty, and acted for most of the great directors of the modern period, among them Alfred Hitchcock, George Cukor, Cecil B. De-Mille, John Ford, John Huston, Fritz Lang, Otto Preminger, Jean Renoir, and Roberto Rossellini. His leading ladies ranged from Norma Shearer to Sophia Loren and included Ingrid Bergman, Madeleine Carroll, Bette Davis, Joan Fontaine, and Hedy Lamarr; among male costars were Yul Brynner, Douglas Fairbanks Jr., Rex Harrison, James Mason, David Niven, Laurence Olivier, and Tyrone Power.

(★ = available on videocassette)

1936

The Man Who Could Work Miracles
82 min.
London Films
Prod: Alexander Korda

Dir: Lothar Mendes
Scr: Lajos Brio, H.G. Wells
Cast: Roland Young, Ralph Richardson, Edward Chapman, Ernest Thesiger, Joan Gardner, Sophie Stewart, Robert Cochran, Lawrence Hanray, George Zucco, George Sanders.

Dishonour Bright

82 min.
Cecil Films
Prod: Herman Fellner, Max Schach
Dir: Tom Walls
Scr: Ben Travers
Cast: Tom Walls, Betty Stockfeld, Eugene Pallette, Diana Churchill, Arthur Wontner, Cecil Parker, George Sanders, Hubert Harben, Henry Oscar, Mabel Terry Lewis.

Find the Lady

70 min.
Fox British
Prod: John Findlay
Dir: Roland Gillette
Scr: Roland Gillette, Edward Dryhurst
Cast: Jack Melford, Althea Henley, George Sanders, Viola Compton, Violet Loxley, Dorothy Vernon, Eric Pavitt, Nancy Pawley, John Warwick, Vera Martyn.

Strange Cargo

68 min.
London Films
Prod: Lawrence Huntington
Dir: Lawrence Huntington
Scr: Gerald Elliott
Cast: George Sanders, Kathleen Kelly, Moore Marriott, George Mozart, Richard Norris, Geoffrey Clarke, Kenneth Warrington, Julien Vedey, Matt Davidson and Adele.

Lloyd's of London
115 min.
Fox
Prod: Darryl F. Zanuck
Dir: Henry King
Scr: Ernest Pascal, Walter Ferris
Cast: Tyrone Power, Madeleine Carroll, Freddie Bartholomew, Sir Guy Standing, George Sanders, C. Aubrey Smith, Virginia Field, Forrester Harvey, Montagu Love, Una O'Connor.

1937

Love Is News
72 min.
Fox
Prod: Harold Wilson, Earl Carroll
Dir: Tay Garnett
Scr: Harry Tugend, Jack Yellen
Cast: Tyrone Power, Loretta Long, Don Ameche, Slim Summerville, Dudley Digges, Walter Catlett, George Sanders, Jane Darwell, Stepin Fetchit, Elisha Cook, Jr.

Slave Ship
100 min.
Fox
Prod: Darryl F. Zanuck
Dir: Tay Garnett
Scr: Sam Hellman, Lamar Trotti, Gladys Lehman
Cast: Warner Baxter, Wallace Beery, Elizabeth Allan, Mickey Rooney, George Sanders, Jane Darwell, Joseph Schildkraut, Arthur Hohl, Minna Gombell, Billy Bevan.

The Lady Escapes
63 min.
Fox

Prod: Leslie Landau
Dir: Eugene Forde
Scr: Don Ettlinger
Cast: Gloria Stuart, Michael Whalen, George Sanders, Cora Wither-
spoon, Gerald Oliver-Smith, June Brewster, Howard Hickman, Joseph
Tozer, Don Alvarado, Maurice Cass.

Lancer Spy
78 min.
Fox
Prod: Samuel G. Engel
Dir: Gregory Ratoff
Scr: Philip Dunne
Cast: Dolores Del Rio, George Sanders, Peter Lorre, Joseph Schild-
kraut, Virginia Field, Sig Rumann, Maurice Moscovitch, Lionel
Atwill, Luther Adler, Fritz Feld.

1938

Four Men and a Prayer
85 min.
Fox
Prod: Darryl F. Zanuck
Dir: John Ford
Scr: Richard Sherman, Sonya Levien, Walter Ferris
Cast: Loretta Young, Richard Greene, George Sanders, David Niven,
C. Aubrey Smith, J. Edward Bromberg, William Henry, John Carra-
dine, Alan Hale, Reginald Denny.

International Settlement
75 min.
Fox
Prod: Darryl F. Zanuck
Dir: Eugene Forde
Scr: Lou Breslaw, John Patrick

Cast: Dolores Del Rio, George Sanders, June Lang, Dick Baldwin, Ruth Terry, John Carradine, Keye Luke, Harold Huber, Leon Ames, Pedro de Cordoba.

1939

Mr. Moto's Last Warning★
74 min.
Fox
Prod: Sol M. Wurtzel
Dir: Norman Foster
Scr: Philip MacDonald
Cast: Peter Lorre, Ricardo Cortez, Virginia Field, John Carradine, George Sanders, Joan Carol, John Davidson, Margaret Irving, Robert Coote.

So This Is London
70 min.
Fox
Prod: Robert T. Kane
Dir: Thornton Freeland
Scr: William Conselman
Cast: Robertson Hare, Alfred Drayton, George Sanders, Berton Churchill, Fay Compton, Carla Lehman, Stewart Granger, Lily Cahill, Mavis Clair, Ethel Revnell.

The Outsider
90 min.
UK
Prod: Walter C. Mycroft
Dir: Paul Stein
Scr: Dudley Leslie
Cast: George Sanders, Mary Maguire, Barbara Blair, Peter Murray Hill, Frederick Leister, Walter Hudd, Kathleen Harrison, Kynaston Reeves, Edmond Breon, Ralph Truman.

The Saint Strikes Back★
67 min.
RKO
Prod: Robert Sisk
Dir: John Farrow
Scr: John Twist
Cast: George Sanders, Wendy Barrie, Barry Fitzgerald, Jonathan Hale, Jerome Cowan, Neil Hamilton, Robert Elliott, Russell Hopton, Edward Gargan, Robert Strange.

The Saint in London★
72 min.
RKO
Prod: William Sistrom
Dir: John Paddy Carstairs
Scr: Lynn Root, Frank Fenton
Cast: George Sanders, Sally Gray, David Burns, Gordon McLeod, Athene Seyler, Henry Oscar, John Abbott, Ralph Truman, Charles Carson, Carl Jaffe.

Nurse Edith Cavell★
98 min.
RKO
Prod: Herbert Wilcox
Dir: Herbert Wilcox
Scr: Michael Hogan
Cast: Anna Neagle, Edna May Oliver, George Sanders, May Robson, ZaSu Pitts, H.B. Warner, Sophie Stewart, Mary Howard, Robert Coote, Martin Kosleck.

Allegheny Uprising★
81 min.
RKO
Prod: P.J. Wolfson
Dir: William Seiter
Scr: P.J. Wolfson

Cast: John Wayne, Claire Trevor, George Sanders, Brian Donlevy, Wilfrid Lawson, Robert Barrat, John F. Hamilton, Moroni Olsen, Eddie Quillan, Chill Wills.

Confessions of a Nazi Spy
102 min.
Warner
Prod: Jack Lord
Dir: Anatole Litvak
Scr: Milton Krims, John Wexley
Cast: Edward G. Robinson, Paul Lukas, George Sanders, Francis Lederer, Henry O'Neill, Lya Lys, James Stephenson, Sig Rumann, Dorothy Tree, Joe Sawyer.

1940

The Saint's Double Trouble
70 min.
RKO
Prod: Cliff Reid
Dir: Jack Hively
Scr: Ben Holmes
Cast: George Sanders, Helene Whitney, Jonathan Hale, Thomas W. Ross, Bela Lugosi, Donald MacBride, John F. Hamilton, Elliott Sullivan.

The Saint Takes Over
69 min.
RKO
Prod: Howard Benedict
Dir: Jack Hively
Scr: Lynn Root, Frank Fenton
Cast: George Sanders, Jonathan Hale, Wendy Barrie, Paul Guilfoyle, Morgan Conway, Robert Emmett Keane, Cyrus W. Kendall, James Burke, Robert Middlemass, Roland Drew.

Green Hell
87 min.
Universal
Prod: Harry Edgington
Dir: James Whale
Scr: Frances Marion
Cast: Douglas Fairbanks, Jr., Joan Bennett, George Sanders, Vincent Price, Alan Hale, Gene Garrick, George Bancroft, John Howard.

Bitter Sweet
94 min.
MGM
Prod: Victor Saville
Dir: W.S. Van Dyke II
Scr: Lesser Samuels
Cast: Jeanette Macdonald, Nelson Eddy, George Sanders, Felix Bressart, Ian Hunter, Fay Holden, Sig Rumann, Herman Bing, Curt Bois.

The Son of Monte Cristo★
102 min.
UA
Prod: Edward Small
Dir: Rowland V. Lee
Scr: George Bruce
Cast: Louis Hayward, Joan Bennett, George Sanders, Florence Bates, Lionel Royce, Montagu Love, Clayton Moore, Ralph Byrd.

The House of the Seven Gables
89 min.
Universal
Prod: Ken Goldsmith
Dir: Joe May
Scr: Lester Cole
Cast: George Sanders, Margaret Lindsay, Vincent Price, Alan Napier, Nan Grey, Cecil Kellaway, Dick Foran, Miles Mander.

Rebecca★
130 min.
Selznick
Prod: David O. Selznick
Dir: Alfred Hitchcock
Scr: Robert E. Sherwood, Joan Harrison
Cast: Laurence Olivier, Joan Fontaine, George Sanders, Judith Anderson, Nigel Bruce, Gladys Cooper, Florence Bates, Reginald Denny, C. Aubrey Smith, Melville Cooper.

Foreign Correspondent★
120 min.
Wanger
Prod: Walter Wanger
Dir: Alfred Hitchcock
Scr: Charles Bennett, Joan Harrison, James Hilton, Robert Benchley
Cast: Joel McCrea, Laraine Day, Herbert Marshall, George Sanders, Albert Basserman, Edmund Gwenn, Eduardo Ciannelli, Robert Benchley, Harry Davenport, Martin Kosleck.

1941

The Saint in Palm Springs
65 min.
RKO
Prod: Howard Benedict
Dir: Jack Hively
Scr: Jerry Cady
Cast: George Sanders, Wendy Barrie, Jonathan Hale, Paul Guilfoyle, Linda Hayes, Ferris Taylor, Harry Shannon, Eddie Dunn.

The Gay Falcon
67 min.
RKO
Prod: Howard Benedict

Dir: Irving Reis
Scr: Lynn Root, Frank Fenton
Cast: George Sanders, Wendy Barrie, Alan Jenkins, Anne Hunter, Gladys Cooper, Edward Brophy, Arthur Shields, Damian O'Flynn, Turhan Bey, Eddie Dunn.

A Date With the Falcon
63 min.
RKO
Prod: Howard Benedict
Dir: Irving Reis
Scr: Lynn Root, Frank Fenton
Cast: George Sanders, Wendy Barrie, James Gleason, Alan Jenkins, Alec Craig, Mona Maris, Victor Kilian, Frank Moran, Russ Clark, Edward Gargan.

Man Hunt
95 min.
Fox
Prod: Kenneth Macgowan
Dir: Fritz Lang
Scr: Dudley Nichols
Cast: Walter Pidgeon, Joan Bennett, George Sanders, John Carradine, Roddy McDowell, Ludwig Stossel, Heather Thatcher, Frederick Worlock, Roger Imhof, Egon Brecher.

Rage in Heaven
82 min.
MGM
Prod: Gottfried Reinhardt
Dir: W.S. Van Dyke II
Scr: Christopher Isherwood, Robert Thoeren
Cast: Robert Montgomery, Ingrid Bergman, George Sanders, Lucile Watson, Oscar Homolka, Philip Merivale, Matthew Boulton, Aubrey Mather.

Sundown★
91 min.
Wanger
Prod: Walter Wanger
Dir: Henry Hathaway
Scr: Barre Lyndon
Cast: Gene Tierney, Bruce Cabot, George Sanders, Harry Carey, Joseph Calleia, Cedric Hardwicke, Carl Esmond, Reginald Gardiner.

1942

The Falcon Takes Over★
67 min.
RKO
Prod: Howard Benedict
Dir: Irving Reis
Scr: Lynn Root, Frank Fenton
Cast: George Sanders, Lynn Bari, James Gleason, Ward Bond, Allen Jenkins, Helen Gilbert, Edward Gargan, Anne Revere, George Cleveland, Hans Conried.

The Falcon's Brother
63 min.
RKO
Prod: Maurice Geraghty
Dir: Stanley Logan
Scr: Stuart Palmer, Craig Rice
Cast: George Sanders, Tom Conway, Jane Randolph, Don Barclay, Cliff Clark, Edward Gargan, Eddie Dunn, Charlotte Wynters, James Newill, Keye Luke.

Son of Fury
98 min.
Fox
Prod: William Perlberg

Dir: John Cromwell
Scr: Philip Dunne
Cast: Tyrone Power, Gene Tierney, George Sanders, Frances Farmer, Elsa Lanchester, Kay Johnson, John Carradine, Harry Davenport, Dudley Digges, Roddy McDowell.

Tales of Manhattan
118 min.
Fox
Prod: Boris Morros, S.P. Eagle (Sam Spiegel)
Dir: Julien Duvivier
Scr: Ben Hecht
Cast: Charles Boyer, Rita Hayworth, Ginger Rogers, Henry Fonda, Charles Laughton, Edward G. Robinson, Paul Robeson, Ethel Waters, George Sanders, Thomas Mitchell.

The Black Swan
85 min.
Fox
Prod: Robert Bassler
Dir: Henry King
Scr: Ben Hecht, Seton Miller
Cast: Tyrone Power, Maureen O'Hara, Laird Cregar, Thomas Mitchell, George Sanders, Anthony Quinn, George Zucco, Edward Ashley, Fortunio Bonanova, Stuart Robertson.

Her Cardboard Lover
93 min.
MGM
Prod: J. Walter Ruben
Dir: George Cukor
Scr: Jacques Deval, John Collier, Anthony Veiller, William H. Wright
Cast: Norma Shearer, Robert Taylor, George Sanders, Frank McHugh, Elizabeth Patterson, Chill Wills.

The Moon and Sixpence
87 min.
UA

Prod: David L. Loew
Dir: Albert Lewin
Scr: Albert Lewin
Cast: George Sanders, Herbert Marshall, Steve Geray, Doris Dudley, Elena Verdugo, Florence Bates, Heather Thatcher, Eric Blore, Albert Basserman.

1943

Quiet Please, Murder
70 min.
Fox
Prod: Ralph Dietrich
Dir: John Larkin
Scr: Joseph MacDonald
Cast: George Sanders, Gail Patrick, Richard Denning, Lynne Roberts, Sidney Blackmer, Kurt Katch, Margaret Brayton, Charles Tannen, Byron Folger, Arthur Space.

They Came to Blow Up America
73 min.
Fox
Prod: Lee Marcus
Dir: Edward Ludwig
Scr: Aubrey Wisberg
Cast: George Sanders, Anna Sten, Ward Bond, Dennis Hoey, Sig Rumann, Ludwig Stossel, Robert Barratt, Poldy Dur, Ralph Byrd, Elsa Janssen.

Paris After Dark
86 min.
Fox
Prod: Andre Daven
Dir: Leonide Moguy
Scr: Harold Buchman

Cast: George Sanders, Philip Dorn, Brenda Marshall, Madeleine LeBeau, Marcel Dalio, Robert Lewis, Henry Rowland, Raymond Coe, Gene Gary, Jean Del Val.

This Land Is Mine★
103 min.
RKO
Prod: Jean Renoir, Dudley Nichols
Dir: Jean Renoir
Scr: Dudley Nichols
Cast: Charles Laughton, Maureen O'Hara, George Sanders, Walter Slezak, Una O'Connor, Kent Smith, Philip Merivale, Thurston Hall, George Coulouris.

Appointment in Berlin
77 min.
Columbia
Prod: Sam Bischoff
Dir: Alfred E. Green
Scr: Horace McCoy, Michael Hogan
Cast: George Sanders, Marguerite Chapman, Gale Sondergaard, Onslow Stevens, Alan Napier, Henry P. Sanders.

1944

The Lodger
84 min.
Fox
Prod: Robert Bassler
Dir: John Brahm
Scr: Barre Lyndon
Cast: Merle Oberon, George Sanders, Laird Cregar, Cedric Hardwicke, Sara Allgood, Aubrey Mather, Queenie Leonard, Doris Lloyd, David Clyde, Helena Pickard.

Action in Arabia

72 min.
RKO
Prod: Maurice Geraghty
Dir: Leonide Moguy
Scr: Philip MacDonald, Herbert Biberman
Cast: George Sanders, Virginia Bruce, Lenore Aubert, Gene Lockhart, Robert Armstrong, H.B. Warner, Alan Napier, Andre Charlot, Marcel Dalio, Robert Andersen.

Summer Storm

106 min.
UA
Prod: Seymour Nebenzal
Dir: Douglas Sirk
Scr: Rowland Leigh
Cast: George Sanders, Linda Darnell, Edward Everett Horton, Anna Lee, Hugo Haas, John Philiber, Sig Rumann, Andre Charlot.

1945

Hangover Square

78 min.
Fox
Prod: Robert Bassler
Dir: John Brahm
Scr: Barre Lyndon
Cast: Laird Cregar, Linda Darnell, George Sanders, Glenn Langan, Faye Marlow, Alan Napier, Frederick Worlock, J.W. Austin, Leyland Hodgson, Clifford Brooke.

The Strange Affair of Uncle Harry

82 min.
Universal
Prod: Joan Harrison

Dir: Robert Siodmak
Scr: Stephen Longstreet, Keith Winter
Cast: George Sanders, Geraldine Fitzgerald, Ella Raines, Sara Allgood, Moyna MacGill, Samuel S. Hinds, Harry Von Zell, Ethel Griffies.

The Picture of Dorian Gray★
110 min.
MGM
Prod: Pandro S. Berman
Dir: Albert Lewin
Scr: Albert Lewin
Cast: George Sanders, Hurd Hatfield, Lowell Gilmore, Angela Lansbury, Donna Reed, Peter Lawford, Richard Fraser, Morton Lowry, Douglas Walton, Miles Mander.

1946

A Scandal in Paris
100 min.
UA
Prod: Arnold Pressburger
Dir: Douglas Sirk
Scr: Ellis St. Joseph
Cast: George Sanders, Signe Hasso, Carol Landis, Akim Tamiroff, Gene Lockhart.

The Strange Woman
100 min.
UA
Prod: Jack Chertok
Dir: Edgar G. Ulmer
Scr: Herb Meadows
Cast: Hedy Lamarr, George Sanders, Louis Hayward, Gene Lockhart, Hillary Brooke.

1947

The Ghost and Mrs. Muir★
104 min.
Fox
Prod: Fred Kohlmar
Dir: Joseph L. Mankiewicz
Scr: Philip Dunne
Cast: Gene Tierney, Rex Harrison, George Sanders, Edna Best, Vanessa Brown, Anna Lee, Robert Coote, Natalie Wood, Isobel Elsom, Victoria Horne.

Forever Amber
140 min.
Fox
Prod: William Perlberg
Dir: Otto Preminger
Scr: Philip Dunne, Ring Lardner, Jr
Cast: Linda Darnell, Cornel Wilde, Richard Greene, George Sanders, Glenn Langan, Richard Haydn, Jessica Tandy, Anne Revere, Jane Ball, Robert Coote.

The Private Affairs of Bel Ami
119 min.
UA
Prod: Ray Heinz
Dir: Albert Lewin
Scr: Albert Lewin
Cast: George Sanders, Angela Lansbury, Ann Dvorak, Frances Dee, John Carradine, Hugo Haas, Marie Wilson, Albert Basserman, Warren William.

Lured
102 min.
UA
Prod: James Nasser

Dir: Douglas Sirk
Scr: Leo Rosten
Cast: Lucille Ball, George Sanders, Charles Coburn, Boris Karloff, Cedric Hardwicke, Alan Mowbray, George Zucco, Joseph Calleia, Robert Coote, Alan Napier.

1949

The Fan
80 min.
Fox
Prod: Otto Preminger
Dir: Otto Preminger
Scr: Walter Reisch, Dorothy Parker, Ross Evans
Cast: Jeanne Crain, Madeleine Carroll, George Sanders, Richard Greene, Martita Hunt, John Sutton, Hugh Dempster, Richard Ney, Virginia McDowall, Hugh Murray.

Samson and Delilah★
128 min.
Paramount
Prod: Cecil B. DeMille
Dir: Cecil B. DeMille
Scr: Jesse Lasky, Jr., Fredric M. Frank
Cast: Hedy Lamarr, Victor Mature, Angela Lansbury, George Sanders, Henry Wilcoxon, Olive Deering, Fay Holden, Russ Tamblyn, Mike Mazurki.

1950

Captain Blackjack★ (Video title: **Blackjack**)
90 min.
UK/FR
Prod: Michael Salkind

Dir: Julien Duvivier
Scr: Julien Duvivier, Charles Spaak
Cast: George Sanders, Agnes Moorehead, Herbert Marshall, Patricia Roc, Marcel Dalio.

All About Eve★
138 min.
Fox
Prod: Darryl F. Zanuck
Dir: Joseph L. Mankiewicz
Scr: Joseph L. Mankiewicz
Cast: Bette Davis, Anne Baxter, George Sanders, Celeste Holm, Gary Merrill, Hugh Marlowe, Gregory Ratoff, Thelma Ritter, Marilyn Monroe, Barbara Bates.

1951

I Can Get It For You Wholesale
93 min.
Fox
Prod: Sol C. Siegel
Dir: Michael Gordon
Scr: Abraham Polonsky
Cast: Susan Hayward, Dan Dailey, George Sanders, Sam Jaffe, Randy Stuart, Mavin Kaplin, Harry von Zell, Barbara Whiting, Vicki Cummings, Ross Elliott.

The Light Touch
107 min.
MGM
Prod: Pandro S. Berman
Dir: Richard Brooks
Scr: Richard Brooks
Cast: Stewart Granger, George Sanders, Pier Angeli, Kurt Kasznar, Larry Keating, Rhys Williams, Norman Lloyd, Mike Mazurki.

1952

Ivanhoe★
106 min.
MGM
Prod: Pandro S. Berman
Dir: Richard Thorpe
Scr: Noel Langley, Aeneas Mackenzie
Cast: Robert Taylor, Joan Fontaine, Elizabeth Taylor, George Sanders, Emlyn Williams, Robert Douglas, Finlay Currie, Felix Aylmer, Francis de Wolff, Guy Rolfe.

Assignment Paris
85 min.
Columbia
Prod: Sam Marx, Jerry Bresler
Dir: Robert Parrish
Scr: William Bowers
Cast: George Sanders, Dana Andrews, Sandra Giglio, Marta Toren, Audrey Totter, Herbert Berghof.

1953

Call Me Madam
115 min.
Fox
Prod: Sol C. Siegel
Dir: Walter Lang
Scr: Arthur Sheekman
Cast: Ethel Merman, Donald O'Connor, Vera-Ellen, George Sanders, Billy De Wolfe, Helmut Dantine, Walter Slezak, Steven Geray, Ludwig Stossel, Lilia Skala.

The Lonely Woman★ (Video title: **Voyage to Italy**)
(Viaggio a Italy)
97 min.

Titanus
Prod: Roberto Rossellini/Sveva-Junior Films
Dir: Roberto Rossellini
Scr: Roberto Rossellini, Vitaliano Brancati
Cast: Ingrid Bergman, George Sanders, Paul Muller, Maria Mauban, Natalia Ray.

1954

Witness to Murder
81 min.
UA
Prod: Chester Erskine
Dir: Roy Rowland
Scr: Chester Erskine
Cast: Barbara Stanwyck, George Sanders, Gary Merrill, Jesse White, Harry Shannon, Claire Carleton.

King Richard and the Crusaders
113 min.
Warner
Prod: Henry Blanke
Dir: David Butler
Scr: John Twist
Cast: Rex Harrison, Virginia Mayo, George Sanders, Laurence Harvey, Robert Douglas, Michael Pate, Paula Raymond, Nick Cravat.

1955

Jupiter's Darling
96 min.
MGM
Prod: George Wells
Dir: George Sidney

Scr: Dorothy Kingsley
Cast: Esther Williams, Howard Keel, George Sanders, Marge and Gower Champion, Richard Haydn, William Demarest.

Moonfleet
87 min.
MGM
Prod: John Houseman
Dir: Fritz Lang
Scr: Margaret Fitts, Jan Lustig
Cast: Stewart Granger, Jon Whiteley, George Sanders, Joan Greenwood, Viveca Lindfors, Liliane Montevecchi, Melville Cooper, Sean McClory, John Hoyt, Alan Napier.

The Scarlet Coat
99 min.
MGM
Prod: Nicholas Nayfack
Dir: John Sturges
Scr: Karl Tunberg
Cast: Cornel Wilde, Michael Wilding, George Sanders, Anne Francis, Robert Douglas, Bobby Driscoll, John McIntire, Rhys Williams, John Dehner, Paul Cavanaugh.

The King's Thief
79 min.
MGM
Prod: Edwin H. Knopf
Dir: Robert Z. Leonard
Scr: Christopher Knopf
Cast: Edmund Purdom, Ann Blyth, George Sanders, David Niven, Melville Cooper, Sean McClory, Isobel Elsom, Rhys Williams, Alan Mowbray, John Dehner.

1956

Never Say Goodbye
96 min.

U-I
Prod: Albert J. Cohen
Dir: Jerry Hopper
Scr: Charles Hoffman
Cast: Rock Hudson, George Sanders, Cornell Borchers, Ray Collins, David Janssen.

While the City Sleeps★
100 min.
RKO
Prod: Bert E. Friedlob
Dir: Fritz Lang
Scr: Casey Robinson
Cast: Vincent Price, Dana Andrews, Thomas Mitchell, George Sanders, James Craig, Rhonda Fleming, Ida Lupino, Howard Duff, Sally Forrest, Robert Warwick.

That Certain Feeling
102 min.
Paramount
Prod: Melvin Frank, Norman Panama
Dir: Norman Panama, Melvin Frank
Scr: Norman Panama, Melvin Frank
Cast: Bob Hope, George Sanders, Eva Marie Saint, Pearl Bailey, Al Capp.

Death of a Scoundrel★
119 min.
RKO
Prod: Charles Martin
Dir: Charles Martin
Scr: Charles Martin
Cast: George Sanders, Yvonne de Carlo, Coleen Gray, Victor Jory, Zsa Zsa Gabor, Nancy Gates, John Hoyt, Tom Conway, Lisa Ferraday, Werner Klemperer.

1957

The Seventh Sin
94 min.
MGM
Prod: David Lewis
Dir: Ronald Neame
Scr: Karl Tunberg
Cast: Eleanor Parker, Jean Pierre Aumont, George Sanders, Bill Travers, Francoise Rosay.

1958

The Whole Truth
85 min.
Columbia
Prod: Jack Clayton
Dir: John Guillermin
Scr: Jonathan Latimer
Cast: Stewart Granger, Donna Reed, George Sanders, Gianna Maria Canale, Michael Shillo, Peter Dyneley, Hy Hazell, Jimmy Thompson, Richard Molinas, John Van Eyssen.

From the Earth to the Moon
100 min.
RKO
Prod: Benedict Bogeaus
Dir: Byron Haskin
Scr: Robert Blees, James Leicester
Cast: Joseph Cotten, George Sanders, Henry Daniell, Carl Esmond, Melville Cooper, Debra Paget, Patric Knowles, Don Dubbins.

1959

That Kind of Woman
92 min.

Paramount
Prod: Ponti-Girosi
Dir: Sidney Lumet
Scr: Walter Bernstein
Cast: Sophia Loren, Tab Hunter, George Sanders, Jack Warden, Barbara Nichols, Keenan Wynn.

A Touch of Larceny
92 min.
Paramount
Prod: Ivan Foxwell
Dir: Guy Hamilton
Scr: Roger MacDougall, Guy Hamilton, Ivan Foxwell
Cast: James Mason, Vera Miles, George Sanders, Robert Flemyng, Ernest Clark, Duncan Lamont, Peter Barkworth, Barbara Hicks, Mavis Villiers.

Solomon and Sheba★
142 min.
UA
Prod: Edward Small
Dir: King Vidor
Scr: Anthony Veiller, Paul Dudley, George Bruce
Cast: Yul Brynner, Gina Lollobrigida, George Sanders, Marisa Pavan, David Farrar, John Crawford, Laurence Naismith, Alejandro Rey, Harry Andrews, Mike Mazurki.

1960

Bluebeard's Ten Honeymoons
93 min.
Anglo-Allied
Prod: Roy Parkinson
Dir: W. Lee Wilder
Scr: Myles Wilder

Cast: George Sanders, Corinne Calvet, Patricia Roc, Ingrid Hafner, Jean Kent, Greta Gynt, Maxine Audley, Selma Vaz Diaz, George Coulouris, Peter Illing.

The Last Voyage
91 min.
MGM
Prod: Andrew Stone, Virginia Stone
Dir: Andrew Stone
Scr: Andrew Stone
Cast: Robert Stack, Dorothy Malone, Edmond O'Brien, George Sanders, Woody Strode, Jack Kruschen, Tammy Marihugh.

Village of the Damned★
78 min.
MGM
Prod: Ronald Kinnoch
Dir: Wolf Rilla
Scr: Stirling Silliphant, Wolf Rilla, Geoffrey Barclay
Cast: George Sanders, Barbara Shelley, Michael Gwynn, Martin Stephens, Laurence Naismith, Richard Warner, Thomas Heathcote, John Phillips, Richard Vernon, Rosamund Greenwood.

1961

Trouble in the Sky
92 min.
British Lion
Prod: Aubrey Baring
Dir: Charles Frend
Scr: Robert Westerby
Cast: Michael Craig, Bernard Lee, Peter Cushing, George Sanders, Elizabeth Seal, Andre Morell, Gordon Jackson, Delphi Lawrence, Noel Willman, Charles Tingwell.

Five Golden Hours
90 min.
Columbia
Prod: Mario Zampi, Fabio Jegher
Dir: Mario Zampi
Scr: Hans Wilhelm
Cast: Ernie Kovacs, Cyd Charisse, George Sanders, Kay Hammond, Dennis Price, Clelia Matania, Reginald Beckwith, Finlay Currie, Martin Benson, Ron Moody.

Call Me Genius
105 min.
Associate British
Prod: W. A. Whitaker
Dir: Robert Day
Scr: Alan Simpson, Ray Galton
Cast: Tony Hancock, George Sanders, Paul Massie, Margrit Saad, Gregoire Aslan, Dennis Price, Irene Handl, Mervyn Johns, John le Mesurier, Liz Frazer.

1962

Operation Snatch
87 min.
Associated British
Prod: Jules Buck
Dir: Robert Day
Scr: Alan Hackney, John Warren, Len Heath
Cast: Terry-Thomas, George Sanders, Lionel Jeffries, Jackie Lane, Lee Montague, Michael Trubshawe, James Villiers, Dinsdale Landen, Jeremy Lloyd, John Meillon.

In Search of the Castaways★
100 min.
Disney

Prod: Hugh Attwooll
Dir: Robert Stevenson
Scr: Lowell S. Hawley
Cast: Maurice Chevalier, Hayley Mills, George Sanders, Wilfred Hyde-White, Michael Anderson, Keith Hamshere, Antonio Cifariello, Wilfred Brambell, Jack Gwillim, Ronald Fraser.

1963

Cairo
91 min.
MGM
Prod: Joseph L. Mankiewicz
Dir: W.S. Van Dyke II
Scr: John McClain
Cast: George Sanders, Richard Johnson, Faten Hamama, John Meillon, Eric Pohlmann, Walter Rilla.

Ecco
(Mondo di Notti)
100 min.
Cresa-Roma /Julia Films
Prod: Francesco Mazzei
Dir: Gianna Proia
Cast: George Sanders (on-screen narrator), Yvon Yve, Leo Campion, Jacque Chazot, Maria Ansaldi, Laura Betti.

The Cracksman
112 min.
ABPC
Prod: W.A. Whittaker
Dir: Peter Graham Scott
Scr: Lew Schwarz, Charlie Drake, Mike Watts
Cast: Charlie Drake, George Sanders, Dennis Price, Nyree Dawn

252

Porter, Finlay Currie, Eddie Byrne, Percy Herbert, Geoffrey Keen, George Cooper, Norman Bird.

1964

Dark Purpose
97 min.
Universal
Prod: Steve Barclay
Dir: George Marshall
Scr: David Harmon, Massimo D'Avack, Steve Barclay
Cast: Shirley Jones, George Sanders, Rossano Brazzi, Micheline Presle, Georgia Moll, Charles Fawcett.

A Shot in the Dark★
103 min.
UA
Prod: Blake Edwards
Dir: Blake Edwards
Scr: Blake Edwards, William Peter Blatty
Cast: Peter Sellers, Elke Sommer, George Sanders, Herbert Lom, Tracy Reed, Graham Stark, Moira Redmond, Vanda Godsell, Maurice Kaufman, Ann Lynn.

The Golden Head
115 min.
Hungarofilm
Prod: Alan Brown
Dir: Richard Thorpe
Scr: Stanley Boulder, Ivan Boldizsar
Cast: George Sanders, Buddy Hackett, Douglas Wilmer, Jess Conrad, Robert Coote.

1965

The Amorous Adventures of Moll Flanders
122 min.

Paramount
Prod: Marcel Hellman
Dir: Terence Young
Scr: Dennis Cannan, Roland Kibbee
Cast: Kim Novak, Richard Johnson, Angela Lansbury, George Sanders, Vittorio de Sica, Leo McKern, Lilli Palmer, Hugh Griffith, Daniel Massey, Cecil Parker.

1966

Trunk to Cairo
99 min.
Noah Films/AI
Prod: Menahem Golan
Dir: Menahem Golan
Scr: Marc Behm, Alexander Ramati
Cast: Audie Murphy, George Sanders, Marianne Koch, Hans Von Borsody, Joseph Yadin, Gila Almagor, Elena Eden.

The Quiller Memorandum★
103 min.
Fox
Prod: Ivan Foxwell
Dir: Michael Anderson
Scr: Harold Pinter
Cast: George Segal, Alec Guinness, Max von Sydow, Senta Berger, George Sanders, Robert Helpmann, Robert Flemyng, Peter Carsten, Edith Schneider, Gunter Meisner.

1967

Warning Shot
100 min.
Paramount

Prod: Buzz Kulik
Dir: Buzz Kulik
Scr: Mann Rubin
Cast: David Janssen, Lillian Gish, Ed Begley, Keenan Wynn, Sam
Wanamaker, Eleanor Parker, Stefanie Powers, Walter Pidgeon, George
Sanders, George Grizzard, Carol O'Connor.

Good Times
91 min.
Columbia
Prod: Lindsley Parsons
Dir: William Friedkin
Scr: Tony Barrett
Cast: Sonny and Cher, George Sanders, Norman Alden, Larry Duran,
Kelly Thordson, Lenny Weinrib, Peter Robbins, Phil Arnold, Edy
Williams, China Lee, Diane Haggerty.

Jungle Book
78 min.
Disney (animated)
Dir: Wolfgang Reitherman
Scr: Terry Gilkyson
Cast (voice only): George Sanders, Phil Harris, Louis Prima, Sebastian
Cabot, Sterling Holloway.

1968

One Step to Hell★
(Rey de Africa)
90 min.
World
Prod: Sandy Howard
Dir: Sandy Howard
Scr: Jack DeWitt, Sandy Howard
Cast: Ty Hardin, Pier Angeli, Rossano Brazzi, George Sanders, Helga

Line, Jorge Rigaud, Dale Cummings, Julio Pena, Charles Fawcett, Alan Collins.

The Best House in London
96 min.
MGM
Prod: Philip Breen, Kurt Unger
Dir: Philip Savile
Scr: Denis Norden
Cast: David Hemmings, George Sanders, Joanna Pettet, Warren Mitchell, Dany Robin, William Rushton.

1969

The Candy Man★
98 min.
Sagittarius
Prod: Herbert J. Leder
Dir: Herbert J. Leder
Scr: Herbert J. Leder
Cast: George Sanders, Leslie Parrish, Gina Roman, Manolo Fabregas.

The Body Stealers
91 min.
GB
Prod: Tony Tenser
Dir: Gerry Levy
Scr: Michael St. Clair, Peter Marcus
Cast: George Sanders, Maurice Evans, Patrick Allen, Neil Connery, Hilary Dwyer, Robert Flemyng, Lorna Wilde, Callan Cuthberton, Michael Culver, Sally Faulkner.

1970

The Kremlin Letter★
123 min.

Fox
Prod: Carter De Haven, Sam Weisenthal
Dir: John Huston
Scr: John Huston, Gladys Hill
Cast: Bibi Andersson, Richard Boone, Nigel Green, Dean Jagger, Lila Kedrova, Michael MacLiammoir, Patrick O'Neal, Barbara Parkins, George Sanders, Max von Sydow.

1971

Doomwatch★
(Released 1976)
92 min.
AVCO EMBASSY
Prod: Tony Tenser
Dir: Peter Sasdy
Scr: Clive Exton
Cast: Ian Bannen, Judy Geeson, John Paul, Simon Oates, George Sanders, Percy Herbert, Geoffrey Keen, Joseph O'Connor.

Endless Night★
99 min.
EMI
Prod: Leslie Gilliat
Dir: Sidney Gilliat
Scr: Sidney Gilliat
Cast: Hayley Mills, Hywel Bennett, George Sanders, Britt Ekland, Per Oscarsson, Lois Maxwell.

1972

Psychomania★
91 min.
Benmar

Prod: Andrew Donally
Dir: Don Sharp
Scr: Armand d'Usseau
Cast: George Sanders, Beryl Reid, Nicky Henson, Robert Hardy.

Bibliography

I. Letters and Manuscripts

Aherne, Brian. Letter to George Sanders, November 1968. Hantsfield, England.

Bloecker, Margaret Sanders. Letters (3) to Lorraine Chanel, December 1970–September 1972. Horsham, England.

Colman, Juliet Benita. Letters (2) to Lorraine Chanel, January–July 1972. London, England; Majorca, Spain.

Graff-Hunter, Enio. Letter to Lorraine Chanel, May 7, 1972. Majorca, Spain.

Pickford, Mary. Letter to George Sanders, August 20, 1936. Hollywood, California.

Sanders, George. Clipping scrapbook, 1934–1949.

Sanders, George. Letter to Brian Aherne, July 8, 1969. Majorca, Spain.

Sanders, George. Letter to Margaret Sanders Bloecker, April 24, 1972. Barcelona, Spain.

Sanders, George. Letters (45) to Lorraine Chanel, 1968–1971. Majorca, Spain; Rome, Italy; Paris, France; Helsinki, Finland.

Sanders, George. Letter to Henry P. Sanders, June 12, 1926. Buenos Aires, Argentina.

Sanders, George. Letters (51) to Margaret Kolbe Sanders, July 12, 1919 to December 10, 1922. Brighton College, Brighton, England.

Sanders, George. Manuscript journal, 1937–1938. Hollywood, California.

Sanders, Margaret Kolbe. Letter to George Sanders, November 25, 1947. Sortavala, Finland.

Sanders, Margaret Kolbe. Manuscript memoirs, 1903–1917.

Sanders (Conway), Thomas. Letters (8) to Margaret Kolbe Sanders, 1917–1918. Bedales School, Petersfield, England.

Sanders (Conway), Thomas. Letters (9) to Margaret Kolbe Sanders, September 28, 1919 to February 6, 1921. Brighton College, Brighton, England.

Sanders (Conway), Thomas. Letter to Henry P. Sanders, August 28, 1921. Worthing, England.

Sanders (Conway), Thomas. Letters (4) to Henry P. Sanders, March 8, 1924 to August 7, 1929. Rhodesia, South Africa.

Waters, Maxine. Letter to Lorraine Chanel, May 2, 1972, Majorca, Spain.

II. Interviews

Angel, Heather. Correspondence interview with author, March 1986.

Ball, Lucille. Correspondence interview with author, May 1986.

Bloecker, Margaret Sanders. Correspondence interviews with author, April–August 1986. Personal interviews with author: June 10, 1986, Walnut Creek, California; September 6, 1986, Horsham, England.

Chanel, Lorraine. Correspondence interviews with author, September 1986; December 1986; July 1987.

Chapman, Marguerite. Correspondence interviews with author, February 1986; April 1986.

Day, Laraine. Correspondence interview with author, March 1986.

Douglas, Robert. Correspondence interview with author, February 1986.

du Maurier, Dame Daphne. Correspondence interview with author, March 1986.

Edwards, Blake. Correspondence interview with author, April 1986.

Fairbanks, Douglas, Jr. Correspondence interviews with author, February–March 1986.

Fontaine, Joan. Telephone interview with author, February 27, 1986. Carmel, California.

Gabor, Eva. Telephone interview with author, June 24, 1986. Beverly Hills, California.

Gabor, Zsa Zsa. Telephone interviews with author, April 3, 5, 6, 1986. Bel Air, California.

Hurwitz, Beatrice, Director of Permissions, Simon & Schuster Publishers. Correspondence with author, May 1986.

Huston, John. Correspondence interview with author, April 1986.

Jones, M.W.D., Archivist, Brighton College, England, correspondence with author, May 1986.

Jones, Shirley. Correspondence interview with author, April 1986.

Kedrova, Lila. Correspondence interview with author, April 1986.

Kidd, Charles, Project Editor, Debrett's Peerage Ltd., London. Personal interview with author, September 9, 1986. London, England.

Knowles, Patric. Correspondence interview with author, March 1986.

Lom, Herbert. Correspondence interview with author, March 1986.

MacAlpine, E.A.M., Headmaster, Bedales School, Petersfield, England. Correspondence with author, May 1986.

Mature, Victor. Correspondence interview with author, February 1986.

Mayo, Virginia. Correspondence interview with author, March 1986.

Mazurki, Mike. Correspondence interview with author, April 1986.

Merrill, Gary. Correspondence interview with author, March 1986.

Mills, Hayley. Correspondence interview with author, August 1986.

Price, Vincent. Correspondence interview with author, March 1986.

Quinn, Anthony. Correspondence interview with author, March 1986.

Raines, Ella. Correspondence interview with author, March 1986.

Sommer, Elke. Correspondence interview with author, February 1986.

Thoresby, Henry. Correspondence interview with author, May 1988.

Tierney, Gene. Correspondence interview with author, February 1986.

Toland, Juliet Colman. Correspondence with author, August–October 1987.

Verdugo, Elena. Correspondence interview with author, March 1986.

von Sydow, Max. Correspondence interview with author, March 1986.

Wilde, Cornel. Correspondence interview with author, February 1986.

III. Printed Sources

Books

Aherne, Brian. *A Dreadful Man* (New York: Simon & Schuster, 1979).

Brown, Peter. *Such Devoted Sisters: Those Fabulous Gabors* (New York: St. Martin's Press, 1985).

Colman, Juliet Benita. *Ronald Colman* (New York: William Morrow & Co., 1975).

Dooley, Roger. *From Scarface to Scarlett* (New York: Harcourt Brace Jovanovitch, 1981).

Everson, William K. *The Detective in Film* (Secaucus, N.J.: Citadel Press, 1972).

Fontaine, Joan. *No Bed of Roses* (New York: William Morrow, 1978).

Gabor, Eva. *Orchids and Salami* (New York: Doubleday, 1954).

Gabor, Jolie (with Cindy Adams). *Jolie* (New York: Mason, Charter, 1975).

Gabor, Zsa Zsa (with Gerold Frank). *Zsa Zsa Gabor: My Story* (New York: World Publishing, 1960).

Guiles, Fred L. *Tyrone Power: The Last Idol* (New York: Doubleday, 1979).

Haskell, Molly. *From Reverence to Rape* (New York: Holt, 1974).

Israel, Lee. *Miss Tallulah Bankhead* (New York: G.P. Putnam's Sons, 1972).

Leamer, Laurence. *As Time Goes By: The Life of Ingrid Bergman* (New York: Harper & Row, 1986).

Maney, Richard. *Fanfare: The Confessions of a Press Agent* (New York: Harper, 1957).

Mellen, Joan. *Big Bad Wolves* (New York: Pantheon, 1977).

Merman, Ethel (with George Eells). *Merman* (New York: Simon & Schuster, 1978).

Morley, Sheridan. *Tales From the Hollywood Raj* (New York: Viking, 1984).

Payn, Graham, and Sheridan Morley. *The Noel Coward Diaries* (Boston: Little, Brown, 1982).

Quinlan, David. *British Sound Films: The Studio Years, 1928–1958* (Totowa, N.J.: Barnes & Noble, 1985).

Rubenstein, Leonard. *The Great Spy Films* (Secaucus, N.J.: Citadel, 1979).

Sanders, George. *Crime on my Hands* (New York: Simon & Schuster, 1944). Inner Sanctum Series.

Sanders, George. *Memoirs of a Professional Cad* (New York: G.P. Putnam's Sons, 1960).

Sanders, George. *Stranger at Home* (New York: Simon & Schuster, 1946). Inner Sanctum Series.

Shipman, David. *The Great Movie Stars: The Golden Years* (New York: Farrar, Strauss & Giroux, 1979).

Spoto, Donald. *The Dark Side of Genius: The Life of Alfred Hitchcock* (New York: Little, Brown, 1983).

Stack, Robert (with Mark Evans). *Straight Shooting* (New York: Macmillan, 1980).

Thomas, Tony. *Cads and Cavaliers: The Film Adventurers* (New York: A.S. Barnes, 1973).

Wiley, Mason, and Damien Bona. *Inside Oscar* (New York: Ballantine Books, 1986).

Zinman, David. *Saturday Afternoon at the Bijou* (New Rochelle, N.Y.: Arlington House, 1973).

Periodicals/Newspapers

Ace, Goodman. "In Memory of George Sanders," *Saturday Review*, May 27, 1972.

"Actor George Sanders Kills Himself in Spain," UPI News Service, April 26, 1972.

Baskette, Kirtley. "Hollywood's Most Baffling Bachelor," (interview) *Modern Screen*, June 1941.

Baskette, Kirtley. "The Strange Case of George Sanders," (interview) *Modern Screen*, April 1942.

Cheatham, Maude. "Portrait of a Puzzle," (interview) *Movie Show*, May 1946.

"La Cocinera y El Ayuda de Camara de George Sanders," *Lecturas* (Barcelona, Spain), May 1972.

"Content with Mediocrity," *Time*, March 28, 1960.

Conway, Tom. "My Brother George and I," *Screenland*, December 1942.

Cook, Alton. "A Spade's a Spade," *Silver Screen*, February 1945.

Darnton, John. "The Consummate Cad," (obit) New York *Times*, April 26, 1972.

Deere, Dorothy. "Blood and Sanders," *Movieland*, November 1943.

Dillon, Franc. "He's Allergic to Skirts," *Movies*, September 1942.

Dodd, Melissa. "Ten Ways to Avoid Matrimony," (interview) *Hollywood Magazine*, January 1938.

Eaton, Harriett. "Too Well Remembered," (interview) *Photoplay*, July, 1947.

Foster, Carl. "The Strictly Private Life of George Sanders," (interview) *Photoplay*, September 1943.

Gabor, Zsa Zsa. "Exactly What I Wanted," *Motion Picture*, July 1949.

"George Sanders Is Revolutionary," (interview) *Photoplay*, February 1944.

"Goodbye, My Love," *Photoplay*, August 1972.

Guerin, Ann. "The End of a Love Affair," *Show*, July 1972.

Hall, Gladys. "George Sanders Puts Women in Their Place," (interview) *Photoplay*, June 1942.

Hall, Gladys. "I Can't Make Anyone Understand Me," (interview) *Silver Screen*, January 1943.

Hall, Gladys. "Things That Keep Sanders Awake," (interview) *Silver Screen*, July 1944.

Holland, Jack. "Actors Are Lousy Lovers," (interview) *Motion Picture*, September 1942.

Kilgallen, Dorothy. "10 Knights in My Hollywood Date Book," *Photoplay*, June 1943.

Lee, Henry. "They Bought $4 Million Pig in Poke," *Sunday News*, March 26, 1967.

Lewis, Patricia. "I'm in Sunny Spain Listening to Sanders on Love," London *Daily Express,* October 3, 1958.

Manners, Mary Jane. "Love Is a Disease," *Silver Screen*, August 1942.

Martin, Pete. "He Sneered His Way to Stardom," (interview) *Saturday Evening Post*, August 8, 1951.

"Milestones," (obit) *Time*, May 8, 1972.

"People," *Time* , April 11, 1969.

Prideaux, Tom. "Happy Encore for Kaufman's Classics," *Life*, November 25, 1966.

Reed, Rex. "Hey There, Georgy Girl," New York *Times*, July 6, 1969.

Riley, Nord. "Sneers for Mr. Sanders, " *Colliers*, November 14, 1942.

Ruddy, J. Maurice. "Film Pictorial Book," *Lloyd's of London*. November 1937.

Sanders, George. "Crime on My Hands," (condensation) *Photoplay*, November 1944; December 1944.

Sanders, George. "If I Weren't An Actor," *Silver Screen*, August 1942.

Sanders, George. "The Role I Liked Best," *Saturday Evening Post*, August 8, 1951.

Sanders, George. "There's a Lot to Like About Women," *Good Housekeeping*, April 1961.

Sheridan, Michael. "Seance With Sanders," *Motion Picture*, July 1944.

"The Strangely Fascinating Mr. Sanders," *Screenland*, September 1942.

"Transition," (obit) *Newsweek*, May 5, 1972.

Wilson, Elizabeth. "Do Ordinary Looking Girls Have the Deepest Passion?" (interview) *Silver Screen*, December 1940.

"Zsa Zsa vs. George," *Motion Picture Annual*, 1954.

Index